Contemporary Studies in Scripture

An exciting new series from Greg Kofford Books featuring authors whose works engage in rigorous textual analyses of the Bible and other LDS scripture. Written by Latter-day Saints for a Latter-day Saint audience, these books utilize the tools of historical criticism, literature, philosophy, and the sciences to celebrate the richness and complexity found in the standard works. This series will provide readers with new and fascinating ways to read, study, and re-read these sacred texts.

Authoring
the Old Testament

Authoring
the Old Testament

Genesis — Deuteronomy

David Bokovoy

GREG KOFFORD BOOKS
SALT LAKE CITY, 2014

Greg Kofford Books
P.O. Box 1362
Draper, UT 84020
www.gregkofford.com
facebook.com/gkbooks

Also available in ebook.

2018   17   16   15   14   5   4   3   2   1

Hardcover ISBN: 978-1-58958-675-8
The Library of Congress cataloged the paperback edition as follows:

Bokovoy, David E., author.
  Authoring the Old Testament : Genesis-Deuteronomy / David Bokovoy.
    pages cm
  Includes bibliographical references and index.
  ISBN 978-1-58958-588-1 (alk. paper)
  1. Bible. Pentateuch--Authorship. 2. Bible. Pentateuch--Criticism, interpretation, etc. 3. Pearl of Great Price. Book of Moses--Criticism, interpretation, etc. 4. Pearl of Great Price. Book of Abraham--Criticism, interpretation, etc. 5. Book of Mormon--Criticism, interpretation, etc. I. Title.
  BS1225.52.B65 2014
  222'.1066--dc23
                            2014001377

To my daughter Kate Bokovoy currently serving a mission in Rancagua, Chile. You exemplify the fact that faith, love, service, and critical thinking are all essential components of developing spirituality.

Contents

Tables

Foreword

Authoring the Old Testament is a welcome introduction, from a faithful Latter-day Saint perspective, to the academic world of Higher Criticism of the Hebrew Bible. As is well known, the Bible is an extremely rich and complex collection of writings. Biblical books report the spoken words of many prophets and historians. They embrace a huge array of subjects, utilizing a host of literary forms and styles, and serving a wealth of purposes past, present, and future.

This important book is a successful stride forward into a very wide arena. Its author, David Bokovoy, openly and humbly acknowledges that this is not, of course, a comprehensive study. Indeed, it would take hundreds of volumes to examine completely the authorship, cultural backgrounds, and textual history of the first five books of the Bible, let alone all of its sixty-six books. And bringing Latter-day Saint scriptures, teachings, and issues into the picture complicates the discussion exponentially.

Rarely do sacred texts—biblical or otherwise—come with a foreword, explaining everything one would like to know about when, where, why, and by whom each text was written. And so there are questions as one strives to be immersed in the worlds of the scriptures. This book wrestles with questions, and even for good questions there are not always clear answers. Matters involving texts and topics that are hundreds or thousands of years old are seldom cut and dry, and much remains debatable and open to discussion. Yet there is value in wrestling with all scriptures—as long as that does not turn into wresting them.

In order to grapple with the vast corpus of biblical material, scholars have fashioned a number of tools. One of those tools, perhaps inaptly, is known as Higher Criticism. Voltaire once said the Holy Roman Empire was neither holy, nor Roman, nor an empire; and likewise one might note that Higher Criticism is neither higher nor critical. A product of Enlightenment thought, it claims no necessarily "higher" moral ground or higher utility than other tools used by various scholars in studying the Bible. Nor is it "critical," either in the sense of being condemning, crucial, or decisive. "Higher" just means above or behind the wording of the text, while the word "criticism" (which comes from the Greek word *kritikos*) has to do with adopting standards, weighing sometimes microscopic evidence, and exercising careful judgment.

Explaining the exploratory nature and the developing operation of many applications of Higher Criticism is the purpose of this book, and it accomplishes this objective boldly and admirably, both in relation to the Bible and Latter-day Saint scripture. Although mastering the tool of Higher Criticism requires years of training and experience, and even though its hypotheses and proposed conclusions need not always be accepted, all readers can understand and take advantage of many of the propositions and insights offered here.

Books about features of the Bible are very much needed within the LDS tradition, which is still a young religion, working out the full implications of the scriptures and doctrines revealed by the Prophet Joseph Smith, as well as identifying avenues through which Mormons may fully communicate with members of all other faith traditions. Many tools, including Higher Criticism, may well prove helpful in this process. Any tool, of course, can be used to build up or to tear down; a drill can drill holes to help fasten things together, or just to poke holes. And a person using a tool must know how and when to use it and when some other tool might yield better results, and this book models ways in which this can be done with discretion.

Many miles lie ahead in this endeavor, and so it is good that this book promises two sequel volumes, one on the histories and prophets, and the other on the writings. Actually, I hope that this book will be the first of many more such books explaining dozens of other exegetical tools and approaches to scripture. With so much ground to cover, it is good that Latter-day Saints need not reinvent every wheel. Biblical scholarship can contribute much to the understanding of LDS scripture, and in due time LDS scripture may return the favor, shedding light on possible meanings, history, reception, and authority of biblical texts.

In the meantime, we all carry on in our daily walk, seeking to be guided by the inspiration found in the revelations of God, as David Bokovoy sincerely hopes this book will engender. While it is good to ponder interpretive questions about the authorship of any text, it is even better to know and embrace the inspiration behind the holy scriptures. For Joseph

Smith, who was himself involved with the authorship of scripture, it was through inspiration that the scriptures radiated the word of God. In his revision of the Bible, Joseph Smith modified the reading of Paul's words as rendered by the King James Version in 2 Timothy 3:16, that "all scripture *is* inspired and is profitable," preferring the insight that "all scripture *given by inspiration of God* is profitable." It was readily evident to Joseph that God may use an array of servants—prophets, scribes, recorders, abridgers, and translators—in bringing forth his word; and still "whether by mine own voice or by the voice of my servants, it is the same" (D&C 1:38).

For all of this, David Bokovoy is to be commended for his breadth of coverage and for his own original contributions. He is a skilled wrestler. He has a thorough grasp of this field of biblical studies, the ability to wisely reduce complex issues to their fundamental elements, and the strength, training, and determination to seek out and offer engaging solutions. While resisting, as I do, some of his holds, readers will be positively served and firmly impressed by the many strengths of this book, coupled with David's genuine dedication to learning "by study and also by faith."

John W. Welch

January 28, 2014

Acknowledgments

It's for myself and my friends my stories are sung.
—Bob Dylan, "Restless Farewell," 1964

Some time ago, I was approached by my friend Loyd Ericson and invited to write a basic introduction to Higher Criticism and the Old Testament for Kofford Books. I was grateful for his confidence that I could successfully produce such a work and agreed that the book was needed. So I responded, "Sure, I would be happy to do that." In my mind, however, I wasn't convinced that now was the right time to undertake such a project. I had a very heavy teaching load and my family was still recovering from my dissertation. After a second visit with Loyd, I realized he was serious about the project, and I determined to give it my immediate attention. I'm grateful to Loyd for his confidence and edits. From start to finish, Loyd was a tremendous help in putting together this volume. I sincerely hope that he is pleased with our efforts.

I need to also immediately express sincere gratitude to my brother Daniel Bokovoy who carefully read through each chapter as it was completed. It was very important to me to write in a way that would help engage a general audience. If this book is at all successful in that goal, it's because of Danny.

I am also grateful to my friends Matt Taylor and Jason Payne with whom I frequently discussed this challenging project. They both gave constant encouragement. As I tried to lay out my objectives, my friend Taylor Petrey read an initial copy of the introduction and offered helpful advice.

I'm also very grateful to my former professor and friend John W. Welch (Jack) for providing the foreword to this volume. His work has meant so much to me and others interested in LDS scholarship. I respect his vision of the need for Mormon Studies to seriously engage academic work on the Bible. I had the privilege to attend his first Society of Biblical

Literature presentation in Boston. This was the first time a Latter-day Saint had offered original research on the Bible in that prestigious venue. It was an inspiring moment. Jack has devoted years of careful study to biblical law, and as one trained in the application of legal principles, he sees many of the issues raised in this book differently than I do. His vision, however, is that we, as Latter-day Saints, should openly address and discuss these complex issues with kindness, faith, and critical analysis. He therefore continues to serve as examples of both a scholar and a saint. I'm fortunate to have him as a friend and mentor.

I feel that it's also important that I express gratitude to my friend and former professor, David Wright, who first helped me to develop a love for studying the Bible critically.

Most of all, I'm grateful to my wife, Carolyn, who supported this highly personal project, as she has every venture I've ever undertaken.

In many ways, this book has been a group effort. I alone, however, am responsible for any mistakes that might appear. It is my sincere hope that this study will help confirm that within Mormonism, spirituality and critical thinking are not only not mutually exclusive paradigms, they are a united undertaking.

Prologue

I showed them . . . that error was in the Bible,
or the translation of the Bible.

—Joseph Smith

This book provides Latter-day Saint readers with an academic investigation into the question, "Who wrote the Bible's first five books?" This series, *Authoring the Old Testament*, presents a basic introduction to biblical scholarship and its relationship to Mormonism. I primarily see this effort as a personal attempt to share with an LDS audience some of the exciting insights I've gained as a student of the "Hebrew Bible."[1] Please note, however, that neither this book, nor this series provides a comprehensive study of the subject.

The present volume specifically explores the making of the Pentateuch (the first five books of the Old Testament). The second volume in the series will provide a basic introduction to the Deuteronomistic History (Joshua, Judges, Samuel, and Kings), as well as the complicated issue of ancient Israelite prophecy. Finally, the third volume will explore the groups of biblical texts known as the "Writings" (Psalms, Proverbs, Ecclesiastes, Song of Solomon, Job, etc.). These three volumes parallel the traditional three-part division of the Old Testament books in both ancient and contemporary forms of Judaism: the Torah, the Prophets, and the Writings.

---

1. Scholars attempt to use "bias-free" language. Since not everyone who accepts this collection of ancient Israelite literature as scripture believes in a "New Testament," scholars use the more neutral term "Hebrew Bible" in reference to the Old Testament. The official *Society of Biblical Literature Handbook of Style* explains this preference with these words: "Bias-free writing respects all cultures, peoples, and religions . . . uncritical use of biblical characterizations such as the *Jews* or the *Pharisees* can perpetuate religious or ethnic stereotypes." Patrick H. Alexander and Shirley Decker-Lucke, *The SBL Handbook of Style: For Ancient Near Eastern, Biblical, and Early Christian Studies*, 17.

Since *Authoring the Old Testament* has been written specifically for an LDS audience, I will connect each volume with both Latter-day Saint thought and the unique books of LDS scripture.[2] In so doing, I am acting as neither critic nor apologist. However, throughout the study, I will offer various paradigms that a believer might adopt to make sense of biblical scholarship in light of his or her spiritual convictions. In this study, I am not trying to convert my reader to Mormonism *per se*, nor to the types of methodologies scholars employ to answer the question, "Who wrote the Old Testament?"

The Hebrew Bible is without question among the most influential writings in the history of the Western world. It is a scribal compilation of a diverse assortment of religious texts written over a thousand-year period. The scholarly consensus holds that these writings, which include various genres such as narratives, laws, poetry, wisdom sayings, prophecy, and apocalyptic texts, were composed from approximately the twelfth through the second centuries BC.[3]

Despite the title of this series, ancient scribes were not *authors* in the contemporary sense. In his study on Near Eastern and biblical scribal activity, Karel van der Toorn explains this distinction by stating that the "making of the Hebrew Bible is owed to the scribal class rather than a limited number of individuals" and that, rather than trying to identify *authors*, we should instead simply seek "to penetrate the mind-set of the scribal elite."[4] Van der Toorn goes on to suggest that scribes were *artisans* rather than *artists*, since unlike modern authors, scribes did not take into consideration intellectual property in the formation of their own literary work.[5] When all is said and done, the Old Testament is a scribal compilation of assorted religious texts, and scribal artisans were very much copiers and preservers of holy tradition.[6]

---

2. I recognize that some readers will no doubt feel tempted to start with the concluding chapters that focus on the implications of Higher Criticism for the Book of Moses, the Book of Abraham, and the Book of Mormon. I hope that my reader will avoid this temptation and instead choose to approach this book like he or she would a detective novel. I believe that it is essential that the reader first understand the "case" before skipping ahead to learn the ending.

3. Marc Zvi Brettler, *Biblical Hebrew for Students of Modern Israeli Hebrew*, 2.

4. See Karel van der Toorn, *Scribal Culture and the Making of the Hebrew Bible*, 5.

5. Ibid.

6. Much of the recent commentary on scribal culture and creativity, including work done by van der Toorn, focuses upon the issue of text critical data, comparing manuscript variants such as those featured in the Septuagint, Masoretic Text, Dead Sea Scrolls, and other minor texts. In addition to van der Toorn, see especially Seth L. Sanders, *The Invention of Hebrew* (Urbana and Chicago: University of Illinois

Recent studies on this topic, however, prove that many biblical scribes produced texts with impressive artistic creativity far beyond that of the basic technical skills required of a mere copyist.[7] The scribes who composed the sources for the Old Testament may not have been "authors" in the exact same way we understand that word today, but they were still authors nonetheless. Presently, most people associate the idea of authorship with individualism and a creation of independent ideas. Scribes were certainly preservers of sacred traditions, but they also used these works (even when recording oral traditions) to create impressive new literary compositions. This book provides evidence that supports this statement.

In its exploration of the question of Old Testament authorship, the present volume provides an introduction to Higher Criticism. Higher Criticism refers to a scholarly attempt to explain inconsistencies in the Bible by identifying its original sources.[8] As an interpretive tool, Higher Criticism constitutes a central part of the historical-critical method. There are many academic approaches scholars use to interpret the Bible, including Form Criticism, Structuralism, Reader-Response Criticism, Deconstruction, Redaction Criticism, and Social-Scientific Criticism (just to name a few).[9] Each of these academic methods has its place; however, this book focuses specifically on Higher Criticism. Over the years there have been many helpful introductions to this topic written for a general au-

---

Press, 2009); and William M. Schniedewind, *How the Bible Became a Book: The Textualization of Ancient Israel* (Cambridge: Cambridge Unversity Press, 2004).

7. Technically, this phenomenon that reveals authorial creativity is known as "inner biblical exegesis." For examples of important work on this subject, see Michael A. Fishbane, *Biblical Interpretation in Ancient Israel* (Oxford: Clarendon Press; Oxford University Press, 1984); Michael A. Fishbane, *Biblical Myth and Rabbinic Mythmaking* (Oxford: Oxford University Press, 2003); Bernard M. Levinson, *Deuteronomy and the Hermeneutics of Legal Innovation* (New York: Oxford University Press, 1997); Bernard M. Levinson, *Legal Revision and Religious Renewal in Ancient Israel* (Cambridge: Cambridge University Press, 2008); Jeffrey Stackert, *Rewriting the Torah: Literary Revision in Deuteornomy and the Holiness Legislation (Forschunmgen Zum Alten Testament)* (Tübingen: Mohr Siebeck, 2007); and David P. Wright, *Inventing God's Law: How the Covenant Code of the Bible Used and Revised the Laws of Hammurabi* (Oxford: Oxford University Press, 2013).

8. In contrast to lower criticism, which in contemporary terms refers to text criticism. Terminology, however, is not used consistently throughout the literature.

9. For an introduction to these various methods, see Adele Berlin and Marc Zvi Brettler, "The Modern Study of the Bible," 2084–96.

dience, and this book is indebted to them all.[10] *Authoring the Old Testament* is unique, though, since it is written specifically for Mormons.

In biblical studies, Historical Criticism seeks to uncover the way in which an original author and an ancient audience would have understood that writer's message. Often contemporary readers of ancient texts assume that ancient authors saw the world in a way that parallels the modern religious experience. But if readers approach a text this way, they fail to allow the original author to share his *own* experience with the divine. In other words, reading modern conceptions into ancient texts limits the original author's ability to tell us what *he* knows. And what he *knows* is often vastly different than our own knowledge. Elder John A. Widtsoe expressed this idea with these words:

> Many Bible accounts that trouble the inexperienced reader become clear and acceptable if the essential meaning of the story is sought out. To read the Bible fairly, it must be read as President Brigham Young suggested: 'Do you read the scriptures, my brethren and sisters, as though you were writing them a thousand, two thousand, or five thousand years ago? Do you read them as though you stood in the place of the men who wrote them?' . . . This is our guide. The scriptures must be read intelligently.[11]

By reading scripture critically, a believer in the text's inspiration can gain an increased understanding of the various ways in which God has touched the hearts and minds of his children.

If this is the reader's first exposure to Historical Criticism, this book will forever transform the way she looks at the Old Testament. It is a secular approach. However, for a believer in holy writ, reading scriptural texts while looking for the diverse (and often contradictory) ways in which authors express their religious views accepts that God speaks to individuals according to their traditions and abilities. This perspective accords with the revelatory process described in the Doctrine and Covenants: "[Revelations] were given unto my servants in their weakness, after the manner of their language, that they might come to understanding" (D&C 1:24). Revelation is highly personal. And apparently, in His efforts to

---

10. See, for example, Richard Elliott Friedman, *Who Wrote the Bible?* (San Francisco: HarperSanFrancisco, 1997); Michael Coogan, *The Old Testament: A Historical and Literary Introduction to the Hebrew Scriptures* (Oxford: Oxford University Press, 2010); John J. Collins, *Introduction to the Hebrew Bible* (Minneapolis: Fortress Press, 2004); and although written for a Jewish audience, see Marc Zvi Brettler, *How to Read the Bible* (Philadelphia: JPS, 2005).

11. John A. Widtsoe, *Evidences And Reconciliations*, section IV.3.

communicate with human beings, God works within the boundaries of culture (2 Ne. 31:3).

Identifying the various ways in which ancient authors interpreted and expressed their experiences with divinity can greatly enhance our own knowledge of the divine, even when (and we might say *especially* when) those ideas contradict our own. Ancient authors' conceptions were often vastly different from those held in the modern era. Therefore, a religious reader gains invaluable insights from ancient sources by identifying themes and ideas that do not reflect his own spiritual views. As a result, this study is not *purely* secular. I believe that there is a deep spiritual component to this endeavor. The Historical Critical method is a useful way for a religious reader to analyze texts.

As we explore the issue of Higher Criticism in the Old Testament, I recognize that some of these scholarly theories may prove uncomfortable to some Latter-day Saint readers. In an academic quest to read the Bible independently from any contemporary theological lens, a certain degree of discomfort for believers is in some ways inevitable. In my own life, however, I have found that this is not a bad thing. I believe that it is healthy for each of us to question our religious assumptions and to continually use the incredible gift God has given us to search for truth: *our brain*. In this process, we should not be afraid to ask questions and entertain challenging topics.

Many years ago, I was a young LDS seminary teacher with a master's degree in Near Eastern and Judaic Studies, and I had a sincere passion for teaching teenagers insights from the Bible. One day I found myself in a class filled with restless students; I could tell from their body language that they had little interest in engaging my lesson on the New Testament. I had nearly given up on gaining their enthusiasm when a normally rambunctious teenage boy slowly raised his hand and *asked a question*.

Though I can no longer recall *what* it was he asked, I'll never forget the boy's response when I was visibly pleased, and sincerely praised him in front of his peers for coming to class with such a fascinating theological question. He said, "Really?! Because when I asked my mom that same question last night she got mad at me for doubting the Church!"

I was shocked! In hindsight, I realize that I have no idea *how* the conversation between this young man and his mother actually took place, and as a general rule, when it comes to teenagers and their perceptions, I'm typically willing to give adults the benefit of the doubt. But unfortunately, from what I've witnessed, it is true that some within the Mormon community strongly oppose critically engaging religious issues.

I have often asked myself the question, what is it about our cultural tradition that leaves some Latter-day Saints with the impression that it is not only *wrong* to express uncertainty about our theology, but that doubts in any form are a result of sin. Under this attitude, it is never right to question such issues as the historicity of scripture, the veracity of the Restoration, or the counsel of our Church leaders. Some of us have bought into the notion that it is immoral to even ask such questions. Yet in reality, nothing could be further from the truth.

In their impressive study, *The God Who Weeps: How Mormonism Makes Sense of Life*, Terryl and Fiona Givens explain the matter in this way:

> The call to faith is a summons to engage the heart, to attune it to resonate in sympathy with principles and values and ideals that we devoutly hope are true and which we have reasonable but not certain grounds for believing to be true. There must be grounds for doubt as well as belief, in order to render the choice more truly a choice, and therefore the more deliberate, and laden with personal vulnerability and investment. An overwhelming preponderance of evidence on either side would make our choice as meaningless as would a loaded gun pointed at our heads. The option to believe must appear on one's personal horizon like the fruit of paradise, perched precariously between sets of demands held in dynamic tension.[12]

Viewed in this light, doubts and uncertainties that arise from serious investigation can be seen as an essential component in our spiritual growth.

We should not, therefore, treat each other (or even ourselves) as sinners when we doubt. In fact, the acceptance of a questioning attitude is exemplified in the biblical passage that sparked the Restoration: "If any of you lack wisdom, let him ask of God, that giveth to all men liberally, and upbraideth not" (James 1:5). Among other things, this famous scriptural line suggests that God will not "upbraid" or "scold" the questioner since *questioning* is an essential part of spiritual and intellectual maturity.

If the revelations in the Doctrine and Covenants teach us anything, it is the power of a good question. Many of these revelations came as a result of theological concerns Joseph Smith developed while carefully working his way through the Bible. Rather than a sign of *sin*, a questioning attitude should be recognized for what it truly is, a desire to obtain truth. This concept was understood by one of the greatest questioning minds

---

12. Terryl Givens and Fiona Givens, *The God Who Weeps: How Mormonism Makes Sense of Life*, 4.

Mormonism has ever produced, Elder B. H. Roberts. Hoping to inspire Latter-day Saints to think critically on religious matters, Elder Roberts expressed the importance of questioning with these words:

> Mental laziness is the vice of men, especially with reference to divine things. Men seem to think that because inspiration and revelation are factors in connection with the things of God, therefore the pain and stress of mental effort are not required; that by some means these elements act somewhat as Elijah's ravens and feed us without effort on our part. To escape this effort, this mental stress to know the things that are, men raise all too readily the ancient bar—"Thus far shalt thou come, but no farther." Man cannot hope to understand the things of God, they plead, or penetrate those things which he has left shrouded in mystery. "Be thou content with the simple faith that accepts without question. To believe, and accept the ordinances, and then live the moral law will doubtless bring men unto salvation; why then should man strive and trouble himself to understand? Much study is still a weariness of the flesh." So men reason; and just now it is much in fashion to laud "the simple faith;" which is content to believe without understanding, or even without much effort to understand. And doubtless many good people regard this course as indicative of reverence—this plea in bar of effort—"thus far and no farther." This sort of "reverence" is easily simulated, and is of such flattering unction, and so pleasant to follow—"soul take thine ease"—that without question it is very often simulated; and falls into the same category as the simulated humility couched in "I don't know," which so often really means "I don't care, and do not intend to trouble myself to find out."[13]

True reverence, as Elder Roberts recognized, is not a *lack* of questioning, but serious study, pondering, and inquiry.

I am writing this book because I believe that as Latter-day Saints, we should strive to understand the way scholars understand the Old Testament. We cannot be afraid to subject our religious texts to serious intellectual investigation. Again, Elder Roberts recognized the importance of this perspective as well. Concerning the Book of Mormon and Higher Criticism, B. H. Roberts wrote:

> The Book of Mormon of necessity must submit to every test, to literary criticism, as well as to every other class of criticism; for our age is above all things critical, and especially critical of sacred literature, and we may not hope that the Book of Mormon will escape closest scrutiny; neither, indeed, is it desirable that it should escape. It is given to the world as a revelation from God. It is a volume of American scripture. Men have a right to test it by the keenest criticism, and to pass severest judgment upon it, and we who accept it as a revela-

---

13. B. H. Roberts, *The Seventy's Course of Theology*, v.

tion from God have every reason to believe that it will endure every test; and the more thoroughly it is investigated, the greater shall be its ultimate triumph. Here it is in the world; let the world make the most of it, or the least of it. It is and will remain true. But it will not do for those who believe it to suppose that they can dismiss objections to this American volume of scripture by the assumption of a lofty air of superiority, and a declaration as to what is enough for us or anybody else to know. The Book of Mormon is presented to the world for its acceptance; and the Latter-day Saints are anxious that their fellow men should believe it. If objections are made to it, to the manner of its translation, with the rest, these objections should be patiently investigated, and the most reasonable explanations possible, given.[14]

Admittedly, this type of analysis creates some problems for some of our traditional paradigms. Some of our assumptions regarding the development of scriptural texts cannot be sustained. Questioning these matters with a critical mind, however, is no sin; neither is struggling with possible inconsistencies within our own religious understandings. According to the *Lectures on Faith*, Jesus Christ himself "was exposed to more powerful contradictions than any man can be" (Lectures on Faith 5:2). And to quote LDS scripture, "art thou greater than he?" (D&C 122:8).

Even though I am writing this book as neither critic nor apologist, I must admit that I am a believer. But I am also a critical biblical scholar. In my academic training and writings, I strive to avoid allowing my own religious views to influence the way I interpret the Bible as an ancient text. I often take the same approach to the LDS scriptures as well. In this effort, I have often felt that walking and writing in both worlds makes me somewhat of an intellectual/spiritual amphibian. Sometimes I approach the text as critic, and other times as religious truth seeker, using the Bible and other scriptural sources as a revelatory tool. I recognize that this is a contradiction. Fortunately, however, when it comes to facing contradictions, I am in good company. It is my sincere hope that this work will allow readers to find "words of wisdom" as they seek learning "even by study and also by faith" (D&C 109:7).

Finally, because I am writing to a Latter-day Saint audience, when possible I will cite from the King James Version (KJV) of the Bible. Any translation is an interpretation, and I would encourage readers to always consider other editions of the Bible in their studies. My use of the KJV in these volumes is designed to show that the observations of Higher Criticism can be applied directly to the Bible typically used by

---

14. B. H. Roberts, "The Translation of the Book of Mormon," 435–36.

LDS readers. Occasionally, I will cite alternative translations. These include the Jewish Publication Society translation (JPS) of the Hebrew and Aramaic in what is known as the Masoretic text.[15] This Jewish version of the Hebrew Bible was first published in a complete form in 1985. I will also occasionally make use of the New Revised Standard Version (NRSV), a translation of the Christian Bible (both Old and New Testaments) first published in 1989. When other editions, including my own translation, are cited, I will provide a note indicating the source.

So . . . who *did* write the Bible's first five books?

---

15. The Masoretic Text (MT) is the authoritative Hebrew version of the Jewish Bible (Christian Old Testament). The MT is widely used as the basis for the translation of the Old Testament in Christian Bibles.

Chapter One

Reading the Bible Critically

Introduction

The Bible opens with two creation stories. The first account, contained in Genesis 1, appears neatly organized into three days of preparation followed by three days of actual formation. Each day concludes with the formulaic expression: "and there was X." By the seventh day, all creation exists in its proper sphere and so, God rests. Then quite dramatically, everything changes. In Genesis 2, "all of a sudden it is as if everything created no longer exists."[1] Creation simply starts all over again.

In some ways, these two accounts are duplicative; each tells a story concerning the creation of animals, plants, and man. On several key issues, however, they contradict each other. For example, while the two stories describe the same events, they place the actions in different sequences. Genesis 1:26–27 states that man and woman were created together on the sixth day, *after* all the animals. The creation story in Genesis 2, however, states that God created man on the *first* day before he created the animals. Finally, after everything else was finished, God created the woman from the man's rib. Thus, in Genesis 1, God creates plants, then animals, and finally man and woman at the same time. In Genesis 2, however, God creates man, plants, animals, and finally woman. Here is the basic outline:

Genesis 1	Genesis 2
plants	man
animals	plants
man and woman	animals
	woman

There's another interesting difference. The creation story in Genesis 1 uses the divine name "Elohim" (translated "God" in the KJV), and the second

---

1. Victor Hurowitz, "P—Understanding the Priestly Source," 30.

story in Genesis 2 uses the divine name "Yahweh Elohim" (translated as "Lᴏʀᴅ God" in the KJV).[2] This vocabulary distinction appears consistently throughout the two accounts.

The chapter and verse divisions of the Bible as presently constituted were added to the original text several centuries after the Book of Genesis was written. The stories themselves, however, feature textual boundaries that signify where the two accounts begin and end. The first story of creation commences with the line: "In the beginning God created the heaven and the earth" (Gen. 1:1). It concludes with the summary statement midway through the fourth verse of the next chapter: "These are the generations of the heavens and of the earth when they were created" (Gen. 2:4a). Literary scholars refer to this editorial technique as "*inclusio*," which means repeating key words from the beginning of a text at its conclusion.[3] The second story begins with the introduction: "In the day that the Lᴏʀᴅ God made the earth and the heavens . . ." (Gen. 2:4b), and continues through chapter three. Thus:

1:1:   "In the beginning God *created the heaven and earth . . .*"

1:2–2:3:   Story of Elohim's creation and rest on the Sabbath day.

2:4a: "These are the generations of *the heavens and of the earth* when they were created."

2:4b: "In the day that the Lᴏʀᴅ God made *the earth and the heavens . . .*"

2:5–3:24: Story of Yahweh's creation (including the "Fall").

Both stories have the same type of beginning. Each one commences with a reference to God creating the "heaven and the earth," but it places the two words in an opposite sequence:

---

2. Known technically as the "tetragrammaton," the divine name Jehovah is a Latinization of the Hebrew name YHWH. Beginning in approximately the exilic time period (sixth century ʙᴄ), instead of pronouncing the name vocally, religious Jews substituted the title "Lord" or *ʾădōnāy*. "As a matter of consequence, the correct pronunciation of the tetragrammaton was gradually lost: the Masoretic form 'Jehovah' is in reality a combination of the consonants of the tetragrammaton with the vocals of *ʾădōnāy*." Karel van der Toorn, "Yahweh," i1711. In this volume, therefore, I will typically use the more correct *Yahweh* for Jehovah.

3. This same literary device appears in Book of Mormon texts; see David E. Bokovoy and John A. Tvedtnes, *Testaments: Links Between the Book of Mormon and the Hebrew Bible*, 117–31.

1:1:   "In the beginning God created the *heaven and earth . . .* "
2:4b: "In the day that the LORD God made the *earth and the heavens . . .*"

Comparing the two lines, it seems that by reversing the sequence in 2:4b, the first account focuses its readers' attention on heaven as the place of God's initial creation.[4] The first account, therefore, seems cosmic or heavenly in its initial focus in contrast to the second one which is much more earthy.

The two separate stories also differ in the way in which God/Yahweh performs the creative acts. In the story found in Genesis 1, God creates by simply speaking a command: "And God said . . ." In Genesis 2, Yahweh creates by physically working with the ground: "And the LORD God formed man of the dust of the ground. . . . And the LORD God planted a garden eastward in Eden" (Gen. 2:7–8). The two accounts even use different verbs to describe God's creation. The verb translated as "created" in 1:1 is the Hebrew verb *br'*, which is a divine verb in the Old Testament that is only used to describe God's creating process (see, for example, Num. 16:30; Ps. 51:12; Isa. 42:15, 43:1, 45:18).[5] In contrast, the second story uses the Hebrew verb *'sh* (translated as "made") to describe Yahweh's creation. In the Old Testament, this verb describes the making or creating process that both humans and gods perform. For example, the same Hebrew verb appears in Genesis 13:4 in reference to Abram's act of "making" an altar, and in reference to the "savory meat" Rebekah "makes" for Isaac in Genesis 27:14.

Perhaps most famously, in Genesis 1:26–27, God commands the first humans to multiply and replenish the earth. However, in the second story, God commands the first humans not to eat the fruit that granted that ability (Gen. 2:16–17). The two stories, therefore, differ in sequence, vocabulary, focus, and even their understanding of God's expectations for his creations.

As a student of the Bible, the Prophet Joseph Smith was sensitive to these issues. Passages in the Doctrine and Covenants illustrate Joseph's awareness and struggles with the two creation stories. In Section 77 the Prophet received an answer to an inquiry he made regarding the Book of Revelation that points toward two different types of creation, one "spiritual" and the other "temporal." Concerning the eventual happiness of man, beast, creep-

---

4. Mark S. Smith, *The Priestly Vision of Genesis 1*, 131.

5. See, for example, Werner H. Schmidt, *Die Schöpfungsgeschichte der Priesterschaft*, 164–67.

ing things, and the fowls of the air (i.e., the objects of creation in Genesis), verse 2 states that God created "that which is spiritual . . . in the likeness of that which is temporal; and that which is temporal in the likeness of that which is spiritual; the spirit of man in the likeness of his person, as also the spirit of the beast and every other creature."[6] This revelation suggests that in the "beginning," two separate types of creations occurred.

We find this concept expressed with even greater clarity in Joseph Smith's own translation of the Bible (the JST). The Book of Moses explains the differences between the two creation stories through a textual addition inserted directly between the two accounts. This addition clarifies what Doctrine and Covenants 77 was suggesting: the story in Genesis 1 describes God creating all things spiritually before they were naturally upon the face of the earth, whereas the events depicted in Genesis 2 refer to a physical or "temporal" creation:

> And now, behold, I say unto you, that these are the generations of the heaven and of the earth, when they were created, in the day that I, the Lord God, made the heaven and the earth, And every plant of the field before it was in the earth, and every herb of the field before it grew. *For I, the Lord God, created all things, of which I have spoken, spiritually, before they were naturally upon the face of the earth.* For I, the Lord God, had not caused it to rain upon the face of the earth. And I, the Lord God, had created all the children of men; and not yet a man to till the ground; for in heaven created I them; and there was not yet flesh upon the earth, neither in the water, neither in the air. (Moses 3:4–5)

This textual insertion (in italics) indicates that the Prophet recognized the contradictions in the Bible's two opening chapters and that these differences existed for a reason. From Joseph's perspective, they could not simply be ignored.

Without question, Joseph Smith loved the Bible. He believed that it was the inspired word of God. Yet Joseph's testimony did not keep him from recognizing that there are serious inconsistencies found within its pages, differences like those witnessed in the first two creation stories. Joseph taught that in the production of the Bible "ignorant translators, careless transcribers, or designing and corrupt priests . . . committed many errors."[7] Throughout his efforts to explicate biblical passages, we find in Joseph's sermons references to alternate translations from the King James Version (including the German), as well as allusions to the original

---

6. See also D&C 29:31–32.

7. Joseph Fielding Smith, comp., *Teachings of the Prophet Joseph Smith*, 327.

Hebrew of the Old Testament.[8] Joseph was a critical reader. "There are many things in the Bible," he declared, "which do not, as they now stand, accord with the revelations of the Holy Ghost to me."[9] And the Prophet was not afraid to point them out.

The Bible as "Privileged" Text

For centuries prior to Joseph Smith, readers of the Bible often interpreted it as a "privileged" text.[10] Scholar James Kugel explains this traditional approach:

> Scripture is perfect and perfectly harmonious. By this I mean, first of all, that there is no mistake in the Bible, and anything that might look like a mistake—the fact that, for example, Gen. 15:13 asserts that the Israelites 'will be oppressed for four hundred years' in Egypt, while Exod. 12:41 speaks of 430 years, whereas a calculation based on biblical genealogies yielded a figure of 210 years—must therefore be an illusion to be clarified by proper interpretation.[11]

This method assumes the Bible is perfectly harmonious and without error, since some, if not all of it, came directly from God. It was believed that the Bible should therefore always be interpreted in a way that either harmonizes or simply ignores inconsistencies. Thus, throughout the centuries prior to Joseph Smith, when biblical texts like Genesis 1 and 2 appeared to contradict each other, qualified professional interpreters (such as scribes, rabbis, or priests) would reinterpret the plain meaning of words for their respective communities in a way that made the Bible conform with both itself and the interpreter's particular religious preference. The Prophet Joseph Smith did not accept this type of interpretive approach. Instead, Joseph turned to what he identified as revelation and scribal errors to explain what he perceived as problems in the text.

And yet, Joseph was not the first critical reader of the Bible to take seriously the types of textual, narrative, and theological discrepancies that

---

8. "I am going to take exceptions to the present translation of the Bible in relation to these matters [interpreting prophecy]. Our latitude and longitude can be determined in the original Hebrew with far greater accuracy than in the English version. There is a grand distinction between the actual meaning of the prophets and the present translations." Ibid., 290–91.

9. Ibid., 310.

10. Adopting the term from Marc Zvi Brettler in *How to Read the Bible*, 1.

11. James Kugel, *The Bible as it Was*, 20.

appear in places like Genesis's two creation stories. As a result of intellectual movements in the seventeenth century, the Western world that Joseph Smith inherited experienced a profound transformation that impacted the way many Americans read the Bible, including the Prophet. European rationalism transformed the traditional approach of interpreting the Bible as privileged text. During this era, several European philosophers who considered reason to be the ultimate source for human knowledge began questioning many long-held assumptions regarding the Bible, including the concept of biblical inerrancy.

Rather than reading the Bible as a scriptural text that requires its own special rules to explain or cover-up inconsistencies, these philosophers interpreted the text according to the standard rules of logic. For example, a slave law in Exodus 21:6 states that some slaves should serve their masters "forever." This statement, however, directly contradicts the slave law in Leviticus 24:40, which states that all slaves must be released every fiftieth year (the year of Jubilee). Not wanting to see these laws as contradictions, Jewish rabbis attempted to reconcile the two passages by stating that the word "forever" really means "practically, but not literally 'forever'"—in other words, simply until the year of Jubilee.[12] In contrast to this approach, which had been adopted by Jewish and Christian interpreters alike, European rationalists such as Thomas Hobbes and Thomas Paine argued that if a text like Exodus 21 said "forever," it should be read as "forever," and that the two laws were simply at odds with one another. In other words, they began to treat the Bible like a *real* book that could contain historical anachronisms and inconsistencies.[13] It was not simply inerrant scripture that needed to be harmonized.

---

12. See Brettler, *How to Read the Bible*, 2.

13. New Testament scholar Bart Ehrman expresses this notion of the Bible as a "real book" rather than inerrant scripture with these words: "Since the Bible is a book, it makes better sense to approach it the way one approaches books. There are certainly books in the world that don't have any mistakes in them. But no one would insist that a particular phone book, chemistry textbook, or car instruction manual has absolutely no mistakes in it before reading it to see whether it does or not. Rather than thinking that the Bible cannot have mistakes, before looking to see if it does, why not see if it does, and only then decide whether it could. . . . If God created an error-free book then it should be without errors. If what we have is not an error-free book, then it is not a book that God has delivered to us without errors." Bart D. Ehrman, *Forged: Writing in the Name of God—Why the Bible's Authors Are Not Who We Think They Are*, 117.

Moses as Biblical Author

According to the traditional Jewish and Christian assumption, the Prophet Moses wrote the Bible's first five books. This tradition developed early in Jewish history. The Bible itself states that Moses stayed on Mount Sinai in the presence of God for forty days and forty nights (Ex. 24:18, 34:28; Deut. 9:9, 10:10). Jewish interpreters came to the conclusion that this was too long of a period for Moses to have only received the laws that the Bible itself identifies as the revelation Moses received from God.[14] Surely, they reasoned, in forty days time, Moses must have received more. Traditions, therefore, developed that Moses received the entire written Pentateuch, Genesis through Deuteronomy, at this time. Eventually, Jewish rabbis even expanded this view to include the entire oral tradition that provided an authoritative interpretation of the written law.

The first book in the Old Testament, traditionally attributed to Moses, is known in English by the name "Genesis" (meaning "Origin"). Genesis receives its name from the Greek translation of the Old Testament known as the Septuagint. Its Hebrew name derives from the book's first word *bereishit*, translated by the English phrase "In the beginning" in the KJV.[15] This is an appropriate title for this work, since Genesis truly is a book about beginnings. It starts with "prehistory," the story of human beings prior to the rise of the "historical" era when the world operated according to the rules and standards of the book's author(s).[16] Genesis 1–11 tells the story of creation and the beginning of human society in mythic terms (with creations, forbidden fruit, talking serpents, and universal floods). Genesis 12 begins the story of Abraham and the historical age, with the beginning of God's chosen family Israel.

The Bible's second book, Exodus, continues this narrative by telling how the family was enslaved in Egypt and eventually freed by impressive miracles performed by Moses. Like the title "Genesis," the English name "Exodus" (meaning "Departure") derives from the early Greek translation of the Old Testament. The Hebrew title, *Sefer ve'eleh shemot* "the book of

---

14. Marc Zvi Brettler, "Torah," 2.

15. See Jon D. Levenson, "Genesis: Introduction," 8–11.

16. Tzvi Abusch has argued regarding the opening chapters of Genesis: "[T]he emergence of the present order is told in terms of the development of the relationship between humankind and God." See Abusch, "Biblical Accounts of Prehistory: Their Meaning and Formation," 2.

'And these are the names'" stems from the text's opening words.[17] In addition to its narrative, Exodus contains a section of laws and a detailed description of the portable temple carried by the Israelites as they journeyed through the wilderness.

The third book in the Bible is known in English by the title "Leviticus," from the Greek *Leuitikos*, meaning "relating to the Levites." Its Hebrew name is *torat kohanim* "the instruction of (or 'for') the priests."[18] In addition to its laws, Leviticus features a detailed account of sacrifices and rituals connected with Israelite temple worship. Unlike the books of Genesis and Exodus, Leviticus is presented as an actual revelation given to the prophet Moses.

The Bible's fourth book is known in English as Numbers. This English name also derives from the Greek Septuagint. The name Numbers refers to the fact that the book's first four chapters feature censuses. Its Hebrew name *Bemidbar* "in the wilderness [of Sinai]," is taken from the fifth Hebrew word in the first chapter.[19] Numbers continues the story of Israel's wilderness travels by recounting some of the remarkable events the Israelites experienced prior to their arrival at the plains of Moab, just opposite of the promised land.

The fifth book in the Bible is referred to in English as Deuteronomy, meaning "Second Law." The book's Hebrew name is *devarim* meaning "words" (and, again, it stems from the book's opening phrase in the original Hebrew).[20] Deuteronomy is presented as the words of Moses spoken to the Israelites immediately prior to their entry into the land of promise. It is both a repetition and revision of many of the earlier biblical laws.

These five books make up what Christian scholars refer to as the "Pentateuch," a Greek term meaning "five books." In ancient and modern Judaism, this collection is known as the "Torah," meaning "Law," or perhaps better "Instruction." But no matter what title the collection was given by early Jews and Christians, tradition held that the prophet Moses was the author of these books and that he had written them all without any error.

European rationalism challenged this long-held assumption. In his highly influential seventeenth-century work, *Leviathan*, Thomas Hobbes cited several biblical passages, including Deuteronomy 34:5–6, as proof that Deuteronomy was not written by Moses. The verses state:

---

17. See Jeffrey H. Tigay, "Exodus: Introduction," 102–7.
18. See Baruch J. Schwartz, "Leviticus Introduction," 203–6.
19. See Nili S. Fox, "Leviticus: Introduction," 281–84.
20. See Bernard M. Levinson, "Deuteronomy: Introduction," 356–63.

So Moses the servant of the LORD died there in the land of Moab, according to the word of the LORD. And he buried him in a valley in the land of Moab, over against Beth-peor: but no man knoweth of his sepulchre unto this day.

Significantly, this same section from Deuteronomy that refers to Moses' death also features the statement, "and there arose not a prophet *since* in Israel like unto Moses" (34:10). Surely, Hobbes reasoned, Moses could not have written these statements concerning himself that specifically point toward future historical events.[21] Hobbes collected additional textual information to support his argument, including the fact that on other occasions the first five books of the Bible state that something or another has occurred "to this day." (See, for example, Deut. 2:22, 3:14.) If Moses had truly written these accounts, how could he refer to an event that happened in his own lifetime as something that continues to occur "to this day"? The language clearly shows that this was not Moses discussing the continuation of things into the future, but is written by someone looking back on history.

Subsequently, others discovered more evidence that refuted the long-held assumption of Mosaic authorship. For example, the first five books of the Bible include the presence of historical anachronisms, allusions to names or events that occur after the death of Moses. British philosopher Thomas Paine discussed some of these anachronisms in his book, *The Age of Reason*. During the time of Moses, the biblical city of Dan was apparently known by the name Laish.[22] Judges 18:27–29 indicates that Laish was renamed "Dan" during the time of the Judges in celebration of the Danite conquest. This event occurred long after Moses's day, and yet, Genesis 14:14 states that Abram, who lived hundreds of years before the Danite conquest, pursued his kinsmen's captives "as far as Dan." Paine recognized that according to the Bible's own internal record, this allusion to Dan could not possibly have been written by Moses, "the humblest man on earth" (Num. 12:3)—an expression which in and of itself indicates that Moses probably did not write *this* particular line.[23]

European rationalists also demonstrated that the Pentateuchal stories feature a variety of strange narrative duplications and changes of style and

---

21. Thomas Hobbes, *Leviathan with Selected Variants from the Latin of 1668*, 252–53.

22. Thomas Paine, *The Age of Reason, Being an Investigation of True and Fabulous Theology (Part 1 and 2)*, 116–17.

23. As Richard Elliott Friedman notes, "normally one would not expect the humblest man on earth to point out that he is the humblest man on earth" in *Who Wrote the Bible?* 18.

language. When the Bible was read as a real book (rather than inerrant scripture), scholars found repetitions and inconsistencies throughout the entire course of the Pentateuch. Abraham enters into two covenants with God (Gen. 15 and 17). Jacob leaves home two different times and for two different reasons (Gen. 27:43–45 and 27:46–28:9). God reveals his name as Yahweh to Moses twice (Ex. 3:13–16 and 6:2–3). Moses and Aaron draw water from the rock two times (Ex. 17:1–7 and Num. 20:1–6), and so on. Therefore, it is not simply creation that is told two different times and in two separate ways, we actually find the same thing happening in biblical story after biblical story. For European rationalists, these repetitions and inconsistencies suggested that the accounts were written by a variety of different authors, not just Moses.

The Legal Collections

The traditional assumption that Moses or any other single individual was the author of the Bible's first five books also proves problematic when considering the types of inconsistencies and contradictions that occur within the Bible's legal collections.[24] In the Pentateuch, biblical laws appear in three distinct literary blocks: first, Exodus 20–23 (the Covenant Code); second, Leviticus and Numbers (the Priestly Code); and third, Deuteronomy 12–26 (the Deuteronomic Code). All three blocks of legal texts feature repetitions. Each block contains laws concerning the Israelite festival calendar, slavery, and asylum (meaning a place offering protection or escape). Two of the collections feature prohibitions against boiling a kid in its mother's own milk; two of them contain altar laws; two include kosher laws, and finally, two of the blocks feature laws regarding tithing. These repetitions are clearly redundant. Why would a single author go to all that effort in producing legal collections just to repeat the same laws over again?

Moreover, the inconsistencies in the laws suggest that these legal blocks derive from separate authors who held different perspectives on how a society should seek to maintain divine order. For instance, the biblical laws concerning slavery contradict one another. The laws in Exodus 21:2–6 address the issue of debt service for Israelite or Hebrew slaves. Verse 2 makes it clear that following six years of service, a male Israelite slave must be set free by his master: "If thou buy an Hebrew servant, six years he shall serve: and in the seventh he shall go out free for nothing."

---

24. For a general survey on interpreting biblical law in Near Eastern contexts, see John W. Welch, *The Legal Cases in the Book of Mormon*, 3–18.

Verse 4 states that if during that time of service, the slave's master gave him a female slave as a wife, and that the two of them had children, only the man would be allowed to go free: "the wife and her children shall [remain] her master's." The slave laws in Exodus go on to state that, "if a man sells his daughter to be a maidservant, she shall not go out as the menservants do" (v. 7). In other words, the law in Exodus states that male slaves are to be eventually set free, but females are not. "This distinction," observed biblical scholar Martin Noth, "may rest on the view that only the man is a person, while the woman on the other hand is a possession."[25]

The notion that upon his release from slavery, a man could not take his wife and children with him, and that female slaves could never go free, appears to have bothered later biblical authors. A careful reading of the slave laws in Leviticus 25:39–55 and Deuteronomy 15:12–18 reveals intentional changes to the earlier laws in Exodus. Deuteronomy 15:12 specifically rejects the standard in Exodus by stating that in the seventh year, all Hebrew slaves, *including women*, are to be set free: "And if thy brother, an Hebrew man, *or an Hebrew woman*, be sold unto thee, and serve thee six years; then in the seventh year thou shalt let him go free from thee." In Exodus, only the male servant needed to pass through the ritual performance of having his ear pierced with an awl if he decided to remain a servant for life (presumably to keep his wife and children), since a female Israelite was already considered a slave "for life." Significantly, in Deuteronomy's revision of the ritual, the law sets female slaves free in the seventh year. Concerning the ear piercing ritual described in Exodus, the text then specifically adds the phrase missing in the earlier law: "and also unto thy maidservant thou shalt do likewise" (Deut. 15:17). These are real differences, and these variations in the concept of justice and slavery in Israelite society suggest the possibility that different authors with conflicting views wrote these texts.

Other disparities in the slave laws exist. The slave law in Deuteronomy states that when a Hebrew slave is set free, the slave owner must provide his former servant with a significant parting gift. This was a merciful law designed to ensure that the impoverished person did not immediately return to debt slavery:

> And when thou sendest him out free from thee, thou shalt not let him go away empty: Thou shalt furnish him liberally out of thy flock, and out of thy floor, and out of thy winepress: of that wherewith the LORD thy God hath blessed

---

25. Martin Noth, *Exodus: A Commentary*, 177.

thee thou shalt give unto him. And thou shalt remember that thou wast a bondman in the land of Egypt, and the LORD thy God. (Deut. 15:13–15)

This directly contradicts the earlier law in Exodus, which states that when a male slave is released from his service after seven years, he shall go out "without taking compensation" (Ex. 21:2).[26]

Both of these slave laws, however, contradict their legal counterpart in the Book of Leviticus. Unlike what we find in Exodus and Deuteronomy, the slave laws in Leviticus place debt release in the calendar year of Jubilee, at the end of seven cycles. This means that debt release took place during the fiftieth year rather than the seventh year of the slave's service (Lev. 25:13). In fact, in the version of the law presented in Leviticus, the text insists that the poor Israelite should not to be considered a slave but instead treated as a laborer. The view found in Leviticus contrasts what appears in Exodus and Deuteronomy—an Israelite cannot be sold as a slave since Israelites were already considered "slaves" to Yahweh.[27]

These types of contradictions are not at all unusual; in fact, they are very much the norm. Since these earlier laws were considered sacred revelations, a later author could not simply toss them aside. Instead, he changed the way audiences read them, which explains why the laws repeat themselves on various topics.[28]

Ancient legal collections from outside of Israel yet created in the biblical world show that laws often served as a type of scribal curriculum for learning to write and process texts. And that often times, a direct literary dependency can be established between separate collections.[29] These biblical laws on slavery

---

26. The Hebrew word *ḥinah* can mean either without "giving" or without "taking" compensation. Though the grammar is ambiguous, since the man's six-year service constituted his "giving," the text clearly refers to the slave not *taking* compensation. The New American Standard Bible translates this: "If you buy a Hebrew slave, he shall serve for six years; but on the seventh he shall go out as a free man without payment."

27. Jeffrey Stackert, *Rewriting the Torah: Literary Revision in Deuteronomy and the Holiness Legislation*, 143.

28. Historically, rather than an account of spiritual versus physical creation, the same process may be happening in the two creation stories in Genesis 1 and 2.

29. For example, the order of marriage laws in the cuneiform collection from Mesopotamia known as the Laws of Eshnunna (ca. 1930 BC), were reused and expanded in various topics in the famous Laws of Hammurabi. The Laws of Hammurabi still preserve the basic structure and sequence of this earlier collection. See B. L. Eichler, "Literary Structure in the Laws of Eshnunna," 83.

appear to reflect this pattern. For instance, the laws in Deuteronomy 12 intentionally revise prior Israelite laws from the Book of Exodus.[30] In Deuteronomy, God commands Israel to centralize sacrificial worship in the city and temple of Jerusalem. This was not consistent with the way ancient Israelites acted in either the biblical narrative or in the archeological record. Instead, we find that for much of their history, Israelites worshiped in the way Lehi did in the Book of Mormon—offering sacrifice in places outside of Jerusalem (1 Ne. 2:7, 5:9, 7:22). The author of the legal material in Deuteronomy wanted to put an end to these types of performances, but faced a difficult task. Earlier biblical legal collections like the laws in Exodus 20:19–23:33 allowed for sacrifice outside of Jerusalem and had already taken on a type of scriptural authority for the Israelite community.[31] Therefore, the scribal authors of texts such as Deuteronomy 12 rewrote the earlier biblical laws that opposed their centralization efforts. For example, compare

> An altar of earth thou shalt make unto me, and shalt sacrifice thereon thy burnt offerings, and thy peace offerings, thy sheep, and thine oxen: *in every place* where I record my name I will come unto thee, and I will bless thee. (Ex. 20:24; emphasis added)[32]

with

> Take heed to thyself that thou offer not thy burnt offerings *in every place* that thou seest: But *in the place* which the LORD shall choose in one of thy tribes, there thou shalt offer thy burnt offerings, and there thou shalt do all that I command thee. (Deut. 12:13–14; emphasis added)

The law in Deuteronomy changed the earlier mandate in Exodus, which allowed sacrifice "in every place" God puts his name, to only "the place" that God chose—Jerusalem. In doing so, it takes the phrase "in every place" from Exodus and uses that exact line to prohibit precisely what

---

30. See, for example, Bernard M. Levinson, *Deuteronomy and the Hermeneutics of Legal Innovation,* 27.

31. "The pursuit of pentateuchal sources is born of a certain fidelity to those patient authors, editors, transmitters, scribes, or copyists who produced the biblical texts. The features in the texts that allow traditions to be traced, sources to be analyzed, and so on, hardly exist by chance. It would have been all too easy for the copyist's pen to have reduced them to uniformity. Today we may argue over the significance of the diversity and duality in the text but we are faithful to the spirit of its authors in trying to recover in all its contours the meaning of the text they created, shaped, and gave to us." Anthony F. Campbell and Mark A. O'Brien, *Sources of the Pentateuch,* xiv.

32. The KJV renders the Hebrew phrase as "in all places."

Exodus *allowed* (i.e., offering sacrifices in places outside of Jerusalem). Because of this literary switch in using the same words from opposing reasons, when a reader goes back and looks at the altar law in Exodus, she can be confused in assuming that the altar law in Deuteronomy and Exodus were written to make the same point.

A similar process occurs with some other biblical laws as well. Exodus 21:12 features a legal statement instituting capital punishment for taking a human life, followed by a series of conditions pertaining to the intentionality of the killer. It appears that this law was also reformulated to reflect the religious standards of later biblical authors. The earlier laws of Exodus identify altars as places of refuge where someone who had unintentionally committed manslaughter could seek asylum:

> He that smiteth a man, so that he die, shall be surely put to death. And if a man lie not in wait, but God deliver him into his hand; then I will appoint thee a place whither he shall flee.[14] But if a man come presumptuously upon his neighbour, to slay him with guile; thou shalt take him from mine altar, that he may die. (Ex. 21:12–13)

The altar was used this way in 1 Kings 1:50–51 and 2:28, where Solomon's enemies Adonijah and Joab flee to the tabernacle and grab "hold on the horns of the altar" in hopes of temporary asylum, though with different results. Interestingly, the Book of Mormon identifies the altar as a place where people could seek deliverance, albeit in a spiritual sense.[33] Alma 15:17 notes that after Alma established the church at Sidom, the people "began to humble themselves before God, and began to assemble themselves together at their sanctuaries to worship God *before the altar*, watching and praying continually, that they might be *delivered from Satan, and from death, and from destruction*." This verse conceptually invokes a long-held Israelite custom by identifying the altar as a location of deliverance from death.[34]

This view, however, is changed in Deuteronomy. Since the later laws of centralization attempted to get rid of all local Israelite altars and replace them with the Jerusalem temple ("the place" God chose for sacrifice), the authors of the laws in Deuteronomy needed to provide a substitute for the altar. So instead of altars serving as places of asylum for a killer, Deuteronomy establishes three cities of refuge:

> Thou shalt separate three cities for thee in the midst of thy land, which the LORD thy God giveth thee to possess it. Thou shalt prepare thee a way,

---

33. See Bokovoy and Tvedtnes, *Testaments*, 166–67.
34. See the analysis on Abraham's escape from the altar in Chapter 8.

and divide the coasts of thy land, which the LORD thy God giveth thee to inherit, into three parts, that every slayer may flee thither. And this is the case of the slayer, which shall flee thither, that he may live: Whoso killeth his neighbour ignorantly, whom he hated not in time past; As when a man goeth into the wood with his neighbour to hew wood, and his hand fetcheth a stroke with the axe to cut down the tree, and the head slippeth from the helve, and lighteth upon his neighbour, that he die; he shall flee unto one of those cities, and live: Lest the avenger of the blood pursue the slayer, while his heart is hot, and overtake him, because the way is long, and slay him; whereas he was not worthy of death, inasmuch as he hated him not in time past. Wherefore I command thee, saying, Thou shalt separate three cities for thee. (Deut. 19:2–7)

These biblical laws reveal a type of evolutionary development. In early Israelite and Judean practice, local altars throughout the land of Israel served as places of asylum where a person could escape death temporally (hence the law in Exodus). Later religious views interpreted these localized altars as "corrupt" since the altars were not in Jerusalem. Thus the law in Deuteronomy was developed to replace the earlier altar-asylum law with "cities" of refuge.

This only scratches the surface with discrepancies and revisions in biblical laws. In the Bible, we find laws such as in Exodus 12:8–9, which states that the Passover offering must be roasted, not boiled (*b-š-l*) in water, while according to Deuteronomy 16:7, the offering *is* to be boiled (*b-š-l*). Some biblical authors felt a need to harmonize these types of discrepancies, just as later Jewish and Christian interpreters of the Bible would for centuries. To harmonize these Passover laws (one which states that the offering should be *roasted* in fire, and the other that the offering should be *boiled* in water), the very late author of Chronicles creatively combined the two statements by writing that "they boiled (*b-š-l*) the Passover offering in fire" (2 Chr. 35:16). But, boiling in fire does not make sense. It does, however, provide a creative solution to the problem of having two different laws giving two different commandments. It seems illogical that these laws were all written by the same author. It makes more sense that they represent different ideas from separate historical time periods in Israelite and Judean history.

The scribes working with these legal texts considered them to be sacred revelations. Rather than throwing out earlier scriptural traditions, later authors altered the sources to reflect their new religious values and to cause audiences to reread the previous legal collections in accordance with these standards. Biblical scholar Michael Fishbane explained this process with words quite similar to those cited earlier from Joseph Smith:

Theological changes [in the Old Testament] underscore the fact that those persons most responsible for maintaining the orthography of the texts tampered with their wording so as to preserve the religious dignity of these documents according to contemporary theological tastes.[35]

Changes to biblical texts are attested both in terms of the actual documents themselves and through the adoption and reformulation of previous words and phrases in the creation of new sources. Ultimately, it was out of sacred respect for this material that scribes compiled these sources into a single narrative.

Conclusion

Throughout the centuries, many people viewed the Bible as an "inerrant" book. However, as Joseph Smith recognized, the Old Testament opens with two separate stories concerning the creation that clearly compete with each other. These types of repetitions and contradictions appear in other places throughout the Pentateuch. Doublets occur with Abraham's covenants with God, Jacob leaving home, God revealing his name to Moses, Moses and Aaron drawing water from the rock, and so forth. The legal blocks in the first five books feature similar repetitions.

Since religious readers of the Bible traditionally assumed that all of this diverse material had been written by Moses, there was a tendency to harmonize the differences found in these various texts. All of this changed, however, with the rise of European rationalism. The more readers deprivileged the Bible and allowed the Old Testament to literally mean what it says, they began to witness that the doublets in the biblical narrative frequently contradict one another. Often the later source shows signs that its author was aware of the previous version of the earlier story or law. The subsequent author tried to intentionally counter the earlier source through his new literary creation.

When combined with the historical anachronisms (including Moses' death) that appear throughout the Pentateuch, it seems likely that these books were written by various individuals long after the Prophet Moses. If we are going to make sense of these issues, we must follow the lead of Joseph Smith and the earlier European rationalists who influenced his world-view and begin an intellectual journey that takes the contradictions between these texts seriously.

---

35. Michael Fishbane, *Biblical Interpretation in Ancient Israel*, 67.

Chapter Two

Documentary Sources in the Pentateuch

Introduction

At approximately the same time that Joseph Smith was trying to make sense of what he saw as errors in the Bible, European scholars influenced by the previous observations of earlier philosophers such as Thomas Hobbes and Thomas Paine were beginning to work out what would eventually become known as the process of Higher Criticism. This refers to an attempt to explain the types of inconsistencies in the Bible we have witnessed so far by identifying original independent textual sources. As an interpretive tool, Higher Criticism is an important part of what scholars today refer to as the historical-critical method, which refers to an approach to biblical interpretation that seeks to read the text "historically," meaning in accordance with its original historic setting, and "critically," meaning independent from any contemporary theological perspective or agenda. As an expression, "Historical Criticism" is the label that we often use today for mainline biblical scholarship that has been done for roughly the past two centuries.[1] Over the years, the historical-critical method allowed scholars to take seriously the kinds of problematic issues discussed in the previous chapter.

During the life of Joseph Smith, this new "enlightened" approach to reading the Bible produced a German school of interpretation in the theology departments of Protestant universities. The most influential member of this intellectual school was the German scholar Julius Wellhausen. In 1878 (thirty-four years after the death of the Prophet Joseph), Wellhausen synthesized previous scholarly discoveries in Higher Criticism through the

---

1. See John J. Collins, *Bible After Babel: Historical Criticism in a Postmodern Age*, 4.

publication of his highly influential book *Prolegomena to the History of Ancient Israel.*[2] Ultimately, Wellhausen's work did for biblical scholarship what Darwin's *Origin of the Species* accomplished for natural science. As Darwin's concept of evolutionary adaptation through natural selection has become central to modern evolutionary theory, so Wellhausen's work on historical criticism provides the foundation for modern scholarly assessments of the Bible.

In order to take seriously the types of textual and theological problems that Joseph Smith and others observed, *Prolegomena* broke up the Bible, especially its first five books, into separate sources that Wellhausen dated to specific times in Israelite history. Wellhausen then put those sources back together according to his own theory regarding the evolution of Israelite religion. Though in the years that followed, not all of Wellhausen's interpretations of the development of various biblical sources have been accepted, as of today almost all contemporary biblical scholars recognize that the first five books of the Old Testament were not written by a single author and that they are in fact a compilation of separate sources composed by different schools of thought.

The Documentary Hypothesis

The approach to biblical interpretation that Wellhausen synthesized has become known as the Documentary Hypothesis. As we discussed in the previous chapter, the Prophet Joseph recognized that the Bible begins with two separate creation accounts. The Documentary Hypothesis holds that the first story (Gen. 1–2:4a) is part of a Priestly source (abbreviated

---

2. Historically, the identification of textual duplicates led to the view of the Pentateuch as an amalgamation of separate sources. An early advocate of this position was Richard Simon (1638–1712). Simon maintained that the Pentateuch consisted of various documents, some of which derived from Moses, but most he attributed to Ezra in the post-exilic period. Following Simon, Jean Astruc (1684–1766) expressed the view that two separate sources appear in the book of Genesis, one that used Elohim (God) and the other the divine name Yahweh (LORD). In his articulation of source criticism, Astruc argued against the traditional view that Moses compiled the Pentateuch. Astruc's analysis prepared the way for further discussion concerning whether these sources were documents or simply fragments combined from other sources. These studies prepared the way for Wellhausen's ground-breaking synthesis of the Documentary Hypothesis. For a basic history, see Anthony F. Campbell and Mark A. O'Brien, *Sources of the Pentateuch: Texts, Introductions, Annotations*, 1–9.

by source critics "P")[3], and the second (Gen. 2:4b–3) is an earlier historical document called by source critics "J" since the author prefers using
the divine name Yahweh (or Jehovah) for deity. According to the theory,
an ancient editor or redactor brought these two separate sources together
to create the opening chapters of Genesis. When the first five books of
the Bible are read in a way that *allows for* instead of *harmonizes* the types
of internal inconsistencies cited in the previous chapter, we witness that
the distinct literary fragments in the Pentateuch can be tied together to
form not just two, but rather four individual strands or sources. When
combined, these independent literary units appear internally consistent
in terms of their respective historical claims, distinct vocabulary, and even
unique theological perspectives.

After extracting these four strands from the Pentateuch, each narrative can be read as an originally independent document that recounts the
entire history of the House of Israel in its own unique way. The attestation
of separate documents explains why we encounter so many doublets in
biblical narratives.[4] As one biblical scholar has explained, unless we have
in the Pentateuch a combination of separate documentary sources,

> Why must we be told twice of the corruption of the antediluvian earth
> (Gen. 6:5, 11–12)? Why should Noah be twice commanded to enter the
> ark (Gen. 6:18, 7:1), and why must he do so twice (Gen. 7:7, 13)? Why
> must we be told twice that all life perished (Gen. 7:21, 22–23)? Why should
> Jacob twice receive the name Israel (Gen. 32:29, 35:10)? Why must Yahweh
> tell Moses twice that he has heard Israel's cry (Ex. 3:7, 6:5)? Do we need
> a new plague of *kinnîm* ['gnats'] (Ex. 7:12–15) before *'ārōb* ['swarm'] (Ex.
> 7:15–28), given the apparent synonymity (see Ps. 105:31)? Why should the
> spies twice describe the giants of Canaan (Num. 13:28, 32–33)? Why are
> the Israelites twice condemned to die in the desert (Num. 14:23, 28–35)? *A
> few redundancies might be attributed to different sensibilities on the part of the
> supplementer, a few inconsistencies to absence of mind. A wholesale pattern of
> redundancy and contradiction is another matter.*[5]

The fact that we can successfully separate these doublets and coherently
read through each individual document on its own suggests that at one
point, the four sources that now appear in the Pentateuch originally existed as independent literary units. Each one was a unique composition,
eventually combined together by an editor to create the Pentateuch.

---

3. An explanation for why this source is "Priestly" will be given in Chapter 3.
4. See Chapter 1.
5. William H. Propp, "The Priestly Source Recovered Intact?" 460; emphasis added.

This process by which the first five books of the Bible appear to have come together should not seem at all strange to Latter-day Saints. In order to understand the Documentary Hypothesis we can use the Book of Mormon as an analogy for what scholars believe is happening in the Bible. According to its claims, the Book of Mormon itself is an ancient religious work produced by Israelite authors via a variety of originally separate documentary sources. Originally, the Book of Mormon began with a documentary source written by the prophet Lehi on what the text refers to as the Large Plates. As editor of his father's work, Nephi provides the following description of the Book of Lehi:

> And upon the plates which I made I did engraven the record of my father, and also our journeyings in the wilderness, and the prophecies of my father; and also many of mine own prophecies have I engraven upon them. (1 Ne. 19:1)

At the same time, however, Nephi produced his *own* documentary version of his father's prophecies and their family's journey into the wilderness known as "the small plates." Nephi explains this in his introduction to his own writings:

> And now I, Nephi, do not make a full account of the things which my father hath written, for he hath written many things which he saw in visions and in dreams; and he also hath written many things which he prophesied and spake unto his children, of which I shall not make a full account. But I shall make an account of my proceedings in my days. Behold, I make an abridgment of the record of my father, upon plates which I have made with mine own hands; wherefore, after I have abridged the record of my father then will I make an account of mine own life. (1 Ne. 1:16–17)

According to these statements, Nephi produced two separate documentary sources covering the same time period and even some of the same spiritual manifestations or visions. On the large plates, Nephi engraved his father's documentary source, and on the small plates, Nephi abridged or edited his father's record, adding the document directly into his own narrative account as a single unit. Eventually, an editor named Mormon brought together both of these documents into a single "book" (i.e., the Book of Mormon).

As editor, Mormon gave the title "Book of Lehi" to his abridgment of Nephi's large plates. Throughout his own abridgment of the large plates, Mormon continued this practice of grouping multiple authors together into a single book that he named after the initial author in the collection. For example, even though the sons of Helaman, Nephi, and Lehi, provided most of the source material Mormon used to produce the Book of Helaman, Mormon still gave the book Helaman's name. In fact, Helaman actually dies near the beginning of the collection (see Hel. 3:37).

The Book of Mormon, therefore, claims to be a collection of separate documentary sources originally written by different authors that at times covered the same historical and religious events, albeit from different perspectives. Editors like Mormon and Nephi redacted or compiled these separate documentary accounts into a single narrative. This is similar to what the evidence suggests happened in terms of the development of the Pentateuch. At some point in time, Israelite scribes produced separate versions of their history (many of which covered the same events), and these documentary sources were eventually brought together by an editor that scholars refer to as a redactor.

Perhaps for Latter-day Saints, one of the best examples of an amalgamated scriptural text that accords with the basic view of the Documentary Hypothesis is Doctrine and Covenants 132. In the *Journal of Mormon History*, Danel Bachman wrote a fascinating article illustrating how the Prophet's revelation on plural marriage is in reality three different documents that have been merged together to create a single literary text.[6] Section 132 provides an answer to three different questions Joseph asked God concerning plural marriage. The first question is identified in verse 1:

> Verily, thus saith the Lord unto you my servant Joseph, that inasmuch as you have inquired of my hand to know and understand wherein I, the Lord, justified my servants Abraham, Isaac, and Jacob, as also Moses, David and Solomon, my servants, as touching the principle and doctrine of their having many wives and concubines.

Bachman provides historical evidence that this question would have been asked by Joseph during his work on the inspired translation of Genesis and other Old Testament passages as early as 1830.

However, in Section 132, this revelation concerning polygamy in the Old Testament, is broken up textually in verses 2 through 28. Based upon comments the Prophet made during a meeting of the Nauvoo City Council, Bachman argues that these verses are a separate revelation that answered a question Joseph had regarding the meaning of Jesus's response to the problem posed by the Sadducees in the Gospel of Matthew:[7]

> Therefore, if a man marry him a wife in the world, and he marry her not by me nor by my word, and he covenant with her so long as he is in the world and she with him, their covenant and marriage are not of force when they are

---

6. Danel W. Bachman, "New Light on an Old Hypothesis: The Ohio Origins of the Revelation on Eternal Marriage," 19–32.

7. See Matthew 22:23–30.

dead, and when they are out of the world; therefore, they are not bound by any law when they are out of the world. Therefore, when they are out of the world they neither marry nor are given in marriage; but are appointed angels in heaven, which angels are ministering servants, to minister for those who are worthy of a far more, and an exceeding, and an eternal weight of glory. For these angels did not abide my law; therefore, they cannot be enlarged, but remain separately and singly, without exaltation, in their saved condition, to all eternity; and from henceforth are not gods, but are angels of God forever and ever. (D&C 132:15–17)

Then, beginning with verse 29, the account returns to the original revelation, answering Joseph's first question:

Abraham received all things, whatsoever he received, by revelation and commandment, by my word, saith the Lord, and hath entered into his exaltation and sitteth upon his throne. . . . God commanded Abraham, and Sarah gave Hagar to Abraham to wife. And why did she do it? Because this was the law; and from Hagar sprang many people. This, therefore, was fulfilling, among other things, the promises. Was Abraham, therefore, under condemnation? Verily I say unto you, Nay; for I, the Lord, commanded it. (D&C 132: 29, 34–35)

Finally, verses 41 through 50 represent a third and separate revelation Joseph received, and Bachman argues that this revelation came to Joseph in Nauvoo, most likely in response to questions he and Emma had regarding the definition of adultery in view of plural marriage. The revelation makes this clear through the line: "And as ye have asked concerning adultery . . ." (v. 41). Bachman's study, therefore, presents modern scripture that partially reflects the development of the Pentateuch according to the Documentary Hypothesis.

The fact is that this process of putting together a single book by splicing together multiple sources is well attested in history. In order to illustrate the Documentary Hypothesis at work, scholars outside the LDS Church have identified a number of real-life examples of a composite source like the Pentateuch in which "various stages of its development can be documented with versions from two or more stages of its history."[8] In these examples, comparing the separate stages of the text to one another allows scholars to witness the ways ancient sources develop over time in a manner that actually parallels precisely what we see happening in the Pentateuch.

---

8. Jeffrey H. Tigay, "The Documentary Hypothesis, Empirical Models and Holistic Interpretation," 120; see also, Jeffrey H. Tigay, *Empirical Models for Biblical Criticism* (Eugene, Ore.: Wipf & Stock Pub, 2005).

The editorial process of bringing together separate, distinct texts into a single literary unit has also been shown to occur, for example, in a variety of ancient Near Eastern sources, including the famous Mesopotamian Epic of Gilgamesh.[9] Yet by simply turning to the Bible itself, we actually can witness this process occurring in terms of the development of real biblical sources.

The Hebrew version of Jeremiah used to produce the King James Version, known as the Masoretic text, is longer than the Greek version found in the Septuagint (the version of the Old Testament used by the early Christian Church).[10] This shows that the biblical Book of Jeremiah was a composite work put together by an editor, and that as a collection of separate sources, the Book of Jeremiah developed over time. Another example from the Bible is the story of David and Goliath in 1 Samuel 17, in which certain problematic verses in the Hebrew text do not appear in the Greek Septuagint.[11] This seems to illustrate, again, that those verses derive from alternate forms of the biblical narrative and that the Hebrew version found in our Bible today derives from a compilation of these separate sources. What is even more interesting in terms of the Documentary Hypothesis is the fact that in the version of the Bible used by the Samaritans, the two independent narratives that tell the story of Moses choosing judges in Exodus 18 and Deuteronomy 1 appear literally spliced together as a single literary unit by an ancient editor (i.e., the exact process theorized by scholars for the development of the Hebrew version of the Pentateuch in the Documentary Hypothesis).[12] Moreover, in the Samaritan version of the Pentateuch, we find the same thing was actually done to the two separate Mount Sinai stories from Exodus 20 and Deuteronomy 5. So not only does the concept of separate documentary sources appearing in the Pentateuch make sense of the types of inconsistencies that appear in the text, the theory can actually be seen at work in sources from the Book of Mormon to the Samaritan Pentateuch.

---

9. See Jeffrey H. Tigay, *The Evolution of the Gilgamesh Epic* (Wauconda, Ill.: Bolchazy-Carducci Publishers, Inc., 2002).

10. The Greek version of Jeremiah is about an eighth shorter than the Hebrew text; however, the Septuagint includes two sections not found in the Hebrew version: the writings of Baruch (Jeremiah's scribe) and a letter attributed to Jeremiah. Later versions of the Septuagint and the Latin Vulgate Bibles eventually separated these portions from the book and included them with the Apocrypha.

11. See Tigay, "The Documentary Hypothesis," 120.

12. See ibid., 123–24.

And in reality, there are many more examples of this same editorial process in terms of other ancient and even modern religious books. In the second century AD, the early Christian apologist and Syrian bishop, Tatian, composed a single biographical narrative about Jesus known as the *Diatessaron* by literally splicing together the four separate gospels of Matthew, Mark, Luke, and John.[13] In his efforts to create a single unified story, Tatian used the same basic technique that scholars believe an editor used to create the first five books of the Bible.[14] In terms of Tatian's composite text, we encounter the story of Jesus' birth this way:

> Then Joseph her husband, being a just man, and not willing to make her a publick example, was minded to put her away privily. But while he thought on these things, behold, the angel of the Lord appeared unto him in a dream, saying, Joseph, thou son of David, fear not to take unto thee Mary thy wife: for that which is conceived in her is of the Holy Ghost. And she shall bring forth a son, and thou shalt call his name JESUS: for he shall save his people from their sins. Now all this was done, that it might be fulfilled which was spoken of the Lord by the prophet, saying, Behold, a virgin shall be with child, and shall bring forth a son, and they shall call his name Emmanuel, which being interpreted is, God with us. Then Joseph being raised from sleep did as the angel of the Lord had bidden him, and took unto him his wife: And knew her not till she had brought forth her firstborn son: and he called his name JESUS. And it came to pass in those days, that there went out a decree from Caesar Augustus, that all the world should be taxed. (And this taxing was first made when Cyrenius was governor of Syria.) And all went to be taxed, every one into his own city. And Joseph also went up from Galilee, out of the city of Nazareth, into Judaea, unto the city of David, which is called Bethlehem; (because he was of the house and lineage of David:) To be taxed with Mary his espoused wife, being great with child. And so it was, that, while they were there, the days were accomplished that she should be

---

13. For an English translation of Tatian that specifies the Gospel sources see Tatian, *The Diatessaron of Tatian*, trans. Hope W. Hogg (Nabu Press, 2009).

14. "Over a century ago, George Foote Moore pointed out that it would have been possible using the Diatessaron alone to distinguish at least parts of the gospel of John both because that gospel featured a number of unique scenes when compared to the synoptics and because it was/is characterized by a particular set of expressions and theological concepts. John in Diatessaron would be equivalent to "P" in the Pentateuch. In both cases, the given 'source'—John or P—can be distinguished from surrounding material in the Diatessaron or Pentateuch respectively partly because the texts in these strata are saturated with a variety of terminological and conceptual elements that are different from the surrounding material." David M. Carr, *The Formation of the Hebrew Bible: A New Reconstruction*, 109.

delivered. And she brought forth her firstborn son, and wrapped him in swaddling clothes, and laid him in a manger; because there was no room for them in the inn.[15]

Readers familiar with the New Testament Gospels will no doubt immediately recognize that in Tatian's efforts to combine separate sources into a unified story concerning Jesus' birth, Tatian took the first segment from Matthew 1:19–25 and the second literary segment from Luke 2:1–7. The two separate versions of Christ's birth now appear as a single narrative. Moreover, the fact that Tatian combined four documentary sources to create his narrative does provide an interesting parallel with the four sources identified in the Documentary Hypothesis.

The same type of process appears in some of the Dead Sea Scrolls, including the famous Temple Scroll from Qumran.[16] The Judean community composed the Temple Scroll by splicing together sections of Deuteronomy with other biblical texts, creating in the process a single composite source from what we know were originally independent works. And more recently, Jewish scholars Hayim Nachran Bialik and Yehoshua Hana Rawnitzki unintentionally produced an anthology of Jewish legends using this same editorial technique.[17] So the Documentary Hypothesis

---

15. For the sake of familiarity for an LDS audience, I have simply given the KJV of these texts that Tatian unites as a single narrative in his book.

16. See Tigay, *Empirical Models for Biblical Criticism*.

17. Tigay drew attention to this modern day example of the Documentary Hypothesis in a response to an assertion presented by Rabbi Yosef Reinman in the *Biblical Archeology Review*: "I wonder how hard Rabbi Reinman looked before concluding that no book was ever composed this way. In fact, there are several examples, from ancient to modern times, of exactly this process. As Biblical scholars have known since the late 19th century, the second-century Syrian bishop Tatian composed the Diatessaron, a single running biography of Jesus, by splicing together the four Gospels using exactly the same techniques supposed by the Documentary Hypothesis. In the same way, in the version of the Torah used by the Samaritans, the two separate versions of Moses' appointment of subordinate judges found in Exodus 18 and Deuteronomy 1 were spliced together in a single narrative. So were the two Mt. Sinai narratives from Exodus 20 and Deuteronomy 5. The Temple Scroll from Qumran was composed by splicing together passages from Deuteronomy and other books of the Bible plus several extrabiblical works. In modern times, the Hebrew writers Hayim Nachrnan Bialik and Yehoshua Hana Rawnitzki composed their classic anthology of Jewish legends (Sefer Ha-Aggadah) by using very similar techniques. In the 1980s I edited a volume, *Empirical Models for Biblical Criticism*, in which several

(and the Book of Mormon for that matter) is not without other examples of religious books derived from a splicing together of various individual sources. And besides, there has to be *some* reason that we have so many repetitions and inconsistencies running throughout the first five books of the Bible. It all makes perfect sense.

The Flood Story as Composite Narrative

Now that we've discussed several known examples of composite sources, let's look at two accounts from the Book of Genesis that scholars believe are composed of separate stories that have been spliced together by an editor. We will begin with the biblical story of Noah and the ark.[18] The basic plot is well known: God is angry with the earth's inhabitants and sends a catastrophic flood; however, to preserve human existence He has Noah and his family construct a massive ark to be filled with animals. Even though this famous story is really quite basic in some respects, as we witnessed with the sequence of creation events in the opening chapters of the Bible, a careful reading of the story (Gen. 6-8:22) reveals a series of significant narrative challenges that require explanation if we are to truly make sense of the account. For example, Genesis 6:19 states that God commanded Noah to bring with him on the ark animals, "two of every sort . . . male and female." However, as the story continues, we read in 7:2 that God commanded Noah to bring with him *not* "two of every kind, male and female," but rather seven pairs of clean animals and two of the unclean (meaning those that could not rightfully be given to God as a sacrifice). This is only one of several inconsistencies in the story.

Genesis 8:6 tells us that the flood lasted for forty days, yet two verses earlier it states that the waters subsided at the end of a hundred and fifty days. Verse 7 indicates that in order to discover if dry land existed, Noah sent out a raven that did not return. Yet verses 8 and 9 tell us that the bird was actually a dove. If we as readers are to understand the flood story, we must account for these internal inconsistencies that create an incoherent

---

colleagues and I presented these and other examples of such methods. The book was reprinted in 2005 by Wipf and Stock Publishers of Eugene, Oregon. There, readers will see that the methods of composition supposed by the Documentary Hypothesis are very far from being outlandish and unparalleled in the history of the world." Tigay, "Documentary Hypothesis Confirmed," 8, 10.

18. Following Friedman's lead for introducing source criticism in his work *Who Wrote the Bible?* 53–60.

narrative flow. It simply comes down to this: as written, the biblical flood story makes very little sense. Was it a raven? Or was it a dove? Did God command Noah to bring two of every animal, or just two of the unclean? This is where the Documentary Hypothesis provides an impressive solution to our problems.

When we seek to identify some sort of consistent plot that accounts for these issues, two individual narrative strands eventually emerge. The mere fact that it is even possible for us to pull out two distinct narratives, directly from this single story provides strong evidence in support of the Documentary Hypothesis at work. To see how separating the biblical passage creates two distinct narratives, read through the story twice. First read the words not in bold as a unit; then return and read through all of the bolded words:

Chapter 6

[5] And the LORD [Yahweh] saw that the wickedness of man was great in the earth, and that every imagination of the thoughts of his heart was only evil continually. [6] And it repented the LORD that he had made man on the earth, and it grieved him at his heart. [7] And the LORD said, I will destroy man whom I have created from the face of the earth; both man, and beast, and the creeping thing, and the fowls of the air; for it repenteth me that I have made them. [8] But Noah found grace in the eyes of the LORD. [9] **These are the generations of Noah: Noah was a just man and perfect in his generations, and Noah walked with God [Elohim]. [10] And Noah begat three sons, Shem, Ham, and Japheth. [11] The earth also was corrupt before God, and the earth was filled with violence. [12] And God looked upon the earth, and, behold, it was corrupt; for all flesh had corrupted his way upon the earth. [13] And God said unto Noah, The end of all flesh is come before me; for the earth is filled with violence through them; and, behold, I will destroy them with the earth. [14] Make thee an ark of gopher wood; rooms shalt thou make in the ark, and shalt pitch it within and without with pitch. [15] And this is the fashion which thou shalt make it of: The length of the ark shall be three hundred cubits, the breadth of it fifty cubits, and the height of it thirty cubits. [16] A window shalt thou make to the ark, and in a cubit shalt thou finish it above; and the door of the ark shalt thou set in the side thereof; with lower, second, and third stories shalt thou make it. [17] And, behold, I, even I, do bring a flood of waters upon the earth, to destroy all flesh, wherein is the breath of life, from under heaven; and every thing that is in the earth shall die (*gw*ʿ). [18] But with thee will I establish my covenant; and thou shalt come into the ark, thou, and thy sons, and thy wife, and thy sons' wives with thee. [19] And of every**

living thing of all flesh, two of every sort shalt thou bring into the ark, to keep them alive with thee; they shall be male and female. ²⁰ Of fowls after their kind, and of cattle after their kind, of every creeping thing of the earth after his kind, two of every sort shall come unto thee, to keep them alive. ²¹ And take thou unto thee of all food that is eaten, and thou shalt gather it to thee; and it shall be for food for thee, and for them. ²² Thus did Noah; according to all that God commanded him, so did he.

Chapter 7

¹ And the Lord said unto Noah, Come thou and all thy house into the ark; for thee have I seen righteous before me in this generation. ² Of every clean beast thou shalt take to thee by sevens, the male and his female: and of beasts that are not clean by two, the male and his female. ³ Of fowls also of the air by sevens, the male and the female; to keep seed alive upon the face of all the earth. ⁴ For yet seven days, and I will cause it to rain upon the earth forty days and forty nights; and every living substance that I have made will I destroy from off the face of the earth. ⁵ And Noah did according unto all that the Lord commanded him. **⁶ And Noah was six hundred years old when the flood of waters was upon the earth**. ⁷ And Noah went in, and his sons, and his wife, and his sons' wives with him, into the ark, because of the waters of the flood. **⁸ Of clean beasts, and of beasts that are not clean, and of fowls, and of every thing that creepeth upon the earth, ⁹ There went in two and two unto Noah into the ark, the male and the female, as God had commanded Noah.** ¹⁰ And it came to pass after seven days, that the waters of the flood were upon the earth. **¹¹ In the six hundredth year of Noah's life, in the second month, the seventeenth day of the month, the same day were all the fountains of the great deep broken up, and the windows of heaven were opened.** ¹² And the rain was upon the earth forty days and forty nights. **¹³ In the selfsame day entered Noah, and Shem, and Ham, and Japheth, the sons of Noah, and Noah's wife, and the three wives of his sons with them, into the ark; ¹⁴ They, and every beast after his kind, and all the cattle after their kind, and every creeping thing that creepeth upon the earth after his kind, and every fowl after his kind, every bird of every sort. ¹⁵ And they went in unto Noah into the ark, two and two of all flesh, wherein is the breath of life. ¹⁶ And they that went in, went in male and female of all flesh, as God had commanded him:** and the Lord shut him in. ¹⁷ And the flood was forty days upon the earth; and the waters increased, and bare up the ark, and it was lift up above the earth. ¹⁸ And the waters prevailed, and were increased greatly upon the earth; and the ark went upon the face of the waters. ¹⁹ And the waters prevailed exceedingly upon the earth; and all the high hills, that were under the whole heaven, were covered. ²⁰ Fifteen cubits upward did the waters prevail; and

the mountains were covered. ²¹ **And all flesh died (*gwʿ*) that moved upon the earth, both of fowl, and of cattle, and of beast, and of every creeping thing that creepeth upon the earth, and every man:** ²² All in whose nostrils was the breath of life, of all that was in the dry land, died (*mwt*). ²³ And every living substance was destroyed which was upon the face of the ground, both man, and cattle, and) the creeping things, and the fowl of the heaven; and they were destroyed from the earth: and Noah only remained alive, and they that were with him in the ark. ²⁴ **And the waters prevailed upon the earth an hundred and fifty days.**

Chapter 8

¹ **And God remembered Noah, and every living thing, and all the cattle that was with him in the ark: and God made a wind to pass over the earth, and the waters asswaged;** ² **The fountains also of the deep and the windows of heaven were stopped,** and the rain from heaven was restrained; ³ And the waters returned from off the earth continually: **and after the end of the hundred and fifty days the waters were abated.** ⁴ **And the ark rested in the seventh month, on the seventeenth day of the month, upon the mountains of Ararat.** ⁵ **And the waters decreased continually until the tenth month: in the tenth month, on the first day of the month, were the tops of the mountains seen.** ⁶ And it came to pass at the end of forty days, that Noah opened the window of the ark which he had made: ⁷ **And he sent forth a raven, which went forth to and fro, until the waters were dried up from off the earth.** ⁸ Also he sent forth a dove from him, to see if the waters were abated from off the face of the ground; ⁹ But the dove found no rest for the sole of her foot, and she returned unto him into the ark, for the waters were on the face of the whole earth: then he put forth his hand, and took her, and pulled her in unto him into the ark. ¹⁰ And he stayed yet other seven days; and again he sent forth the dove out of the ark; ¹¹ And the dove came in to him in the evening; and, lo, in her mouth was an olive leaf pluckt off: so Noah knew that the waters were abated from off the earth. ¹² And he stayed yet other seven days; and sent forth the dove; which returned not again unto him any more. ¹³ **And it came to pass in the six hundredth and first year, in the first month, the first day of the month, the waters were dried up from off the earth:** and Noah removed the covering of the ark, and looked, and, behold, the face of the ground was dry. ¹⁴ **And in the second month, on the seven and twentieth day of the month, was the earth dried.** ¹⁵ **And God spake unto Noah, saying,** ¹⁶ **Go forth of the ark, thou, and thy wife, and thy sons, and thy sons' wives with thee.** ¹⁷ **Bring forth with thee every living thing that is with thee, of all flesh, both of fowl, and of cattle, and of every creeping thing that creepeth upon the earth; that they may breed**

abundantly in the earth, and be fruitful, and multiply upon the earth. [18] **And Noah went forth, and his sons, and his wife, and his sons' wives with him:** [19] **Every beast, every creeping thing, and every fowl, and whatsoever creepeth upon the earth, after their kinds, went forth out of the ark.** [20] And Noah builded an altar unto the LORD; and took of every clean beast, and of every clean fowl, and offered burnt offerings on the altar. [21] And the LORD smelled a sweet savour; and the LORD said in his heart, I will not again curse the ground any more for man's sake; for the imagination of man's heart is evil from his youth; neither will I again smite any more every thing living, as I have done. [22] While the earth remaineth, seedtime and harvest, and cold and heat, and summer and winter, and day and night shall not cease.

Notice that we can read two separate stories in this one section and that both stories when separated actually make sense. How is this possible unless we really *do* have two separate narratives that have been simply spliced together by an editor? More importantly dividing the flood account into two separate narratives actually resolves all of our problems. The inconsistencies disappear.

Now that the two individual accounts have been separated according to their respective plots and the story's internal problems have been resolved, it is possible for us to dig deeper and uncover each story's unique themes and vocabulary distinctions. In examining these distinct narratives, a variety of secondary elements that are unique to each strand (such as themes, styles, and vocabulary) immediately jump out. Notice that throughout the entire narrative, the second (bolded) source consistently uses the divine name Elohim (translated as "God" in the KJV), whereas the other strand consistently uses the divine name Yahweh (translated as "LORD"). Surely this cannot be a mere coincidence. The second (bolded) narrative refers to the sex of the animals as "male and female" (Gen. 6:19; 7:9, 16), whereas the first narrative uses the terms "the male and his female" (7:2), as well as "male and female." Although in the KJV both narratives use "die" or "died," the bolded document in 6:17 and 7:21 technically states that everything "expired" (*gw'*), while the first strand in 7:22 indicates that everything "died" (*mwt*). This is all highly impressive evidence of textual division. When all is said and done, by extracting two separate stories from the account, we can read each narrative as a coherent document with entirely consistent vocabulary from start to finish, including use of the divine name.

We must remember that this reading stems from a result of problems within the text that require *some* sort of explanation. Genesis 7:4 and 7:12 state that it rained forty days (and nights) whereas 7:24 and 8:3 speak of 150 days, and part of the story indicates that God required Noah to bring two of every animals while another section states that the Lord required Noah to bring seven, and so on. The existence of two separate narratives within the account provides the best solution to these types of narrative inconsistencies. Only after the two stories are untwined, are we as readers able to step back and witness the bigger picture of the incredible thematic and vocabulary unity that arise when the flood story in Genesis is seen as two independent narratives combined by an editor into a single literary unit.

The issue here is not simply that we have two distinct versions of the flood story that have been spliced together. When we compare these two stories side by side, we actually witness the same thing happening here that occurs in the biblical laws—namely, one of the flood stories appears to be aware of the earlier version and is reacting to it. With Deuteronomy, we saw this in terms of the altar laws and asylum, in the flood stories, we see this happening in terms of narrative detail or plot. One of the keys to understanding the way in which these two accounts relate to one another is the second narrative in Genesis 7:8–9:

> Of clean beasts, and of beasts that are not clean, and of fowls, and of every thing that creepeth upon the earth, there went in two and two unto Noah into the ark, the male and the female, as God had commanded Noah.

Here, the source emphasizes that Noah took not only two of every creature with him upon the ark, but specifically two of every clean animal. Again, the word "clean" means something that is fit for sacrifice. So the account really wants its readers to know that Noah *only* needed two clean animals. Only two—*not* seven! In this later revised version Noah would not be offering a sacrifice, and, therefore, would not need additional clean animals for sacrificial offerings. This emphasis seems to be a reaction to the assertion of the earlier source, which states that God gave Noah the following command in 7:2:

> Of every clean beast thou shalt take to thee by sevens, the male and his female: and of beasts that are not clean by two, the male and his female.

The reason that this earlier source has Noah bringing seven of every clean male and female animal species is so that Noah could offer sacrifices following the flood. And this is precisely what Noah did at the end of the source in Genesis 8:20:

> And Noah builded an altar unto the LORD; and took of every clean beast, and of every clean fowl, and offered burnt offerings on the altar.

So it would seem that the second (bolded) source was not only aware of the tradition in which Noah brought seven of every clean animal and offered sacrifice, but that its author chose to give special emphasis to the claim that no additional clean animals were brought onto the ark. After all, the account could have simply just said that Noah brought two of *every* animal. Why go to the effort to specify that Noah brought two of the clean and unclean? Instead, the author goes to great length to make sure we know this, taking the time to distinguish between the two categories; in doing so, he seems to want to correct the earlier version that tells us that Noah brought with him seven of each of the clean and two of each of the unclean.

There is even *more* evidence supporting the conclusion that the second (bolded) source is aware of the other. In Genesis 6:5a, the first documentary source (not bolded) provides a justification for God's decision to flood the earth with this statement:

> And the LORD (Yahweh) *saw* (*r'h*) *that* (*ky*) the wickedness of man was great *in the earth* (*b'rṣ*).

On the other hand, the second (bolded) source seems to be aware of this issue, and it provides its own justification for the flood with a similar statement based upon Genesis 6:12:

> And God (Elohim) *looked* (*r'h*) upon the earth, and, behold, it was corrupt; *for* (*ky*) all flesh had corrupted his way *upon the earth* (*'l hrṣ*).

Even though they use different names for God, the two statements share a lot in common.[19] Both stories depict God performing the act of *seeing* via the exact same Hebrew word (*r'h*). They also both use the same Hebrew word (translated as "that" in the first example and "for" in the second) to identify the evil (*ky*). Finally, both statements include a reference to the evil occurring *on* or *in* the earth. Since these statements derive from two separate narratives, these literary connections surely cannot constitute a mere coincidence. Clearly, one of the accounts knows the other one.

Though subtle, the difference between 6:5a and 6:12 proves quite profound and seems to reflect a specific religious view connected with the issue of sacrifice that led the second source to intentionally change the number of animals in the story. 6:12a features a unique perspective on sin and its ability to "pollute" the earth.[20] Unlike in 6:5a, God sees the

---

19. See the analysis provided by David P. Wright, "Profane Versus Sacrifical Slaughter: The Priestly Recasting of the Yahwist Flood Story," 1–20.

20. Ibid.

effect of sin in 6:12a as a contaminating like force: "God looked upon the earth, and, behold, it was corrupt." Humanity's ability to "corrupt" (*šḥt*) the earth through sin anticipates later Priestly concerns in the Pentateuch regarding sacrifice and human capacity to pollute holy ground, including the tabernacle.[21] All of this makes perfect sense. When we divide up the rest of Genesis in this same manner, we see that the first story derives from a document that has animal sacrifice beginning with Cain and Abel. The second source, however, concerned with Priestly issues and the ability of human sin to pollute the ground does not have animal sacrifice at the beginning of human history; it instead presents this ordinance as an act first introduced by God to Moses and Aaron (i.e., later on in Exodus and Leviticus). That is why we have the clean and unclean difference.

Even more remarkable is the unique way in which these two separate stories conceptualize God. Not only do they each use different divine names (Yahweh and Elohim), but the first source pictures a God who can experience human emotion, including great sadness and even regret (Gen. 6:6–7). The view of deity is really quite similar to the one featured in Joseph Smith's Book of Moses, where Enoch sees God literally weeping over his creations (Moses 7:49).[22] Later in the same biblical source, Yahweh appears in human-like fashion, taking the time to personally close the ark (Gen. 7:16); and like a man seduced by the smell of a good barbeque meal, Yahweh appears in the account's conclusion showing feelings that can be affected by the smell of smoked meat rising through the air (8:21). All of this stands in contrast to the depiction of God in the second narrative, where deity is clearly far less human-like in his actions and certainly much more distant or removed. And when we divide up the Pentateuchal stories according to their individual plots, we find that these types of differences remain consistent throughout each individual retelling of the rise of the House of Israel.

We can actually go back now and look at the first two stories in the Bible that we discussed at the beginning of Chapter 1. Notice that the first creation story, Genesis 1–2:4a, uses the divine name Elohim (translated as "God") all throughout the narrative, just like the second (bolded) story witnessed in the biblical flood narrative. In contrast, the second creation story, beginning in Genesis 2:4b, uses the divine name Yahweh. It's not a

---

21. Ibid.

22. For an exploration of this theological view within Mormonism, see Terryl Givens and Fiona Givens, *The God Who Weeps: How Mormonism Makes Sense of Life* (Salt Lake City: Ensign Peak, 2012).

coincidence that the picture of God Elohim in Genesis 1 is a lot like the view of Elohim in the Priestly version of the flood story, where God is distant and removed—not at all human-like in his other worldly actions. He speaks and the elements obey. The account even goes so far as to use a special unique Hebrew verb for God's creative act to distinguish it from examples of human creation: *bara* (*br*). In contrast, Yahweh (the same name used in the flood story for the God who literally comes down and shuts the door of the ark for Noah) is a lot more human-like in the second creation story. He physically plants a garden, gets down and dirty (so to speak) in the formation of man from the soil, and even chooses to walk around the garden during the cool of the day. The reason that these pairs of stories use the same divine names and feature the same conceptualizations of deity is that they derive from the same documentary sources that have been spliced together to create the Book of Genesis.

Challenges to the Theory

Returning to the flood story, in previous decades some conservative scholars felt a need to argue against the Documentary Hypothesis and make a case for the story's overall textual unity in order to support their theological assumptions regarding the Bible. Israeli scholar Umberto Cassuto, for example, articulated a number of reasons why the story should be treated from his perspective as a single unit.[23] Cassuto claimed to find a "finished structure" in the story of Noah which "cannot possibly be the outcome of the synthesis of fragments culled from various sources; for from such a process there could not have emerged a work so beautiful and harmonious in all its parts and details."[24] The problem with this assessment, however, is that "beauty" is in the eye of the beholder. It certainly cannot be used as an argument for original textual unity. Additionally, if anything, Cassuto's argument serves against the idea that the flood narrative is a collection of various fragments.[25] This says nothing for the fact that the narrative is a

---

23. For a history of early Jewish opposition to the Documentary Hypothesis, see Baruch Schwartz, "The Pentateuch as Scripture and the Challenge of Biblical Criticism: Responses Among Modern Jewish Thinkers and Scholars," 203–29.

24. Umberto Cassuto, *A Commentary on the Book of Genesis Part II: From Noah to Abraham*, 34.

25. In recent years, some European scholars have argued that rather than "documents," much of the Pentateuch is comprised of literary fragments written by different authors. Due to the way that the four major strands can be extracted

synthesis of two separate documents that tell two different versions of the history of the world that can easily be separated from one another and read coherently as individual source threads. While in his efforts, Cassuto provided some interesting literary observations, ultimately the issue still comes down to the fact that his literary analysis leaves readers with a serious problem: if the text was written by the same person as a single narrative, we have no way to make sense of all of the inconsistencies in the plot.

Cassuto's literary efforts to defend the idea of textual unity were then followed by an attempt by biblical scholar F. I. Andersen to identify a chiastic reading of the flood story.[26] The term *chiasmus* refers to a poetic literary device that occasionally appears as a form of poetic repetition in the Bible.[27] Chiasmus is a type of poetic reversal as seen, for example, in the literary form, "the first shall be last and the last shall be first." We won't take the time to reproduce Andersen's chiastic model here. Suffice it to say that at first glance, Andersen's chiastic diagrams look impressive, but on closer examination, many difficulties in his proposed structures quickly emerge. These difficulties include issues regarding the demarcation of literary units and an arbitrary selection on his part of certain types of words as significant, while simply dismissing others (this is actually a frequent problem with attempts to identify extended chiastic structures in the scriptures).[28] As a result, Andersen's structures seem imposed rather than a reflection of true authorial intent.

---

and read as a consistent unit, these theories have failed to affect the North American and Israeli scholarly consensus. The so-called Fragmentary Hypothesis was inaugurated by Johann Severin Vater in his work *Commentar über den Pentateuch: Mit Einleitungen zu den einzelnen Abschnitten, der eingeschalteten Übersetzung von Dr. Alexander Geddes's merkwurdigeren critischen und exegetischen Anmerkungen, und einer Abhandlung über Moses und Verfasser des Pentateuchs*, see especially 393–94. However, as Konrad Schmid notes regarding this recent European trend, "The newer contributions to Pentateuchal research from Europe do not aim at overthrowing the Documentary Hypothesis, rather, they strive to understand the composition of the Pentateuch in the most appropriate terms, which . . . includes 'documentary' elements as well." Konrad Schmid, "Has European Scholarship Abandoned the Documentary Hypothesis? Some Reminders on Its History and Remarks on Its Current Status," 17–18.

26. F. I. Andersen, *The Sentence in Biblical Hebrew*, 39–40, 59.

27. See the studies presented in John W. Welch, ed., *Chiasmus in Antiquity: Structures, Analysis, Exegesis* (Provo: FARMS, 1998).

28. For a complete critique of Andersen's chiastic theory for the flood story, see J. A. Emerton, "An Examination of Some Attempts to Defend the Unity of the

Andersen's analysis was quickly followed by Gordon Wenham, who likewise argued for the unity of the flood narrative by creating his own chiastic structure.[29] The mere fact that entirely different chiastic structures can be seen in this single story probably tells us something about their legitimacy. Like Andersen's effort, Wenham's lengthy chiastic analysis is highly problematic, since many of the events in his lines do not naturally correspond with one another (a point that Wenham himself acknowledges); even more importantly, the length of the units used to create his chiasm vary considerably between about half a verse to several verses. This suggests that if there was truly a single author of the flood story, that author was not nearly as interested in creating the type of symmetry or literary balance that Wenham's structure demands.

In this basic introduction to source criticism, we will not consider in detail the various reasons why the efforts of conservative scholars arguing for textual unity prove problematic. In the end, none of these theories, no matter how intricate, successfully resolves the problem of serious narrative inconsistencies in the biblical account that require some sort of explanation. They simply are there—and they are real.[30]

Thus far, the best way scholars have been able to successfully explain the inconsistencies in the story of Noah's flood is by separating the account into two individual sources. The mere fact that we can even do *that* and not only have the separate stories make sense, but actually witness a strong thematic and vocabulary consistency within the two sources, provides compelling evidence that the documentary analysis of the flood story is correct.

Joseph as Redacted Narrative

Another example of an edited story in Genesis that can be identified as a compilation of two separate sources is the well-known account of Joseph who was sold into slavery by his brothers.[31] According to the story,

---

Flood Narrative in Genesis: Part II," 1–21.

29. G. J. Wenham, "The Coherence of the Flood Narrative," 336–48.

30. In this introduction, we've only considered a few arguments posed by those defending more traditional understandings of the biblical texts. Those readers interested in following up on these criticisms should refer to the footnotes and suggestions for further reading at the conclusion of this book.

31. This section benefits from the analysis provided in Joel S. Baden, *The Composition of the Pentateuch: Renewing the Documentary Hypothesis*, 1–44.

Joseph's father Jacob loved him far more than he did any of Joseph's older siblings. One day, as a result of their intense jealously, Joseph's brothers decided to throw him into a pit. Then one of Joseph's brothers stepped forward and pled for Joseph's life. A band of traders took Joseph to Egypt, and his brothers provided their father Jacob with a torn coat as evidence of Joseph's demise. As readers, we know this story so well, that when we see the actual account in the Bible, our familiarity with the basic narrative often keeps us from witnessing the significant internal problems that the biblical account possesses. But they are there. Just like they were in the biblical flood story.

To begin with, the story mentions the presence of two different groups of foreigners involved in the sale of Joseph: Ishmaelites and Midianites. Genesis 37 presents Judah telling his brothers, "Come, and let us sell [Joseph] to the Ishmeelites, and let not our hand be upon him; for he is our brother and our flesh" (v. 27). The account then indicates that Judah's brothers accepted his proposal. However, before the brothers could even begin the transaction, the subsequent verse states that Midianite merchants arrived upon the scene and that they "lifted up Joseph out of the pit." If we read the story straight through, it would seem that the Midianites interfered with Joseph's brothers' plot and that the Midianites sold Joseph to the Ishmaelites. Verse 28 then states that the Ishmaelites took Joseph with them into Egypt and that they sold Joseph as a slave for "twenty pieces of silver."

This is all a bit problematic in terms of narrative flow, to say the least, but what makes the account even *more* confusing is the fact that its conclusion directly contradicts what we are told in verse 28 about the Ishmaelites, stating that "the Midianites sold [Joseph] into Egypt unto Potiphar, an officer of Pharaoh's, and captain of the guard" (v. 36). And if this wasn't confusing enough, Genesis 39:1 states, "Joseph was brought down to Egypt; and Potiphar, an officer of Pharaoh, captain of the guard, an Egyptian, bought him of the hands *of the Ishmeelites*, which had brought him down thither." What is happening here? Did Ishmaelites or Midianites sell Joseph? When read carefully, the text is actually filled with all sorts of contradictions that need to be explained in order for the story to make sense. Who sold Joseph? And why did the brothers allow the Midianites to take their brother out of the pit when they, that is the brothers, were planning on selling Joseph?

The story features a variety of strange repetitions, awkward transitions, and highly confusing narrative gaps. For example, the brothers seem to come to the conclusion to kill Joseph two separate times, once in Genesis

37:18 and again in verse 20. Reuben's plan to save Joseph by throwing him into a pit (v. 22) is actually the *exact* same plan that the brothers come up with to kill Joseph and dispose of his body (v. 20). Finally, both Reuben and Judah present the same basic argument for not killing Joseph (vv. 22, 27). In sum, when the story is read carefully with attention paid to not only repetitions but also direct contradictions, interpreting the narrative as a single unit leaves readers with what one biblical scholar aptly described as "insurmountable literary problems."[32]

As interpreters, we have to make sense of these issues, and the best way is to simply do what we did with the flood story and divide up the account according to a consistent narrative plot. Once again, this is precisely what the Documentary Hypothesis does. Dividing the account into separate sources works perfectly and resolves our narrative challenges (just as it did for the flood story). However, as we witnessed in terms of the flood story in Genesis, some conservative scholars who have tried to see the story of Joseph as a literary whole have presented complicated arguments for textual unity based on literary analyses of the account. In one of the most famous examples of this effort, J. P. Fokkelmann attempted to do the exact same thing with the story of Joseph that F. I. Andersen and Gordon Wenham did with the flood account: to find a chiastic structure that suggests single authorship.[33] As we saw with Andersen's analysis, however, while such readings can prove interesting, they simply do not address the primary problem of major contradictions in the story. Ultimately, reading chiastic structures into these biblical narratives leaves the serious narrative difficulties unaccounted.

Paying attention to the details, however, allows scholars to extract two separate documents that have been edited together to read as one. One version of the story of Joseph features Reuben trying to convince his brothers to spare Joseph's life; in the other, the brother is Judah. One source depicts the brothers selling Joseph to a group of Ishmaelite traders who bring Joseph down into Egypt; the other depicts a group of Midianite merchants. Thus, through a careful reading of the narrative plots, the two separate stories can easily be separated from one another. As with the story of the flood, reading the respective plots as independent narratives is the only viable solution to resolve the major problems in the text:

---

32. Baden, *Composition of the Pentateuch*, 13.
33. J. P. Fokkelmann, *Reading Biblical Narrative: An Introductory Guide*, 80.

Genesis 37:18–36

¹⁸ And when they saw him afar off, even before he came near unto them, they conspired against him to slay him. ¹⁹ And they said one to another, Behold, this dreamer cometh. ²⁰ Come now therefore, and let us slay him, and cast him into some pit, and we will say, Some evil beast hath devoured him: and we shall see what will become of his dreams. **²¹ And Reuben heard it, and he delivered him out of their hands; and said, Let us not kill him. ²² And Reuben said unto them, Shed no blood, but cast him into this pit that is in the wilderness, and lay no hand upon him; that he might rid him out of their hands, to deliver him to his father again.** ²³ And it came to pass, when Joseph was come unto his brethren, that they stript Joseph out of his coat, his coat of many colours that was on him; **²⁴ And they took him, and cast him into a pit: and the pit was empty, there was no water in it. ²⁵ And they sat down to eat bread:** and they lifted up their eyes and looked, and, behold, a company of Ishmeelites came from Gilead with their camels bearing spicery and balm and myrrh, going to carry it down to Egypt. ²⁶ And Judah said unto his brethren, What profit is it if we slay our brother, and conceal his blood? ²⁷ Come, and let us sell him to the Ishmeelites, and let not our hand be upon him; for he is our brother and our flesh. And his brethren were content. **²⁸ Then there passed by Midianites merchantmen; and they drew and lifted up Joseph out of the pit,** and [they] sold Joseph to the Ishmeelites for twenty pieces of silver: and they brought Joseph into Egypt. **²⁹ And Reuben returned unto the pit; and, behold, Joseph was not in the pit; and he rent his clothes. ³⁰ And he returned unto his brethren, and said, The child is not; and I, whither shall I go?** ³¹ And they took Joseph's coat, and killed a kid of the goats, and dipped the coat in the blood; ³² And they sent the coat of many colours, and they brought it to their father; and said, This have we found: know now whether it be thy son's coat or no. ³³ And he knew it, and said, It is my son's coat; an evil beast hath devoured him; Joseph is without doubt rent in pieces. ³⁴ And Jacob rent his clothes, and put sackcloth upon his loins, and mourned for his son many days. ³⁵ And all his sons and all his daughters rose up to comfort him; but he refused to be comforted; and he said, For I will go down into the grave unto my son mourning. Thus his father wept for him. **³⁶ And the Midianites sold him into Egypt unto Potiphar, an officer of Pharaoh's, and captain of the guard.**

The fact that we can, as demonstrated above, successfully extract two independent stories here that when read separately, not only make better sense, but actually produce a thematic and vocabulary consistency between them provides another compelling witness that separate documentary sources have been spliced together to create the biblical story of Joseph.

Conclusion

The Prophet Joseph Smith felt convinced that the Bible, including its opening books, came to us through scribal activities. He recognized that there were simply too many theological and narrative inconsistencies for this not to be the case. The Documentary Hypothesis is a crucial observation made by scholars taking the Old Testament seriously as a *real* book and recognizing many of the same inconsistencies. By extracting separate scribal sources out of the Bible's first five books, scholars are able to explain why these problems appear. They are the result of the fact that the Pentateuch was produced by various authors who held different views regarding not only Israelite history, but even of God.

Thus far in our analysis, we've really only looked at two major stories from the Book of Genesis. But dividing them up into separate sources is not only possible and resolves their difficulties, it enables us to read each account—each "document"—as coherent independent narratives. We can effectively take the same type of approach to the rest of the Pentateuch and answer almost all of the problems that for many years, critical readers like Joseph Smith have witnessed happening in the Bible's first five books. So Joseph was right. The Pentateuch *is* a scribal compilation. It is composed of separate documentary sources that feature some genuine differences.

Chapter Three

Identifying the Sources

Introduction

In so far as separate documentary sources exist in the Pentateuch, we are left with some interesting questions: what are these documents, who wrote them, and how did they come together in their current form? This is where documentary analysis in the Pentateuch admittedly becomes challenging. It is much easier to identify the separate sources than it is to actually use the documents to recreate a textual history. Scholars have proposed a variety of competing theories to make sense of the data, each of which has its strengths and weaknesses. As it stands now, there is not a consensus to allow us to answer these questions in detail. But the fact that scholars debate some of the specifics pertaining to the history of the sources should not be interpreted as evidence for the theory's weakness. Today, virtually all biblical scholars agree with the fact that separate sources appear in the Pentateuch, and despite the academic debates concerning historical dating and specific textual parameters, there is much that can be known concerning these sources.

Even though tradition held that Moses was the author of the Bible's first five books, the books themselves never directly make that claim. The authorship of Genesis, Exodus, and Numbers is intentionally left anonymous. Leviticus and Deuteronomy are presented as revelations given to Moses, but even these books do not declare that they were written by the Prophet himself. At most, Leviticus and Deuteronomy present themselves as a type of scribal compilation that records the words spoken and sometimes written by Moses.

Archaeologists have uncovered thousands of documents from the world of the Bible. In these texts we almost never encounter an instance in which an author signs his name as the creator of the work.[1] This is one

---

1. Karel van der Toorn, *Scribal Culture: The Making of the Hebrew Bible*, 31–32.

of many ways that ancient Near Eastern books (including those in the Bible) differ from contemporary literary works.[2] The type of anonymity that we encounter in the first five books of the Bible was the norm in Near Eastern literature until the Hellenistic era (ca 321 BC), when later authors were influenced by Greek concepts of authorship. Therefore, the authors of the documentary sources in the Pentateuch are not identified in their sources, nor should we expect them to be.

Picking up on the synthesis of documentary analysis presented by Julius Wellhausen, most contemporary scholars continue to refer to the four major documentary threads in the Pentateuch by the abbreviations P, J, E, and D. These sources were most likely the product of scribal schools, rather than individual authors. When extracted and read separately, each source tells the history of the House of Israel in its own unique way. They also present contradictory views concerning God, humanity, and the universe. The distinct perspectives and vocabulary witnessed in each documentary tradition provides scholars with compelling evidence in support of the Documentary Hypothesis. This chapter explores the unique religious and literary characteristics witnessed in each source and places the documents into a historical context.

The Priestly Source (P)

Scholars refer to the first documentary source that appears in the Bible as "P" (an abbreviation for _Priestly_). Because P is so different from the other documents in the Pentateuch, it is without question the easiest source to identify. Since the time of Wellhausen, biblical scholars have arrived at a virtual consensus on which portions of the Bible derive from this ancient Judean scribal work.[3] P receives its name due to its emphasis on

---

2. Modern books typically contain a title page separated from the main body of the text, which presents the name of the author, the book's publisher, and its publication date. Ancient Near Eastern documents often have a similar feature referred to as a colophon. A colophon is a scribal statement inserted into the conclusion of a text. Most of the examples of these types of documents derive from Mesopotamia. The original author or creator of the story or document is never given. At most, Mesopotamian colophons contain a note identifying the name of the scribal copyist. For a consideration of colophons in the Book of Mormon, see David E. Bokovoy and John A. Tvedtnes, _Testaments: Links Between the Book of Mormon and the Hebrew Bible_, 106–16.

3. David M. Carr, _The Formation of the Hebrew Bible: A New Reconstruction_, 110.

rituals and theology connected with Israelite priests, including dietary law (see Gen. 9:4–6). P features detailed accounts of priestly clothing, temple architecture, sacred objects, and regulations connected with ritual purity.

Scholars debate over the exact date that this source was originally written, though the consensus holds that an early stage of P was probably composed during the sixth century BC.[4] With its elaborate depiction of priestly ordinances and rituals, P was most likely produced by priestly scribes seeking to preserve their understanding of Israelite history and the details pertaining to their temple worship. This may have been in response to the Babylonian destruction of the Jerusalem temple in 586 BC and the Judean exile.

P runs mainly from Genesis through Numbers. However, many scholars believe that some of P appears in Deuteronomy, including its final chapter (Deut. 34).[5] Since the Pentateuch begins with P's creation story and ends with a Priestly account of Moses' death (thereby framing the Pentateuch with P), many scholars believe that a Priestly editor was responsible for compiling the Bible's first five books. As a literary unit, P begins with an account of the creation of the world (Gen. 1–2:4a) and then narrates the subsequent events of "prehistory" (the time before the historical era of the original author), the story of the patriarchs, the Exodus from Egypt, and the Israelite wanderings in the wilderness. Then, after describing these events, P finally concludes with the death of Moses.

Scholars sensibly identify the first creation story in the Bible with P. Like the second flood narrative (the one that was in bold in Chapter 2), the account of creation in Genesis 1 through 2:4a shares much in common with themes that appear in later sections from the Bible concerning sacrifice, the tabernacle, and the importance of maintaining holiness boundaries. Naturally, these are issues that would have deeply concerned a priestly author connected with the Jerusalem temple. Thus, it is in P's version of the flood story that Noah does not bring sacrificial animals into the ark, since he is not technically a priest. P also skips the story of Cain and Abel, which appears in Genesis 4 and describes the first sacrificial offerings.

All of this makes sense. When we read P as a literary unit, its version of Israelite history assumes that sacrifices began when God instituted the rituals at Mount Sinai to be performed by Aaron, the first High Priest. P therefore omits the story of Cain and Abel and makes certain that Noah, a non-priest, only brought two clean animals as well as two that were not (Gen. 7:8).

---

4. Michael Coogan, *The Old Testament: A Historical and Literary Introduction to the Hebrew Scriptures*, 53.

5. Ibid.

Many of the rituals performed by Israelite priests were designed to help maintain proper religious boundaries. Priests were guardians of holy places, time, objects, and individuals. Priestly rites were specifically designed to "put difference between holy and unholy, and between unclean and clean" (Lev. 10:10). It is interesting, therefore, that Genesis 1 focuses upon the importance of the Sabbath day as holy time separated from the other days in the week. This perspective parallels other parts within P where God expresses concern over the separate nature of holiness. "I will maintain my holiness by those who are near me," God states within the priestly source, "and I will maintain my honor before all the people" (Lev. 10:3; my translation).

In fact, P's creation story goes as far as depicting God as a type of holy priest. God creates by separating and establishing proper boundaries, such as light from dark, waters above from waters below, and dry land from water. Similarly, biblical priests helped distinguish ritual boundaries between things clean versus unclean. Biblical scholar Mark Smith explained this priestly perception of God in Genesis 1:

> Like the high priest who turns to the people of the Temple and blesses them, God pronounces the divine blessing over all creatures that have God's life force in them. God's blessing at the primordial beginning of the world will continue for all time.[6]

In P, therefore, God shares much in common with the nature and work of a biblical priest. This specific view of deity is significantly different from the image readers encounter in the Bible's second creation story. God is not simply a gardener like he is in Genesis 2, working with the soil to produce both vegetation and man; instead, God is a priest and the universe is his temple.

Moreover, the creation in Genesis 1 directly parallels the biblical account of building the tabernacle, the predecessor to the temple (the work place of the priest). The story of Israel's experience with Moses at Mount Sinai serves as the primary focus of P's narrative. At Sinai, God revealed his instructions for building his temple/tabernacle and the work that priests would perform within its walls. Israel was to surround the tabernacle, keeping temple ritual as a focus as the people journeyed towards the promised land.

The connection between creation in Genesis 1 and the construction of the tabernacle in P appears through a repetition of key words and phrases in both accounts. Thus, when we read P as a unified documentary source,

---

6. Mark S. Smith, *The Priestly Vision of Genesis 1*, 109.

we find that creation in Genesis 1 foreshadows the creation of the tabernacle in Exodus 39–40. Here are a few of the connections:

1. God gives his instructions for building the tabernacle in six segments with each one beginning with the statement "The LORD said to Moses" (Ex. 25:1; 30:11, 17, 22, 34; 31:1). This parallels the six days of creation in Genesis 1 organized around the expression "And God said . . . " (vv. 3, 6, 9, 11, 14, 20, 24, 26, 28, 29).

2. The seventh creative act in Exodus 31:12 introduces the command to keep the Sabbath day holy. This parallels the six-segment creation formula of God speaking and then resting on the seventh day, His Sabbath, in Genesis 1.

3. At the conclusion to the story of creating the tabernacle, the account ends with the formulaic statement: "Thus was all the work of the tabernacle of the tent of the congregation finished (*klh*)" (Ex. 39:32; see also Ex. 40:33). This parallels the end of the creation of the universe in Genesis 1–2:4a which concludes with the formulaic statement: "And on the seventh day God ended (*klh*) his work which he had made" (Gen. 2:2), with both statements using the exact same Hebrew word.

4. At the conclusion of the tabernacle story, the account states that Moses surveyed his work by *looking*: "And Moses did look (*r'h*) upon all the work, and, behold, they have done it as the LORD had commanded" (Ex. 39:43). We see the same thing happening in Genesis 1 after each creative work: "And God saw (*r'h*) the light, that it was good: and God divided the light from the darkness" (Gen. 1:4). Again, both statements use the exact same Hebrew word.

5. Upon completing the creation of the tabernacle, Moses blessed his people: "And Moses did look upon all the work . . . and Moses blessed (*brk*) them" (Ex. 39:43). Again, we see the same thing happening in Genesis 1, using the same language: "And God blessed (*brk*) them . . ."[7]

These connections read as if the same person wrote the two stories concerning creation and the building of the tabernacle. This observation provides more evidence that a priestly author produced Genesis 1–2:4a. Creation in Genesis 1–2:4a lays the ground work for the specific concerns that an

---

7. See the analysis provided in Smith, *The Priestly Vision of Genesis 1*, 76–77.

Old Testament priestly writer would have in working with holy festivals in a calendar cycle, as well as both Sabbath day and temple worship.

What's more, when P is put together as a documentary source, it omits the biblical stories of Israel's experience at Sinai with Moses receiving the Ten Commandments (as well as the later incident with the golden calf). From P's perspective, none of these events took place. Instead, P's narrative focuses its attention solely upon the tabernacle narrative. Thus, only after God dwells among the Israelites in a portable temple where priestly ordinances can be performed, does God give the Israelites a series of laws. When he does, the laws are those of Leviticus.

In addition to these observations, when we extract P's unique narrative plot, distinct religious themes and literary features become more apparent. For example, more than any other documentary source, P relies heavily on literary structure. As a sacrificial system must maintain proper boundaries, so too, P's narrative maintains distinct textual boundaries. P's creation story appears bracketed with a tight *inclusio* that repeats some of the key words from the beginning of the text in its conclusion in Genesis 2:4a.[8] After creation, P originally continued with the genealogy list in Genesis 5. By connecting 5:1–2 with 2:4a, P would have read:

> In the beginning God created the heaven and the earth. . . . [P's creation story.] These are the generations of the heavens and of the earth when they were created. This is the book of the generations of Adam. In the day that God created man, in the likeness of God made he him; Male and female created he them; and blessed them, and called their name Adam, in the day when they were created . . . [P's story of Adam].

P starts with the creation of the world, where its depiction of the creation of human beings appears in Genesis 1:26–27:

> And God said, Let us make man in our image, after our likeness: and let them have dominion over the fish of the sea, and over the fowl of the air, and over the cattle, and over all the earth, and over every creeping thing that creepeth upon the earth. So God created man in his own image, in the image of God created he him; male and female created he them.

This clearly differs from the second creation story in Genesis 2, where man and woman were created on separate days. In that account the Lord created the man, then he created the animals, and finally the woman out of the man's rib. As we've discussed, the language, themes, and even structure in the creation account in Genesis 1 are all very different from what ap-

---

8. See the analysis presented in Chapter 1 of the present study.

pears in Genesis 2. Instead, Genesis 1 directly parallels the vocabulary and themes found in Genesis 5:1–2.

As the original continuation of P's narrative, Genesis 5:1–2 can be interpreted poetically to read:

> This is the scroll of the generations of Adam.
> On the day God created Adam
> He made him in the likeness of God.
> He created them male and female.
> He blessed them, male and female.
> He called their name Adam
> On the day they were created.

Genesis 5:1–2 parallels the creation of the first humans in 1:26–27. When these two texts are placed back together, textual units can be identified as Genesis 5 introduces a new literary unit in P concerning the man Adam while conceptually referring back to the creation narrative in Genesis 1. The tight textual boundaries within P then continue through all of the "these are the generation . . ." statements in Genesis that signify new literary sections, all of which introduce new units within the text and belong to P.[9] The other sources do not have these same types of textual markers.

In terms of its unique themes, P also contains multiple genealogy lists, which would have served as an important priestly concern, since only those with the proper ancestral lineage could serve as priests. Not surprisingly, the priestly source in Exodus gives special attention and focus to Aaron, the great High Priest. P, for example, tells us that Aaron married a woman from the house of Judah (Ex. 6:23). With this statement, P establishes a familial connection between the royal Davidic monarchy and the Priestly family.[10] This relationship would no doubt elevate the political importance of the priestly caste.

Moreover, in P's story of the Exodus, it is not simply Moses, the prophet, who works wonders in order to deliver Israel from Egypt. Aaron too, the great High Priest of Israel, plays a prominent role. For instance, in Exodus 4:17 (a non-Priestly segment), God tells Moses that Moses's staff (i.e., the very one in his hand) will be used to perform signs in Pharaoh's court: "And thou shalt *take this rod in thine hand*, wherewith thou shalt

---

9. See Matthew A. Thomas, *These Are the Generations: Identity, Covenant, and the 'Toledot' Formula* (New York: T&T Clark, 2011).

10. The most compelling theory is that P was written during the pre-exilic period even though it was not finalized until the Persian era.

do signs" (Ex. 4:17). This statement, however, is directly countered in P's portrayal of staff-miracles, which highlights the role of Aaron. Instead of Moses's staff being used to perform God's signs (the way God intended in Exodus 4:17), it is Aaron's:

> And the LORD spake unto Moses and unto Aaron, saying, When Pharaoh shall speak unto you, saying, Shew a miracle for you: then thou shalt say unto Aaron, Take thy rod, and cast it before Pharaoh, and it shall become a serpent. And Moses and Aaron went in unto Pharaoh, and they did so as the LORD had commanded: and *Aaron cast down his rod* before Pharaoh, and before his servants, and it became a serpent. Then Pharaoh also called the wise men and the sorcerers: now the magicians of Egypt, they also did in like manner with their enchantments. For they cast down every man his rod, and they became serpents: but *Aaron's rod* swallowed up their rods. (Ex. 7:8–12)

This view of Aaron, Israel's great High Priest, as the one who assumed the role of casting down the rod before Pharaoh stands in contrast to the tradition that Moses himself threw down the rod. Of course it would make sense for a priestly author to tell the story of the Exodus with Aaron as an impressive hero. These types of features that appear consistently throughout the narrative when P is extracted and read as a documentary source provide impressive evidence that this segment within the Pentateuch was an originally independent narrative spliced directly into the Bible's first five books.

The Holiness School (H)

For many years, biblical scholars have recognized that a unique collection of priestly laws appears within Leviticus 17–26. Though part of P, this collection stands out from the rest of the priestly source in its linguistic and stylistic features. Although the literary units in this block are introduced with the Priestly formula "the Lord spoke to Moses saying," these sayings are presented as direct speech by God to Israel, together with frequent interjections of the statement "I am the Lord your God."[11] The academic consensus holds that this collection is an originally independent priestly compilation.

Beginning with the work of German scholar August Klostermann in 1893, it has been customary for biblical scholars to refer to this body of legislation as the "Holiness Code."[12] This collection is designated by the letter H (for *holiness*) in order to distinguish it from the other priestly

---

11. John J. Collins, *Introduction to the Hebrew Bible*, 148.
12. August Klostermann, *Der Pentateuch*, 368–418.

material in the Pentateuch. For many years, scholars assumed that this block was produced after P was written and was inserted into P by a later editor. However, subsequent studies have shown that the unique themes and rhetoric that appear in this holiness block extend beyond the laws in Leviticus 17–26.

In 1995, Israeli scholar Israel Knohl published an important study on this issue entitled *The Sanctuary of Silence: The Priestly Torah and the Holiness School*.[13] In his study, Knohl effectively illustrated that H is in reality a literary unit that appears dispersed within P. He further argued that these two sources originally derived from two independent priestly schools. One is the standard P school, which produced what Knohl labeled the "Priestly Torah," and the other H school, which Knohl called the "Holiness School." Knohl showed that the work of the Holiness School clearly postdates the writing of the Priestly Torah. He went on to suggest that this Holiness School was the priestly caste responsible for blending their work into P in order to create the final version of this document. Knohl also argued that the Holiness School then edited the entire Pentateuch.

The difference between P proper and H is subtle but can nevertheless be identified. The Priestly Torah focuses upon priestly ordinances designed to maintain holiness through ritual activity. In contrast, the Holiness School shows a greater concern with how holiness as a state of being relates to humans, places, objects, times, and ultimately God himself.[14] Anything that is unholy or "impure" threatens the quality of holiness. In sum, the primary distinction between P and H is that in P proper, the state of holiness is specifically achieved through proper ritual performances; in H, holiness is achieved primarily through moral behavior rather than ritual.

P's primary view of holiness is demonstrated in Leviticus 11–15. The laws in this section of the Priestly Torah are not what we would consider ethical or even moral behaviors. Instead, they deal with ritual impurity and describe the conditions under which a person is considered unfit to approach the holy altar. These conditions include corpse contamination, male or female sexual emissions, and scale disease (biblical leprosy). All throughout P, holiness is a quality maintained through proper ritual performances.

According to the ideal of holiness in H, Israel could achieve and maintain holiness by keeping God's commandments. "Sanctify yourselves therefore, and be ye holy: for I am the LORD your God," states the Holiness

---

13. Israel Knohl, *The Sanctuary of Silence: The Priestly Torah and the Holiness School* (Minneapolis: Fortress Press, 1995).

14. David P. Wright, "Holiness in Leviticus and Beyond," 352.

School legislation, "and ye shall keep my statutes, and do them: I am the LORD which sanctify you" (Lev. 20:7–8). Whereas most of P places special emphasis upon the status of the priestly caste as "holy," H democratizes the quality of holiness as a divine attribute available to all Israel. This is seen quite clearly, for example, in Leviticus 19:2: "Speak unto all the congregation of the children of Israel, and say unto them, Ye shall be holy: for I the LORD your God am holy." On the other hand, in P the special status of Aaron and his decedents as vessels of holiness appears expressed in a variety of sections. This view appears exemplified through the priestly story in Numbers concerning a Levite named Korah. Aaron was a descendent of Levi, and even though only Aaron's sons could serve as priests proper, the entire tribe of Levi held specific responsibilities in biblical rituals. The Levites functioned as a type of priestly caste, although their holiness and therefore access to divinity in the temple was less than that of a priest; they were designated to serve the higher priestly caste. Numbers 18 suggests that this relationship between Priests and Levites was worked out quite amicably. Numbers 8, however, provides hints of another view.

The account states that the Levite Korah rebelled against Moses and Aaron. Korah and his followers approached Moses and Aaron, complaining:

> Ye take too much upon you, seeing all the congregation are holy, every one of them, and the LORD is among them: wherefore then lift ye up yourselves above the congregation of the LORD? (Num. 16:3)

The story then states that Moses addressed his response to the "sons of Levi" with these words:

> Hear, I pray you, ye sons of Levi: Seemeth it but a small thing unto you, that the God of Israel hath separated you from the congregation of Israel, to bring you near to himself to do the service of the tabernacle of the LORD, and to stand before the congregation to minister unto them? And he hath brought thee near to him, and all thy brethren the sons of Levi with thee: and seek ye the priesthood also? (Num. 16:8–10)

This conflict between Priest and Levites is resolved when the earth opens and consumes Korah and his followers. Through this story, the priestly account makes clear that when it comes to the quality of holiness, Aaron and his decedents held the absolute divine rite. From the priestly perspective, God created a system to control his temple performances. This system defined some Israelites holier than others and the priests themselves held the highest role.

Bringing P back together as a documentary unit, we find that the Priestly source (both P and H combined) covers the rise of the House of

Israel from the creation in Genesis 1, to the flood account, the patriarchs, the Exodus, the construction of the tabernacle, the Israelite wanderings in the wilderness, and finally the death of Moses. P tells this story in accordance with its own unique religious and even political agenda.

There is no doubt that an emphasis throughout P upon rituals and holiness, which were important ideas to the Judean school, was responsible for this narrative. Yet P is not simply a ritual narrative. Writing to an audience facing the prospect of Babylonian captivity (or perhaps even already in exile), P addresses the feelings of those who may have felt abandoned by their God. As such, "the Priestly document is a powerful affirmation of faith in God's unconditional commitment to Israel," states authors Anthony Campbell and Mark O'Brien, "which, although delayed by human fragility, will never be deflected from the ultimate goal of God's love."[15]

The Yahwistic Source (J)

Genesis begins with the priestly source and its story about creation. Then, when the text references the divine name Yahweh in Genesis 2:4b, readers encounter a second documentary source telling its own unique story. Again, following Wellhausen's lead, scholars refer to this documentary narrative by the letter J because the source typically refers to the divine name of God as Yahweh (or Jehovah) in the original Hebrew.

J was likely written by Judean scribes from the Southern kingdom of Judah, as many of the geographical references in its narrative focus upon the Southern territory.[16] Judah was the dominant Southern tribe and the name given to the Southern kingdom at the time of the divided monarchy. The tribe was named after Jacob/Israel's oldest son Judah, who appears as a prominent character in J's patriarchal narratives. It was Judah, for example, not Reuben, who was the brother who tried to save Joseph in the second source we explored in Genesis 37.[17] For many years, scholars have followed Wellhausen's original proposal that J is the oldest documentary source in the Pentateuch, written sometime during the tenth or possibly ninth century BC. However, subsequent studies on the J material have presented arguments that portions of J cannot be earlier than the seventh century BC.

---

15. Anthony F. Campbell and Mark A. O'Brien, *Sources of the Pentateuch: Texts, Introductions, Annotations*, 22.

16. Coogan, *The Old Testament*, 52.

17. See the analysis provided in Chapter 2.

If correct, this would date the final version of the source to a time period shortly before the Book of Mormon story told by Nephi begins.[18]

Like P, J also begins with a creation story. From that point, J covers the same basic narrative plot found in P concerning the patriarchs and the rise of the House of Israel (though P was clearly written after J).[19] These two separate accounts were then woven together by an editor into a single literary unit. The first fourteen chapters of Genesis move back and forth between these separate documentary sources. Despite the fact that these two narratives have been spliced together, it is easy for scholars to distinguish P from J. Until Exodus 6, P uses the divine name Elohim, whereas J uses Yahweh. Also, J is far less concerned with priestly issues then P. As we've seen, J presents information (like Abel and Noah offering sacrifices) that directly challenges P's vision regarding the origins of the sacrificial system. Not being of priestly origin, J is also much less interested in textual boundaries and literary structure than P. Instead, J shows more concern in explaining how things in the world began. For this reason, J contains several statements such as "therefore the place was called X," as well as entire narratives discussing the beginning of institutions and human culture, including those found in J's story of Eden.

As discussed in the previous chapter, J depicts God in a manner different than P in the flood stories. In J God is Yahweh, a deity who can experience human emotion. Yahweh "regrets" that he made man in J, and man's wickedness causes Him to feel "sad" (Gen. 6:6). In J's creation story, God is a gardener who physically works with soil in order to create (Gen. 2:8) and chooses to literally walk in his garden during the cool of the day in order to escape the heat (Gen. 3:8).

Since God is so human-like in J, there is a real threat that humans will actually *become* gods, something that Yahweh does not wish to see happen. In J, God works hard to maintain a boundary separating humans from gods. This boundary, however, especially in the opening portions of J, is constantly at risk as humans seek to overstep their proper limits. When we put the documentary source together in accordance with a coherent literary flow, we find that this unique theme emerges right from the beginning.

According to J's creation story, Yahweh created man to physically resemble Himself so that the man could help deity with His garden (Gen.

---

18. Campbell and O'Brien, *Sources of the Pentateuch*, 10.

19. Latter-day Saints might look toward the Small and Large Plates in the Book of Mormon narrative as an analogy for two different accounts covering the same material from two different angles; see the analysis provided in Chapter 1.

2:15). However, in order to keep the man and woman from actually becoming gods, Yahweh gave the first humans a command not to eat the fruit that would grant them knowledge. In the account, the serpent points this out to the woman, telling her that she won't really die by eating the fruit but will instead become just like the gods:

> And the serpent said unto the woman, Ye shall not surely die: For God doth know that in the day ye eat thereof, then your eyes shall be opened, and ye shall be as gods, knowing good and evil. (Gen. 3:4–5)

The implication of the serpent's statement is that Yahweh is keeping the true power of the fruit hidden from the humans so that they will not become fully divine, since the humans already physically resembled the gods in order to assist Yahweh in His labors. Eventually, Yahweh confirms the legitimacy of the serpent's assessment when he speaks to the other non-specified deities in his council:

> And the LORD God said, Behold, the man is become as one of us, to know good and evil: and now, lest he put forth his hand, and take also of the tree of life, and eat, and live for ever. (Gen. 3:22)

Thus, in J God does not want humans to become like him. This view directly contradicts the perspective concerning God found in Genesis 1, (i.e., P), where God created the humans to rule like he rules, and to have dominion like he has dominion (Gen. 1:26–27). P's idea that God created humans in his image and likeness, and that human maleness and femaleness were inherent in creation from the beginning, seem to be an attempt to directly counter J's earlier creation theology.

When we read J as a separate documentary source, we encounter this same theme in J's other accounts in prehistory. In J, the separation between gods and humans appears breached when mortal women have sexual relations with the "Sons of God," who in ancient conceptions were considered divine beings in Yahweh's court or assembly (Gen. 6:1–4).[20] In J, the humans attempt to breach the barrier between God and man by building a tower that will allow human access to heaven (Gen. 11:1–9). Thus, while Latter-day Saints connect well theologically with J's religious view that God is like a man, there is an important distinction. Latter-day Saints believe that an anthropomorphic God created humans so that they might *become* divine beings.

Dividing the opening two chapters of Genesis into their respective sources solves many problems for a Latter-day Saint audience. Often read-

---

20. See David E. Bokovoy, "'Ye Really Are Gods': A Response to Michael Heiser Concerning the LDS Use of Psalm 82 and the Gospel of John," 267–313.

ers struggle to make sense of the fact that God gave the first humans a command in Genesis 1 to "be fruitful, and multiply" (v. 28), yet in Genesis 2, he commanded the humans *not* to eat the fruit that would have granted them this very ability. Latter-day Saints often reconcile this contradiction by asserting that God needed to create a situation in which agency could exist by giving two conflicting commands. This reading certainly contains merit as a theological concept. However, combining this construct with an historical awareness of the two separate traditions that produced these distinct accounts resolves much of the dissonance readers often sense.

As the narrative continues, we find that the J source has its own unique view concerning the story of Israel. Mark O'Brien and Anthony Campbell explain:

> The Yahwist [authors of J] narrative is thought of a selection from the storehouse of Israel's stories and traditions, arranged and interpreted to express a particular communication concerning Israel in the Yahwist's time. . . . The Yahwist's purpose in assembling this rich and varied material was to proclaim that Israel was the LORD's chosen mediator to bring salvation and blessing to the troubled humanity described in Genesis 2–11.[21]

From J's perspective, Abraham and his decedents were chosen by Yahweh to bless the nations of the earth. "I will make of thee a great nation, and I will bless thee," states Yahweh concerning Abraham in J, "and in thee shall all families of the earth be blessed" (Gen. 12:2–3). The mythic stories in J's prehistory illustrate the world's need for this blessing. However, as the narrative moves forward, Israel often proves too weak to provide it. In its view of the Exodus story, J recounts traditions concerning Israel's rebellion against Moses and Yahweh in the wilderness. Therefore, the beauty of the J narrative is that even in the midst of such weakness, we find Yahweh's divine blessing at work in the lives of his people.

The Elohist Source (E)

The first several chapters of the Bible switch back and forth between P and J. However, at Genesis 15, the Bible moves to a third and separate documentary thread that was spliced into the Book of Genesis by an unknown editor. Once again, following Wellhausen's lead, critical scholars refer to this new source by the letter E (an abbreviation of *Elohist*) in light of the fact that this documentary thread prefers to use the term *Elohim*

---

21. Campbell and O'Brien, *Sources of the Pentateuch*, 91.

for Israel's deity.[22] Admittedly, despite its unique focus, E is the most challenging source to identify in the Pentateuch.

Though each of the three sources P, J, and E can be extracted and read through as continuous narratives, E seems to be the least well preserved in the Pentateuch. The biblical Redactor who spliced these separate documents together may not have added the entire E source as it was originally written. Some scholars have argued that the editor primarily chose to include portions of E in the creation of the Pentateuch when E featured stories that a parallel version did not exist in J, such as the story of Abraham's near sacrifice of Isaac in Genesis 22.[23] This angle makes sense of the fact that E appears primarily clustered toward the end of the patriarchal narratives as a way of perhaps filling out or enriching the J narrative.[24]

In chapter 15, E begins with God making a covenant with Abraham. From that point, its story continues the same basic narrative plot presented by P and J. Unlike P and J, however, E does not contain a story of creation or an account of prehistory. Instead, E features a much tighter focus on Israel as a people, ignoring P and J's stories of origin.[25] This highly specified concentration is shown in E's version of the blessing of Balaam from the Book of Numbers. Concerning Israel we read: "the people shall dwell alone, and shall not be reckoned among the nations" (Num. 23:9). The term translated as "to be reckoned" in this passage comes from a root meaning "to consider," or "to take into account."[26] From E's perspective, if a story is not specifically an "Israelite" account (like the stories of creation, Cain, Abel, Noah, etc.), then it was simply not worth addressing.

---

22. For challenges in distinguishing E from other sources, see Carr, *The Formation of the Hebrew Bible*, 110.

23. Campbell and O'Brien, *Sources of the Pentateuch*, 162.

24. Many scholars believe that J and E were combined as a literary unit into a JE document prior to being combined with P by the biblical redactor. Though his proposal that P never knew J is highly problematic, Joel Baden's recent study on source criticism makes a compelling case that the JE narrative never existed and that E is an individual documentary narrative. See Joel S. Baden, *J, E, and the Redaction of the Pentateuch* (Tübingen: Mohr Siebeck, 2009).

25. Another example might be in how Mormons understood the Restoration—they originally would begin the story with Moroni and the plates to emphasize miracles and a restored gospel, but have since began the story with the First Vision to emphasize a restored Church.

26. For the Hebrew root, see Ludwig Koehler and Walter Baumgartner, *The Hebrew and Aramaic Lexicon of the Old Testament*, 1:360.

According to the biblical history of Israel, the once unified twelve tribes of Israel split into two separate factions after the death of King Solomon. Solomon's son Rehoboam continued the Davidic monarchy in the Southern kingdom of Judah, primarily consisting of the tribes Judah and Benjamin. The kingdom in the North, known historically as Israel, consisted primarily of the other ten tribes and was first ruled over by a man named Jeroboam.

Though sharing a common heritage, these two kingdoms were often at political and religious odds with one another, and each had its own scribal traditions. The first two documentary sources that appear in Genesis (P and J) were clearly produced by Judean scribes in the Southern kingdom. E, however, shows signs that it was written in the North, probably in the ninth century BC.[27] This dating would make E earlier than not only P, but also J (at least in its final form). E tells Israel's family story in a way that gives special emphasis to sacred Northern sites such as Bethel (Gen. 18:11–12, 17–18, 20–22; 35:1–8). Also, the E sections of the Pentateuch share many significant religious themes with other biblical books known to have been produced by Northern authors, including the prophet Hosea, as well as the Samuel and Elijah stories in the Deuteronomistic History.[28] These themes include a unique emphasis on God's covenant with Israel, the presentation of Moses in an especially positive light, and strong religious warnings against idolatry. The focus upon Northern traditions and imagery is one of the observations that allows scholars to distinguish E from P even though both sources use the same divine title.

E is further unique in that it shows a much greater interest in the issue of prophecy than the other two documents. For example, in the story of Abimelech taking Abraham's wife Sarah into his house, God saves Sarah by manifesting himself to Abimelech through a dream. In this dream, Abraham is specifically called a prophet:

> Now therefore restore the man his wife; for he is a prophet, and he shall pray for thee, and thou shalt live: and if thou restore her not, know thou that thou shalt surely die, thou, and all that are thine. (Gen. 20:7)

This makes E unique, since neither Abraham nor any of the other patriarchs in Genesis are ever specifically referred to as a "prophet" in either J or P. Hence, unlike the other traditions, the E source focuses upon the prophetic leadership of four of Israel's ancestors: Abraham, Jacob, Joseph, and Moses.

---

27. See the basic summary provided by Alan W. Jenks, "Elohist," 2:481–83.

28. The Deuteronomistic History will be given detailed consideration in the subsequent volume, *Authoring the Old Testaments: The Prophets*.

Throughout the documentary strand, E either implicitly or explicitly refers to each of these men as prophets who receive revelation from God.

Interestingly, in E, however, this prophetic revelation almost always comes in a unique and indirect way. E regularly presents God revealing his divine will by means of dreams or vision rather than direct appearances. "And God came to Laban the Syrian *in a dream* by night," states the documentary narrative in E, "and said unto him, Take heed that thou speak not to Jacob either good or bad" (Gen. 31:24). These types of spiritual manifestations in E contrast with the more direct way in which God reveals himself in J. In comparison to the way E depicts God speaking to people in dreams, we find that in J, the human-like Yahweh appears to Abraham, walks with the patriarch, and even negotiates directly with Abraham regarding the stipulations for destroying Sodom and Gomorrah:

> And the LORD said, Because the cry of Sodom and Gomorrah is great, and because their sin is very grievous; I will go down now, and see whether they have done altogether according to the cry of it, which is come unto me; and if not, I will know. And the men turned their faces from thence, and went toward Sodom: but Abraham stood yet before the LORD. And Abraham drew near, and said, Wilt thou also destroy the righteous with the wicked? (Gen. 18:20–23)

E, on the other hand, places emphasis upon the role of prophecy and indirect communications with God in a way that stands apart from the other sources.

Along this line, E also has frequent references to angels or divine messengers appearing to man rather than God himself. We see this, for example, in E's story of Hagar and Ishmael in the wilderness:

> And God heard the voice of the lad; and the angel of God called Hagar out of heaven, and said unto her, What aileth thee, Hagar? fear not; for God hath heard the voice of the lad where he is. (Gen. 21:17)

This same theological trend continues in E's story of the Exodus, where, for example, God provides Moses with the reassurance: "Behold, I send an Angel before thee, to keep thee in the way, and to bring thee into the place which I have prepared" (Ex. 23:20). Thus in revealing himself through angels and dreams rather than personal visits, God in E is much more distant or removed and far less personal than what we find in P and J. He does manifest himself, however, through his mediators. Like P and J, E is ultimately a documentary source that seeks in its own way to recount the rise of the House of Israel and God's sacred interactions with his chosen people.

Yahweh versus Elohim

In terms of the first three sources, P and E tend to use the title Elohim or God whereas J uses the divine name Yahweh to refer to God. The individual and unique perspectives concerning deity in P, J, and E can be further seen in the manner in which the first three sources depict how the God of Israel revealed to humankind His personal name. Though contemporary Latter-day Saints typically make a rigid distinction between the two divine names, Elohim (God the Father) and Jehovah (the pre-mortal Jesus), this same view does not appear in the Old Testament. Instead, the names are often used interchangeably for the same deity.

Our current tradition of referring to *Elohim* as the Father and *Jehovah* as the premortal Son came about in 1916, when the First Presidency of the Church under the direction of Joseph F. Smith presented a doctrinal statement that designated Elohim as the Father and Jehovah as the premortal Jesus.[29] This was done to ensure a clarity of expression within the Church. However, as Latter-day Saints, we cannot retroactively read this designation into pre-1916 Church hymns and sermons, which often use the two names interchangeably for both the Father and the Son.[30] For example, in the Kirtland temple dedicatory prayer, we see Joseph Smith praying to God the Father: "O Jehovah, have mercy upon this people, and as all men sin forgive the transgressions of thy people, and let them be blotted out forever" (D&C 109:34). If we, as Latter-day Saints, cannot retroactively read early LDS hymns and sermons in accordance with the 1916 declaration, we certainly cannot expect to do so in the Old Testament.

Until Exodus 6, the Priestly source always uses the word *Elohim* as a reference to the God of Israel. P explains that the name Yahweh was not revealed to humanity until the time of Moses. Instead, the early patriarchs knew God by the name El Shaddai:

---

29. The official declaration refers to God the Eternal Father, "whom we designate by the exalted name-title 'Elohim,'" and Jesus Christ, "whom we also know as Jehovah;" see James R. Clark, *Messages of the First Presidency of the Church of Jesus Christ of Latter-day Saints*, 26–34. For a consideration of these issues, see Ryan Conrad Davis and Paul Y. Hoskisson, "Usage of the Title Elohim," 113–35.

30. Consider the analysis provided by Charles R. Harrell, *This is My Doctrine: The Development of Mormon Theology*, 173–75.

And I appeared unto Abraham, unto Isaac, and unto Jacob, by the name of God Almighty (El Shaddai), but by my name JEHOVAH [YAHWEH] was I not known to them. (Ex. 6:3)[31]

This provides important evidence that with this extracted narrative, we're dealing with an originally independent documentary source. God never refers to himself in P's early narratives by the divine name Yahweh. Instead, both God and the patriarchs specifically call God by the sacred title El Shaddai:

And when Abram was ninety years old and nine, the LORD appeared to Abram, and said unto him, I am the Almighty God (El Shaddai); walk before me, and be thou perfect. (Gen. 17:1)

And Isaac called Jacob, and blessed him, and charged him, and said unto him. . . . God Almighty (El Shaddai) bless thee, and make thee fruitful, and multiply thee, that thou mayest be a multitude of people. (Gen. 28:1–3)

And God said unto [Jacob], I am God Almighty (El Shaddai): be fruitful and multiply; a nation and a company of nations shall be of thee, and kings shall come out of thy loins. (Gen. 35:11)

And Jacob said unto Joseph, God Almighty (El Shaddai) appeared unto me at Luz in the land of Canaan, and blessed me. (Gen. 48:3)

So in P's version of Israel's history, it is not until Exodus 6 that God chooses to make known his name as *Yahweh*. Before that the documentary source either uses the generic term Elohim "God" or El Shaddai to refer to the God of the Old Testament.

The same is true for E, which begins in Genesis 15 with the story of God entering into, what Latter-day Saints refer to as, the Abrahamic Covenant.[32] This is one of E's major themes. However, the Elohist source presents God revealing to Moses his divine name three chapters earlier than the priestly version in Exodus 6. E's version of this experience appears in Exodus 3:14–15. Here the revelation came as a direct response to Moses' question to God: "What is your name?"

---

31. From this point forward in Exodus through Numbers, the presence of the name Yahweh in a passage cannot be interpreted as an indication that the passage is part of J, even though the presence of Elohim continues to be an indication that a text is not J.

32. For a defense of the Elohist source see Axel Graupner, *Der Elohist: Gegenwart und Wirksamkeit des transzendenten Gottes in der Geschichte*, (Neukirchen-Vluyn: Neukirchener Verglag, 2002); Tzemah Yoreh, *The First Book of God* (Berlin: de Gruyter, 2010); Joel Burnett, *A Reassessment of Biblical Elohim* (Atlanta: Scholars, 2001).

> And God said unto Moses, I AM THAT I AM: and he said, Thus shalt thou say unto the children of Israel, I AM hath sent me unto you. And God said moreover unto Moses, Thus shalt thou say unto the children of Israel, The LORD God [Yahweh Elohim] of your fathers, the God of Abraham, the God of Isaac, and the God of Jacob, hath sent me unto you: this is my name for ever, and this is my memorial unto all generations.

When we extract the E source from the first two books and read it as a documentary whole, this is the first time that E's God is linked with the divine name Yahweh.

The account depicts Moses' concern that when he appears as a prophet unto the children of Israel, they will want to know which God sent him:

> When I come unto the children of Israel, and say unto them, The God of your fathers hath sent me unto you; and they shall say to me, What is his name? what shall I say unto them? (Ex. 3:13)

Since the E source never presents a Patriarch or even the narrator referring to Israel's deity by the name Yahweh, we cannot assume that the Israelites' question was simply a test to make sure that Moses represented their one true familial God. Again, E never uses this name and provides no indication up to this point that Yahweh is the God of Israel's fathers.

Instead, this question assumes that while living in Egypt, the Israelites would have revered multiple gods and would have therefore wanted to know which deity Moses represented. As one historian explains:

> The Exodus group first got to know the god Yahweh in connection with its liberation by Moses (Ex. 3:13, 15; 6:2). That certainly does not mean that before that the group had no religion; even if we know nothing about the pre-Yahwistic religion of this group, we can begin from the assumption that it too had its family gods and shared in the worship of Egyptian or Semitic gods in the region. What came about through the liberation from Egypt was not the relationship to God as such but the special tie to the god Yahweh.[33]

According to E's logic, when the Children of Israel asked Moses for the name of the God of their fathers, they asked this question because they had historically worshipped so many different gods, especially while in Egypt. This same view regarding Israelite religion in Egypt appears supported by various sources including Joshua's famous invitation presented to the new Israelite generation entering the promised land:

---

33. Rainer Albertz, *A History of Israelite Religion in the Old Testament Period: From the Beginnings to the End of the Monarchy*, 49.

> Now therefore fear the LORD, and serve him in sincerity and in truth: and put away the gods which your fathers serve on the other side of the flood, and in Egypt; and serve ye the LORD. (Josh. 24:14)

There were many gods of the fathers, and the Israelites would want to know the name of the specific deity Moses represented. E depicts Moses anticipating this question in order to connect the title Elohim used throughout its historical narrative with the deity Yahweh.

The expression "Yahweh Elohim (LORD God) of your Fathers" that appears in God's response to Moses' question is consistent with the fact that E uses the title "Elohim (God) of my father" in reference to deity:

> And [Jacob] said unto them, I see your father's countenance, that it is not toward me as before; but the *God (Elohim) of my father* hath been with me. (Gen. 31:5)

> Except the *God (Elohim) of my father*, the God of Abraham, and the fear of Isaac, had been with me, surely thou hadst sent me away now empty. God hath seen mine affliction and the labour of my hands, and rebuked thee yesternight. (Gen. 31:42)

> And Israel took his journey with all that he had, and came to Beer-sheba, and offered sacrifices unto the *God (Elohim) of his father* Isaac. (Gen. 46:1)

In Exodus 3, the E source uses the expression "Elohim (God) of his/my father," and for the first time, connects the phrase with the divine name Yahweh revealed to Moses in response to his question.

This exchange shows us that there are two separate incidents where God reveals his name to Moses. One occurs in Exodus 3 and the other in Exodus 6. As with elsewhere in the Bible these two versions or doublets provide strong evidence of separate sources, specifically P and E.

In contrast to these two versions of Israelite history, J's narrator regularly uses the divine name Yahweh, and its characters use this as God's name at the earliest stages of human history. Directly following J's genealogy of early humans and its famous Cain and Abel story, J contains a line that directly contradicts the view of P and E on the divine name: "then [meaning at this point] began men to call upon the name of the LORD [Yahweh]" (Gen. 4:26). Hence, the Documentary Hypothesis not only resolves the difficult narrative and legal collection issues we encounter throughout the Pentateuch, separating biblical sources from one another allows readers to make sense of the various conflicting statements regarding deity, including his name.

The Deuteronomic Source (D)

The fourth documentary source in the Pentateuch appears in the Book of Deuteronomy and is hence referred to by the abbreviation "D." D is presented as the final speech of Moses to the Children of Israel before his death and, like the other three sources, it seeks to document the rise of the House of Israel. Unlike the other texts, however, there is very little narrative in D. Instead, the story of God's promises to the patriarchs, the escape from Egypt, the desert wanderings, and the revelation given through Moses are simply summarized as part of Moses' final sermon. Most of the source focuses upon a presentation of laws that both parallel and modify earlier legal collections. The name "Deuteronomy" stems from a Greek origin that means "second law." And this title provides an effective summary of the source's basic content.

It is clear that Moses was not the author of this document. D's textual framework is presented in a third person formula, "These are the words that Moses addressed to all Israel *on the other side* of the Jordan" (JPS Deut. 1:1; emphasis added), by an author living in the land of Israel (the west side of the Jordan River instead of the east where Moses died). And the account depicts Moses' death and burial in the book's final chapter, making it impossible from a critical perspective to attribute the text to Moses himself.[34]

We can also rule out Mosaic authorship of Deuteronomy due to the types of issues and influences that appear throughout the source. During the seventh century BC, the Assyrian empire from Mesopotamia controlled the kingdoms of Israel and Judah. Not only do we find Assyrian influences in D suggesting a compositional date long after the time period of Moses, but D intentionally reworks earlier biblical laws found in E.[35] D also responds to many of the Priestly writings to the point that we can identify an evolution in religious ideas by comparing these two sources.

We saw that in P proper, holiness was a sacred status achieved primarily through proper ritual performances. Later in H, the idea of holiness is democratized as a state that all Israel could achieve through both ritual and obedience to moral law. Holiness, however, was not a preexisting state but something that could, from H's perspective, be obtained through moral conduct. In contrast, Deuteronomy defines the people as holy from the beginning, before any act of obedience or ritual performance—simply because Israel was chosen by God:

---

34. See the analysis in Chapter 1.
35. See, for example, the analysis of slave laws discussed in Chapter 2.

H: "Sanctify yourselves therefore, and *be ye holy*: for I am the LORD your God" (Lev. 20:7).

H: "And *ye shall be holy* unto me: for I the LORD am holy, and have severed you from other people, that ye should be mine" (Lev. 20:26).

H: "Speak unto the children of Israel, and bid them that they make them fringes in the borders of their garments. . . . That ye may remember, and *do all my commandments, and be holy* unto your God" (Num. 15:38–40).

D: "For *thou art an holy people* unto the LORD thy God: the LORD thy God hath chosen thee to be a special people unto himself, above all people that are upon the face of the earth" (Deut. 7:6).

D: "For *thou art an holy people* unto the LORD thy God, and the LORD hath chosen thee to be a peculiar people unto himself, above all the nations that are upon the earth" (Deut. 14:2).

D: "Ye shall not eat of any thing that dieth of itself: thou shalt give it unto the stranger that is in thy gates, that he may eat it; or thou mayest sell it unto an alien: for *thou art an holy people* unto the LORD thy God" (Deut. 14:21).

These texts illustrate a fundamental thematic difference that appears consistently between D and H and suggests an evolution in religious views.

The current consensus on Deuteronomy is that, like E, the book was originally created by an Israelite scribal school from the Northern kingdom, as it tends to focus its attention on Northern issues.[36] In fact, D lacks any formal references to the Southern Davidic dynasty that ruled in Jerusalem. Also, like E, Deuteronomy places considerable emphasis upon the role of prophecy. D provides rules that allow Israel to identify a true prophet of God (Deut. 18:15–22). While we do not encounter any references to "prophets" in the earlier legal collections in the Pentateuch, prophecy appears as a major focus of chapters 13 and 18. Furthermore, in the Book of Deuteronomy, the law is both spoken and interpreted by Moses, the prophetic mediator. Whereas the law given to Israel at Mount Sinai in Exodus, Leviticus, and Numbers was spoken by God only.

In terms of its religious message, Deuteronomy shares many themes in common with the Book of Hosea. Hosea was a prophet of the Northern kingdom who specifically emphasized God's love for Israel as well as the

---

36. For an introduction and basic survey on the origins and developments of Deuteronomy, including its historical ties to the Northern kingdom, see Coogan, *The Old Testament*, 183–84.

importance of exclusive worship of Yahweh and the need for social reform. Interestingly, these are the very points that D emphasizes.[37]

Further, rather than using "Sinai" to refer to the place where the law was given, as J and P do, Deuteronomy follows E (and therefore the Northern trend) by referring to God's holy mountain as "Horeb":

> J: "And the LORD came down upon mount *Sinai*, on the top of the mount: and the LORD called Moses up to the top of the mount; and Moses went up" (Ex. 19:20).

> E: "Now Moses kept the flock of Jethro his father in law, the priest of Midian: and he led the flock to the backside of the desert, and came to the mountain of God, even to *Horeb*" (Ex. 3:1).

> D: "The LORD our God spake unto us in *Horeb*, saying, Ye have dwelt long enough in this mount" (Deut. 1:6).

> D: "And when we departed from *Horeb*" (Deut. 1:19).

> D: "Specially the day that thou stoodest before the LORD thy God in *Horeb*" (Deut. 4:10).

> D: "Take ye therefore good heed unto yourselves; for ye saw no manner of similitude on the day that the LORD spake unto you in *Horeb*" (Deut. 4:15).

This is really quite significant. It shows that there were two different traditions in ancient Israel regarding the holy mountain of God that Moses ascended and where Israel entered into a sacred covenant to serve their deity. In the North, these events are described as occurring on a mountain named Horeb, whereas Southern authors connected the experience with a mountain named Sinai. Again, all of this points to separate historical sources appearing in the Pentateuch, with E and D having a strong Northern influence.

Scholars refer to the Northern scribal community responsible for this source as the "Deuteronomic School."[38] This group of Israelite scribes passionately believed that Israel needed to return to what they perceived as Israel's original faith by worshipping Yahweh, the true God of Israel, at a single national shrine. This scribal community began creating their own version of Israelite history and Moses' sermons prior to the Northern kingdom's fall to the Assyrians in 722 BC. Eventually the Deuteronomists were among the exiles from the North that flooded the Southern kingdom of

---

37. I will address such issues in greater detail in *Authoring the Old Testament: The Prophets*.

38. See *Authoring the Old Testament: The Prophets*.

Judah at the time of the Assyrian conquest. These Israelite religious reformers brought with them the sacred records they had created and copied, including an early form of Deuteronomy. The Deuteronomistic scribes then established relations with the Jerusalem priesthood and the school's views eventually sparked the religious reforms of King Hezekiah (715–687 BC).

Most scholars believe that an early form of the Book of Deuteronomy also served as the inspiration for King Josiah's reforms. 2 Kings 22 presents the story of Josiah's workmen discovering a lost "book of the law" in the temple that Josiah's people had long forgotten. When the words of the book were read to Josiah, he rent his clothes as a sign of anguish and commanded the priests:

> Go ye, inquire of the LORD for me, and for the people, and for all Judah, concerning the words of this book that is found: for great is the wrath of the LORD that is kindled against us, because our fathers have not hearkened unto the words of this book, to do according unto all that which is written concerning us. (2 Kgs. 22:13)

Upon discovering this "Law of Moses" (Deuteronomy), Josiah sought to centralize Israelite religious performances at the temple in Jerusalem, "the place God had chosen to put his name." According to the biblical account in 2 Kings, Josiah destroyed all of the localized religious shrines to other gods, as well as all other traditional places of worshipping Yahweh outside of Jerusalem.

D changed earlier biblical laws to reflect its authors' outlook on the importance of centralizing worship into a single place (i.e., the temple of Jerusalem).[39] In terms of its unique religious views, we could define D by the word "one": there is *one* God, whose name rests on the *one* acceptable temple, the *one* place where people can offer an acceptable sacrifice, who chose *one* people to serve as his *one* covenant partner. For D, it is all about the "one." Significantly, D features the Jewish declaration of faith known as the *Shema*: "Hear O Israel the LORD our God is one" (Deut. 6:4).

As a source text, D takes up most of the Book of Deuteronomy. (Remember the book shows signs of Priestly influence including the final chapter.) Deuteronomy is very unique in its theological views regarding God. In D, God is much less human-like than he appears in any of the other Pentateuchal sources—including P, which depicts God as less human-like than J. In this sense, D approaches the theological standard for Judaism and most forms of Christianity. For example, Deuteronomy

---

39. See the analysis provided on altar laws in Chapter 2.

4:12 tells its readers that when Israel approached the holy mountain, they did not *see* a God with a body; they only *heard* a voice: "ye heard the voice of the words, but saw no similitude (*tmwnh*); only ye heard a voice." The Hebrew word in this passage translated as "similitude" literally means "form," and refers to a physical manifestation.[40] Later in the sermon, the fact that Israel did not see a physical, corporeal God provides the author's justification for the biblical prohibition against idolatry:

> Take ye therefore good heed unto yourselves; for ye saw no manner of similitude (*tmwnh*) on the day that the LORD spake unto you in Horeb out of the midst of the fire: Lest ye corrupt yourselves, and make you a graven image, the similitude (*tmwnh*) of any figure, the likeness of male or female. (Deut. 4:15–16)

In other words, D argues that since Israel did not see God with a physical form, no one should ever use a physical form to represent God. In D, the Israelites cannot see God because God does not have a physical body.[41]

This religious view contrasts with earlier biblical sources including Exodus 24:9–11, where Moses, Aaron, Nadab, Abihu, and seventy elders of Israel ascended Mount Sinai and literally *saw* the "God of Israel" (v. 10).[42] According to that narrative, these men not only saw God's feet and

---

40. For the Hebrew root, see Koehler and Baumgartner, *The Hebrew and Aramaic Lexicon*, 2:1746–47.

41. Latter-day Saint readers will recognize that this image of God in D is really quite opposite to the way God is depicted in the Doctrine and Covenants: "The Father has a body of flesh and bones as tangible as man's" (D&C 130:22). These conceptions, however, actually took Joseph Smith and the early Church leaders a little while to work through as well. The Lectures on Faith given to the Kirtland School of the Prophets and originally included in the Doctrine and Covenants contain an earlier LDS conception: "There are two personages who constitute the great, matchless, governing, and supreme power over all things—by whom all things were created and made that are created and made, whether visible or invisible; whether in heaven, on earth, or in the earth, under the earth, or throughout the immensity of space. They are the Father and the Son: *The Father being a personage of spirit, glory, and power, possessing all perfection and fullness. The Son, who was in the bosom of the Father, a personage of tabernacle*, made or fashioned like unto man, or being in the form and likeness of man" (Lectures on Faith 5.2).

42. Historically, most source critics have assumed that Exodus 24:1–15 derives from the Elohist source; see, for example, William Henry Propp, *Exodus 19–40: A New Translation with Introduction and Commentary*, 107; Richard Elliott Friedman, *The Bible with Sources Revealed: A New View into the Five Books of Moses*, 160–61. Several, however, see redactional development in the pericope. Carr, for example, sees Exodus 24:3–8 as a late text that "links P and non-P

hand, God literally joined with these men in eating a communal meal.[43] In this source, God was physical, had a body, and could use it just like a human being. Thus, the anti-anthropomorphic statements in D stand out from the religious views in other Pentateuchal strands.

In earlier biblical sources, God not only had a physical body, but his body could be found in holy places such as a temple or a mountain. D counters this perspective by implementing what scholars refer to as a "Name Theology." For instance, we find that in the Priestly version of creation, God created men and women to physically resemble himself:

> And God said, Let us make man in our image, after our likeness: and let them have dominion over the fish of the sea, and over the fowl of the air, and over the cattle, and over all the earth, and over every creeping thing that creepeth upon the earth. So God created man in his own image, in the image of God created he him; male and female created he them. (Gen. 1:26–27)

God has a corporeal, physical form in P's theology (much like he does in LDS views), and human beings were created in his divine image and likeness. Later in P, its author makes this point clear by using the Hebrew

---

elements of the Exodus Sinai narrative;" See David Carr, "Response to W.M. Schniedewind, *How the Bible Became a Book: The Textualization of Ancient Israel*," 1–20. Ska sees 24:3–8 as a late unified pericope; see Jean Louis Ska, "From History Writing to Library Building: The End of History and the Birth of the Book," 160–69. Baden's analysis, however, is without the phrase "they ate and drank," Ex. 24:1–2, 9–11bA is J; 24:3–8, 11bB ("they ate and drank"), 12–15, 18b is E; and 24:16–18a is P; see Baden, *J, E, and the Redaction of the Pentateuch*, 186n 146, 140, 180, 184n 142, 186n 147, 195, 218, 372. For a similar reading, see Baruch J. Schwartz, "The Visit of Jethro: A Case of Chronological Displacement?: The Source-Critical Solution," 29–48. Wright, in his study on the CC, agrees with Baden and Schwartz that 24:1–2, 9–11bA is not E; see David P. Wright, *Inventing God's Law: How the Covenant Code of the Bible Used and Revised the Laws of Hammurabi*, 497, n. 76 and 498, n. 79. For my views on the relationship between E and J see below.

43. Admittedly, such explicit anthropomorphic depictions do not reflect the views typically witnessed in later biblical texts. With regard to the Exodus 24 pericope, Mark Smith writes, "this sort of anthropomorphism is exceptional, and if other anthropomorphisms of God are any indication, they seem more at home in the milieu of Israelite religion in the period up to the eighth century." Mark S. Smith, *The Memoirs of God: History, Memory, and the Experience of the Divine in Ancient Israel*, 143. Smith bases his dating on his view of the creation of the Yahwist source discussed in chapter one of his study.

term *kavod* translated as "glory" in the KJV. References to the *kavod* or "Glory of God" appear all throughout the Priestly source:

> And Moses and Aaron went into the tabernacle of the congregation, and came out, and blessed the people: and *the glory of the LORD* appeared unto all the people. (Lev. 9:23)

> But all the congregation bade stone them with stones. And *the glory of the LORD* appeared in the tabernacle of the congregation before all the children of Israel. (Num. 14:10)

Scholars typically understand these Priestly references to God's Glory as something physical or corporeal. For example, concerning the *kavod* of God, biblical scholar Moshe Weinfeld has written, "the underlying imagery of the concept of God's Glory, the '*Kabod* of Yahweh,' embedded in Priestly tradition is drawn in corporeal and not abstract terms."[44] This point comes through in the writings of the prophet Ezekiel who shares many of P's theological perspectives. In Ezekiel's opening vision, we read that the Judean prophet saw God in the likeness of a man, and that this physical form was God's Glory:

> Upon the likeness of the throne was the likeness as the appearance of a man above upon it. And I saw as the colour of amber, as the appearance of fire round about within it, from the appearance of his loins even upward, and from the appearance of his loins even downward, I saw as it were the appearance of fire, and it had brightness round about. As the appearance of the bow that is in the cloud in the day of rain, so was the appearance of the brightness round about. *This was the appearance of the likeness of the glory of the LORD.* (Ezek. 1:26–28)

Since all throughout P, God's *kavod* appears manifested in the tabernacle and temple, God dwelt among his people Israel in a literal sense:

> And I will sanctify the tabernacle of the congregation, and the altar: I will sanctify also both Aaron and his sons, to minister to me in the priest's office. And *I will dwell* among the children of Israel, and will be their God. (Ex. 29:44–45)

> And I will set my tabernacle among you: and my soul shall not abhor you. And *I will walk among you*, and will be your God, and ye shall be my people. (Lev. 26:11–12)

> And they gathered themselves together against Moses and against Aaron, and said unto them, Ye take too much upon you, seeing all the congregation are holy, every one of them, and *the LORD is among them*: wherefore then lift ye up yourselves above the congregation of the LORD? (Num. 16:3)

---

44. Moshe Weinfeld, *Deuteronomy and the Deuteronomic School*, 201.

This theological view that God has a physical body and literally *dwells* in the temple proved distasteful as a religious concept to the authors of Deuteronomy. Instead, D replaces the early concept of God dwelling in his temple with Name Theology.

In Deuteronomy, the Israelites neither see God nor hear his voice speaking to them from Horeb or the temple. Instead His voice comes from heaven where he dwells:

> Out of heaven he made thee to hear his voice, that he might instruct thee: and upon earth he shewed thee his great fire; and thou heardest his words out of the midst of the fire. (Deut. 4:36)[45]

> Look down from *thy holy habitation, from heaven*, and bless thy people Israel, and the land which thou hast given us, as thou swarest unto our fathers, a land that floweth with milk and honey. (Deut. 26:15)

Thus, one of the ways in which D stands out as a unique Pentateuchal source is through an emphasis upon God's *name* dwelling in his temple and rejection of the earlier priestly perspective regarding the temple as the literal house of God.[46] Unlike the earlier biblical sources, particularly P, there is not a single reference in Deuteronomy (or later Deuteronomic literature, for that matter) to either God dwelling in the temple or to the idea of building a house for God. In D, it is always His *name* that dwells in the temple:

> But unto the place which the LORD your God shall choose out of all your tribes *to put his name there*. (Deut. 12:5)

> Then there shall be a place which the LORD your God shall choose *to cause his name to dwell there*. (Deut. 12:11)

> If the place which the LORD thy God hath chosen *to put his name there* be too far from thee. (Deut. 12:21)

> And thou shalt eat before the LORD thy God, in the place which he shall choose *to place his name there*. (Deut. 14:23)

> Which the LORD thy God shall choose *to set his name there*. (Deut. 14:24)

---

45. Granted, there are some earlier hints within D of an ability to see God (Deut. 5:4), and that his voice came from Sinai (Deut. 5:21). Geller has shown that the final form of D, however, went to great lengths to suppress these views. He writes, "The purpose of Deut. 4.36 is to purify the Deuteronomic doctrine of transcendence by stripping away the last shred of immanence that even the older Deuteronomic thinkers had allowed to cling to." Stephen A. Geller, "Fiery Wisdom: Logos and Lexis in Deuteronomy 4," 116.

46. Weinfeld, *Deuteronomy and the Deuteronomic School*, 193.

In the place which the LORD shall choose *to place his name there.* (Deut. 16:2)

But at the place which the LORD thy God shall choose *to place his name in.* (Deut. 16:6)

In the place which the LORD thy God hath chosen *to place his name there.* (Deut. 16:11)

All of these statements from D emphasize the different theological views of God that the authors of Deuteronomy held of God not having a physical body.

From a literary perspective, D is given over the course of a single day, with Moses retelling the same history of Israel that appears in the other three sources. D is a rhetorical source written to convince its audience to adopt the authors' depiction of the past as a guide for religious performances in the present. The text seeks to accomplish this agenda by giving emphasis through repetition of the same concepts and phrases over and over again: law, commandments, statues, ordinances, decrees, one, love, the place, etc. D is also unusual and stands out from the other documents as it has multiple literary sermons and religious exhortations unlike anything we encounter in the other three strands.

Conclusion

Although each of the four documents in the Pentateuch tells the same basic story, each one features its own unique ways of conceptualizing history and God. The differences between these four strands of material are significant and appear consistently throughout the sources when we extract each one from the Pentateuch and put them back together again into four separate documents in accordance with their respective literary plots. This explains the doublets and inconsistencies we encounter all throughout the Pentateuch. Although scholars continue to debate some of the issues surrounding specific textual parameters, one would be hard pressed to find a biblical scholar who does not accept the fact that the Pentateuch is composed of separate religious schools of thought in Judean and Israelite history.

TABLE 3.1 SUMMARY OF DISTINGUISHING CHARACTERISTICS

	Elohist (E)	Yahwist (J)	Priestly (P)	Deuteronomic (D)
Chapter Locations	Gen. 15–Ex., Num.	Gen. 2–4, Gen. 6–Ex., Num.	Gen.1, Gen. 5–Deut.	Deut.
Divine Name	Elohim	Yahweh	Elohim	Both
View of God	Distant, yet anthropomorphic; uses angels and dreams as mediators	Highly anthropomorphic	Dwells in temple; corporeal	Dwells in heaven; neither anthropomorphic, nor corporeal
Unique Emphasis	Prophets	Eiologies; sacrificial worship exists prior to Aaron	Rituals, dietary law and temple worship; sacrificial system begins with Aaron	Centralization and Jerusalem temple
Literary Style	Most fragmentary of the four documents	Loose literary structures and textual boundaries	Tight textual structures and multiple genealogy lists	Sermons provide literary structure
God and Israel	Emphasizes God's covenant with Israel and strong warnings against idolatry	God does not want humans to become like Him nor gain sexual knowledge	God wants humans to become like Him and reproduce	Israel is holy from the beginning since chosen by Yahweh
Historical Focus	Ignores human history and focuses only on Israel	Discusses creation and rise of human institutions and culture	Familial connection between Priestly caste and the Davidic monarchy	God is one and the temple is the one place he may be properly worshipped
Emphasized Figure	Moses	Judah	Aaron as mediator	Moses as prophetic mediator
Divine Mountain	Horeb	Sinai	Sinai	Horeb
Religious Focus	Fear of God; creating a kingdom of priests and a holy nation	Faith in Yahweh	Ritual purity	Faith in Yahweh according to Deuteronomic law

Chapter Four

Dating the Sources

Introduction

For nearly 130 years, the academic consensus has been that separate historical sources appear in the books of the Pentateuch, which were not written by Moses or any other single author, but were instead produced by Israelite and Judean scribes. However, some critics wishing to preserve a more traditional model for understanding the Pentateuch have argued that the Documentary Hypothesis is circular in its reasoning, that this approach to the Bible commits the logical fallacy of simply *assuming* what it is trying to *prove*. These critics suppose that those who espouse the hypothesis as an explanation for the development of the Pentateuch simply assign distinct fragments to a particular source based upon their thematic and structural features. In other words, they believe that since J prefers to use the divine name Jehovah, source critics simply identify a literary section where the name Yahweh appears as J; or since the Priestly source likes to emphasize the importance of Aaron's role in the Exodus, scholars identify every positive mention of Aaron to P; or every depiction we encounter of Moses as a prophet to E, etc.

If this approach was the method by which scholars identified the separate strands in the Pentateuch, then the critics of the theory would be justified in challenging the scholarly consensus. The Documentary Hypothesis would be a circular analysis: J likes origin stories, therefore an origin story is J; P likes genealogy lists, therefore a genealogy list is P. The truth is, however, that the identification of these unique literary themes within the various sources constitutes a secondary, rather than a primary feature of the analysis.

The literary and religious themes we discussed in the previous chapter are not the most compelling identifying feature of a documentary source. Instead, these themes appear only after the document has been identified as a literary unit based upon plots, doublets, and inconsistencies. To identify a specific source, scholars look for the document's story and the way in which its plot is told through a narrative continuity. In other words, one of the basic criteria used to identify a particular source text is simply its readability. *Does the story make sense?* This readability factor provides one of the most compelling arguments for the existence of the documentary sources. "When the sources are separated from one another," writes biblical scholar Richard Elliott Friedman, "we can read each source as a flowing, sensible text; that is, the story continues without a break."[1]

Throughout the Pentateuch, we encounter inconsistencies like the flood and Joseph stories that we are able to separate in order to make two different yet coherent narratives. Only after scholars have done this do they find that the plot they have put together to answer the story's internal problems contains the unique theological and vocabulary connections in each documentary source. These secondary elements provide a strong additional witness that scholars have put the sources together correctly. But they are not the primary focus. As Joel Baden explains regarding this process, the analysis must "be carried out on the basis of the narrative consistencies and contradictions; we cannot start with the diversity of theme or language and divide the text on these bases."[2]

Only after a consistent narrative plot is identified do we find issues such as themes, style, vocabulary, and even historical setting of the source as strong secondary support. As Baden puts it,

> What makes the theory compelling is not that it resolves only the narrative problems, but that the secondary elements of theme and style fit beautifully into the source division revealed by the narrative analysis. We see in the individual documents a confluence of all the literary aspects: the separation

---

1. Richard Elliott Friedman, *The Bible With its Sources Revealed: A New View into the Five Books of Moses*, 13. However, see the critique and analysis provided recently by David Carr, *The Formation of the Hebrew Bible: A New Reconstruction*, 111. Carr argues that one of the problems with this approach is the "documented evidence that scribes did not preserve their source documents unaltered and without gaps, particularly in cases of conflation of parallel sources," 112. However, despite his skepticism, Carr notes "even if the reconstructed strata have significant gaps, their relative readability stands as a significant argument that they once existed separate from their present context in some form," 117; for Carr, only after a text is assigned to a stratum on other grounds such as doublets, contradictions, and word/phrase usage should the relative readability of the strand be used as evidence that the source once existed as a separate literary document.

2. Joel S. Baden, *The Composition of the Pentateuch: Renewing the Documentary Hypothesis*, 30.

of the narrative, the identification of coherent themes, and consistent style align, so that there is a convergence of evidence.[3]

Though there are still some questions that remain, this theory is the best way scholars have come up with to make sense of the data we have. For biblical scholarship, the concept of separate literary sources in the Pentateuch has proven to be as much of a compelling "scientific" discovery as evolution itself. This chapter continues our exploration of the authorship of these sources by considering their compositional dating in light of external factors concerning the history of Israel.

Dating the Sources through Biblical Hebrew

The ability to assess the relative dating of the languages that appear in the Bible provides one of the most useful pieces of information for helping scholars understand the relationship of the Pentateuchal sources to one another. Most of the books in the Old Testament were written in a language that we refer to as Biblical Hebrew. Rather than an actual language that was written by a group of people at a specific time, Biblical Hebrew is in fact a scholarly construct based on the books of the Old Testament, and it represents a compilation of separate languages or dialects spoken by Israelites over an extended period (a small portion of the Old Testament was actually written in Aramaic, a Semitic language closely related to Hebrew).[4] The books of the Old Testament only provide us with a partial representation of the various forms of Hebrew originally spoken in ancient Israel. Scholars are able to distinguish these separate dialects of Hebrew based upon issues of chronology, geography, and even literary genre (for example, poetry versus prose).

Languages develop over time. Consider how different English is today than the dialect used by the Prophet Joseph Smith and his contemporaries. If we go back further in time, back to 1611 (i.e., the age in which the King James Version of the Bible was translated), we find that *that* form of English differs significantly from Joseph Smith's nineteenth century speech. And of course, going back even further into the literary history of English, we encounter examples of "Old English," the type that appears in the epic poem of Beowulf dating sometime between the eighth

---

3. Ibid., 31.

4. See the analysis provided by Marc Zvi Brettler, *Biblical Hebrew for Students of Modern Israeli Hebrew*, 1–4.

and the early eleventh centuries AD. Despite the fact that Beowulf is technically written in English, when a contemporary English speaker tries to read the poem in its original dialect, she will find the task very difficult; it would certainly be much more difficult than trying to understand the seventeenth-century King James dialect, which even in its time was deliberately composed with archaic English grammar and phraseology.

Since all languages evolve over time, grammatical forms and linguistic constructs provide helpful clues regarding the original date of the text. This is true for the documentary sources that appear in the Pentateuch. Scholars refer to the technical study of the manner in which languages evolve over time as *diachronic* analysis.

The scholarly consensus holds that the Old Testament includes literary works composed by Israelite and Judean scribes over an approximately thousand-year period from about the twelfth to the second centuries BC.[5] This is roughly the same amount of time between our current form of English and the Old English of Beowulf. The Book of Mormon also covers a similar period of Nephite history, where we find Lehi and his family leaving Jerusalem with a Hebrew dialect and Moroni, a thousand years later, acknowledging that the dialect his people used in his day had been modified:

> If our plates had been sufficiently large we should have written in Hebrew; but the Hebrew hath been altered by us also; and if we could have written in Hebrew, behold, ye would have had no imperfection in our record. (Morm. 9:35)

This transformation reflects our modern understanding of linguistic evolution. However, in contrast to English, Hebrew has "exhibited a remarkable uniformity over time."[6] So there really isn't as much distinction between the oldest forms of Hebrew and say Mishnaic Hebrew (first through fourth centuries AD), as there is in contemporary American English versus Beowulf. Nonetheless, there is a diversity of Hebrew dialects in the Old Testament and a diachronic analysis helps us to date the documentary sources in the Pentateuch.

The era in which many Old Testament texts were written includes the period between 586 and 538 BC. These are the years immediately after the Book of Mormon narrative begins. This is important to note, since during this historical period, important linguistic and religious changes took place in Judea, as a large portion of the population was taken captive into

---

5. Brettler, *Biblical Hebrew*, 2; rather than written texts, the earliest forms derive from oral poetic compositions.

6. Bruce K. Waltke and M. O'Connor, *An Introduction to Biblical Hebrew Syntax*, 4.

Babylon. The Babylonian exile had a tremendous impact upon the way in which the Hebrew language developed. As one linguist has observed:

> The Babylonian exile marks the beginning of a new stage in the development of Hebrew. The spoken and written languages had been drifting apart before the exile, and the social and political turmoil brought about by the fall of Jerusalem and the destruction of the First Temple produced a significant change in the linguitic *status quo*.[7]

During this era, Hebrew came under the direct influence of Aramaic, the administrative language used by early Near Eastern empires such as the Babylonians and Persians as the *lingua franca* or "working language." As a result, Aramaic eventually became the day-to-day language used in Israel during the Second Temple period (539 BC–70 AD). This explains why some of the late historical books in the Old Testament, like Esther and portions of Daniel, were written in Aramaic instead of Hebrew. Utilizing this Aramaic influence, scholars are able to distinguish between pre-exilic Hebrew (before 586 BC) and post-exilic Hebrew (after 538 BC, when the Jews returned from captivity). The middle section of exilic-Hebrew can also be identified as a transitional dialect between the two stages.

Additionally, there are important differences between the very earliest layers of Biblical Hebrew and the most common dialect that appears in the Old Testament. Scholars refer to the most common form of the language in the Old Testament as "Standard Hebrew." The earlier forms of Hebrew appear in biblical poems, such as the Song of Deborah in Judges 5 and Moses' Song of the Sea in Exodus 15.[8]

Separating the individual Pentateuchal texts according to their respective narratives, a diachronic analysis can help us determine the historical relationship of the sources to one another. As summarized by biblical scholar Richard Elliott Friedman, a diachronic analysis of the Hebrew in the documentary sources reveals:

1. The Hebrew of J and E comes from the earliest stage of biblical Hebrew.
2. The Hebrew of P comes from a later stage of the language.

---

7. Angel Saenz-Badillos, *A History of the Hebrew Language*, 112.

8. "Some poetic passages of the Hebrew Bible (e.g., Exodus 15; Judges 5) have been dated to this early period [the transition from LB III to Iron I, i.e., 1400–1200 BC] on the basis of certain archaic features of their language, but no extrabiblical text identifiable as Hebrew survives from this period." Gene M. Schramm, "Languages (Hebrew)," 205.

3. The Hebrew of the Deuteronomistic texts comes from a still later stage of the language.
4. P comes from an earlier stage of Hebrew than the Hebrew of the book of Ezekiel (which derives from the time of the Babylonian exile).
5. All of these main sources come from a stage of Hebrew known as Classical or "Standard" Biblical Hebrew, which is earlier than the Hebrew of the post-exilic, Persian period (known as Late Biblical Hebrew).[9]

Thus, it appears that E (or possibly J) was the first documentary source. P was written thereafter, which makes sense in light of the way P reacted to J's stories about creation and the flood. The Hebrew in D is later than that of P, which connects with D's rejection of the earlier Priestly concept of God literally dwelling in his temple. We also see various texts within D that show an awareness of P including Deuteronomy 4:16–19:

> [Do not] corrupt yourselves, and make you a graven image, the similitude of any figure, the likeness of male or female, the likeness of any beast that is on the earth, the likeness of any winged fowl that flieth in the air, the likeness of any thing that creepeth on the ground, the likeness of any fish that is in the waters beneath the earth: And lest thou lift up thine eyes unto heaven, and when thou seest the sun, and the moon, and the stars, even all the host of heaven, shouldest be driven to worship them, and serve them.

In a commandment prohibiting the construction of a religious idol, this passage specifically reverses the order of Priestly creation in Genesis. Scholars refer to the citation of an earlier biblical passage in reverse order as Seidel's Law.[10] The use of Seidel's Law in this passage parallels our modern use of quotation marks. It shows that the author of Deuteronomy 4:16–19 knew the priestly story of creation and confirms the validity of the linguistic analysis that shows the Hebrew in D is later than the Hebrew in P.

It is fairly simple to provide a relative dating for the Pentateuchal sources based upon thematic and linguistic observations. The issue becomes tricky in pinpointing the actual years these sources were written. As

---

9. Richard Elliott Friedman, *The Bible With its Sources Revealed*, 7–8.

10. The technique of using inverted quotations in biblical sources was first discussed academically by biblical scholar Moshe Seidel in "Parallels between Isaiah and Psalms," 149–72, 272–80, 335–55 (Hebrew); for an analysis of this device in the Book of Mormon, see David E. Bokovoy and John A. Tvedtnes, *Testaments: Links Between the Book of Mormon and the Hebrew Bible*, 56–60.

expected, there exists considerable academic debate. In fact, new theories are constantly being presented, requiring the Documentary Hypothesis to have some flexibility.

However, there are some issues for which we have a general scholarly consensus. Currently, many scholars are "agnostic on whether there was any writing of biblical materials in tenth-century Judah, given the uncertainties surrounding it."[11] Archaeological evidence suggests that writing itself was probably only beginning to take place in Israel and Judah during this time period. According to biblical scholar Seth Sanders,

> In the tenth-century the first records of an inland script appear in Israel, but they are in an unstandardized Canaanite. We have alphabetic writing and official seals from the probable period of the United Monarchy in the tenth century but the writing is not yet Hebrew and the seals are wordless. Standardized local script-languages appear in monumental form hand in hand with local states in the Levant by the late ninth century. The first deliberate vernaculars are royal tools. Hebrew arose alongside these written language and was produced in both the north and south of Israel by the beginning of the eighth century BCE. through the sixth century BCE.[12]

This means that during the time period of Saul, David, and Solomon, a written form of Hebrew was only beginning to take shape; when it developed, the written form of Hebrew derived from the earlier Phoenician script. David Carr has made this clear in his most recent analysis of the Pentateuchal sources:

> It is plausible to suggest that these early kingdoms [Judah and Israel] developed a preliminary literary system. . . . A combination of archaeological and biblical evidence, critically read, suggests the emergence of a new kind of textual system in the tenth and ninth centuries, one built on the Phoenician script (and potentially depending on other elements of the Phoenician system), one influenced in some ways by Egyptian educational-literary prototypes, and one shared between the Southern and Northern highlands, along with some areas of the Transjordan that were dominated at times by Israel-Judah (e.g., Moab).[13]

Ultimately, what this means is that biblical figures such as Abraham, Isaac, Jacob, and Moses, whom the texts have living prior to the time of the divided monarchy, most likely did not possess an actual written language. If they did, it certainly would not have been Hebrew, and we would have no

---

11. Carr, *The Formation of the Hebrew Bible*, 359.
12. Seth L. Sanders, *The Invention of Hebrew*, 106.
13. Carr, *The Formation of the Hebrew Bible*, 385.

idea what that script could have been. One could make an argument that Moses might have known how to write in an Egyptian hieroglyphic script, or Abraham might have known some form of early cuneiform; however, this seems highly unlikely given the complexity of these systems and the fact that such knowledge was restricted to those devoted to years of highly technical scribal education. Moreover, the linguistic evidence behind the biblical sources show no signs whatsoever that biblical sources could have been originally written in a language other than Hebrew.

Ancient Israelite Literacy

Throughout history, most people did not have time nor the opportunity to go to school and learn to read and write complicated ancient scripts. They were far too busy taking care of crops, working, and trying to survive. Expansive literacy is largely a privilege of the modern industrial world. Even after the alphabet had been developed, and prior to the days of the printing press, the literacy rate in Europe at the end of the middle ages was only about a quarter of the population. Karel van der Toorn explains the issue of ancient literacy in these terms:

> The great civilizations of antiquity were oral cultures. Though the figures differ depending on place and period, literacy was always restricted to a small segment of society. The Mesopotamians were the first humans to write, but less than 5 percent of the populations were actually literate. In Egypt the rate of literacy was slightly higher than in Mesopotamia, but even the most generous estimates put it as no more than 7 percent of the population. In the classical world the situation was not much different. Greece had an overall literacy rate of about 10 percent, yet it was still predominately an oral culture, rhetoric being the foundation and eloquence the aim of education.[14]

So the vast majority of ancient Israelite and Judean people could not read, nor did they even possess a written Hebrew script until the ninth century BC (after the time period of King David).[15]

This archaeological assessment reflects the fact that neither the act of writing itself, nor references to actual written texts, holds an important place in the books of Genesis, Exodus, Leviticus, and Numbers and that

---

14. Karel van der Toorn, *Scribal Culture and the Making of the Hebrew Bible*, 10.

15. Recent archaeological discoveries leave open the possibility that a Hebrew script may have developed as early as the tenth century BC, but given that these inscriptions are fragmentary and written with Phoenician script, scholars debate whether they should be called "Hebrew."

writing and the production of written scriptural texts was not an important feature of early Israelite history.[16] The authors of the Bible's first three books did not conceptualize a time period when inspired prophets such as Abraham or Moses wrote scriptural texts.

Instead, even in the Book of Exodus, the focus of transmitting revelation from God is on *orality* rather than *textuality*. Significantly, when God originally gives Moses the Ten Commandments in Exodus, the Lord did not *write* the law, but instead simply *spoke* the words: "And God *spake* all these words, saying . . ." (Ex. 20:1). Then in terms of sharing that revelation, Exodus reports that the Israelites specifically asked Moses to *speak* to them, rather than *write* God's words: "And they said unto Moses, Speak thou with us, and we will hear: but let not God speak with us, lest we die" (v. 19).

This lack of emphasis on writing revelation is historically significant. William Schniedewind expresses the matter this way:

> It is truly an astonishing observation that writing has no role in the revelation at Mount Sinai in Exodus 19. Writing has no role in the description of the giving of the Ten Commandments in Exodus 20. Writing has no role in the so-called Covenant Code in Exodus 21–23. Somehow the story of the revelation in Exodus 19–23 seems unaware that the Torah is a text.[17]

Schniedewind has observed that the act of writing does not occur in the account until after the completion of the covenant in Exodus 24:4. When it finally does, the allusion to an actual written text happens not because God commanded Moses to record the event, but only as an afterthought. It is as if at some point, writing down the words of God just seemed the thing to do: "and Moses wrote all the words of the Lord."[18] Even this reference to writing, according to Schniedewind, is probably a later textual addition to Exodus that was made in order to connect its law with Deuteronomy and the religious reforms of King Josiah (see 2 Kgs. 23:2, 21).

Still, taking this statement seriously in Exodus 24:4, a plain literary reading of this passage would only indicate that Moses wrote down the "Book of the Covenant" (Ex. 21–23) and the Ten Commandments (Ex. 20), not the entire Pentateuch. Outside of this reference, the only other place in these books that depicts Moses as a scriptural author is the conclusion to the Book of Deuteronomy.

---

16. William M. Schniedewind, *How the Bible Became a Book: The Textualization of Ancient Israel*, 81–82.

17. Ibid., 121.

18. Ibid., 122.

> And Moses wrote this law, and delivered it unto the priests the sons of Levi, which bare the ark of the covenant of the Lord, and unto all the elders of Israel. (Deut. 31:9)

As we have seen, Deuteronomy is both linguistically and conceptually later than the other Pentateuchal strands. This statement, therefore, provides evidence for the developing appreciation of written scriptural texts in Judean religious conceptions.

When we consider still later Jewish religious texts, we encounter an even greater emphasis upon the written scriptural word in a way that begins to parallel our own modern perception. From this historical perspective, it is interesting to compare the lack of emphasis upon writing down scriptural texts in the first four books of the Pentateuch with what we encounter in the second century Jewish text known as Jubilees:

> Set your mind on every thing which I shall tell you on this mountain, and write it in a book so that their descendants might see that I have not abandoned them on account of all of the evil which they have done. (Jubilees 1:5)

The statement that Moses created the Torah as a written revelation parallels the view in Joseph Smith's Book of Moses (a text we will explore in light of Higher Criticism in Chapter 7).

In a way, the Book of Mormon seems to reflect some of these concepts on literacy. Nephi would have produced his record during a time period when the notion of writing sacred scripture had only recently begun to take shape in ancient Judean culture and when very few people would have received the scribal training necessary to produce a complex literary work. Nephi begins his account with what seems to be an almost immediate apologetic need to explain to his readers how he is able to perform this extraordinary deed:

> I, Nephi, having been born of goodly parents, therefore I was taught somewhat in all the learning of my father . . . therefore I make a record of my proceedings in my days. Yea, I make a record in the language of my father, which consists of the learning of the Jews and the language of the Egyptians. (1 Ne. 1:1)

It is difficult to access with any precision what we are to understand by "learning" of the Jews and the "language" of the Egyptians. In Joseph Smith's day, the word "learning" was used to describe "the knowledge of principles or facts received by instruction or study." It would be logical to associate this term, therefore, with Jewish scribal practices or techniques. "Language" was also defined as "the expression of ideas by words or significant sounds, for the communication of thoughts."[19] Thus, we could assume that Nephi had been trained in Judean scribal skills by his father and that he produced his record using Egyptian words and phrases. This, however, would have been a highly unusual skill in and around Jerusalem at his time and would mean that Nephi was quite privileged in terms of literacy.[20]

Assyrian Influence On Scribalization

The concept of a Pentateuch or Torah that we find both in Judaism and in later Old Testament books such as Ezra and Nehemiah began with Deuteronomy and the Josianic writers.[21] In terms of its initial sources, most scholars believe that the Pentateuch took its preliminary shape in Jerusalem during the late eighth century BC.[22] This was the period of the prophet Isaiah and the Judean king Hezekiah. This does not mean that scholars assume that no form of Old Testament scriptural texts existed prior to this point. Instead, it suggests that with the emergence of Jerusalem as an important political center, together with the rise of the Assyrian empire, Judean scribes at this time began to collect and record Israelite oral traditions, as well as compose new religious literature. These writings eventually made their way into the pages of our Old Testament.[23]

During this historical period, the rise of the Assyrian empire led to the development of scribalization in the ancient Near East, and this movement greatly affected the Southern kingdom of Judah. The Assyrians used writing to record detailed information as a political tool to help govern conquered territories. In addition to scribalization and the increased development of written texts, the Assyrian empire had another significant impact upon Judea and the eventual creation of the Bible: the rise of the Assyrian empire

---

19. Noah Webster, *American Dictionary of the English Language* (1828).

20. For an analysis of Nephi as trained Judean scribe, see Brant Gardner, "Musings on the Makings of Mormon's Book: Preliminary: Nephi as Author."

21. Schniedewind, *How the Bible Became a Book*, 121.

22. Ibid., 5. However, as discussed in the previous chapter, recall that the individual documentary sources were still being written and revised through the exilic era. The Pentateuch as we know it was probably not produced until the Persian era (550–330 BC).

23. Yet David Carr writes in his most recent assessment, "though there were potential early cores behind separate Pentateuchal traditions, such as the ancestral or Exodus-Moses traditions, most specialists in the study of the Pentateuch now think that the first proto-Pentateuchal narrative, one extending from creation to Moses, dated to the exile at the earliest." Carr, *The Formation of the Hebrew Bible*, 359.

transformed the political landscape of the ancient world by creating urban-ization (meaning the physical growth of urban population centers).[24] We see this process occurring in terms of the Old Testament King Hezekiah whom the Bible presents as responsible for several government building projects during this era, including fortifications (the broad wall of Jerusalem), water projects (his famous tunnel), and even a new government center (Ramat Rahel). Urbanization served as a means for the development of even greater scribal skills in ancient cities such as Jerusalem.

All of this provided an important context for the creation of the bibli-cal sources, which tell the history of the House of Israel. From a histori-cal perspective, Israelite scribes trained and influenced by their Assyrian conquerors were the authors who produced the written sources used to create the Pentateuch.

In trying to assign specific dates to these sources, it is in some ways easiest to begin with the J source.[25] Conceptually, J's human-like por-trayal of God reflects an early Israelite religious perception, similar to the ones we encounter in other ancient Near Eastern sources. Often dated by scholars to the tenth or ninth centuries BC, J has long been considered "the most ancient historiographic work of the Bible."[26] However, more recent evidence suggests that J perhaps developed as a response to the view of national history and Assyrian imperialism witnessed in the Covenant Code and its accompanying E narrative.[27] This means that it is quite likely

---

24. On the urbanization of Jerusalem during this time period, see Schniedewind, *How the Bible Became a Book*, 68–73.

25. To reveal my own feeling on the matter, I currently believe that the documentary sources were developed in the following sequential order: E, J, P, D. Before we conclude this section, it is important to note that although scholars will continue to debate this historical issue, the dating of the Pentateuchal sources does not affect the legitimacy of the Hypothesis.

26. Albert de Pury, "Yahwist ("J") Source," 1013.

27. In his analysis on the relationship between the Laws of Hammurabi and the Covenant Code (Ex. 20:19–23:33), David P. Wright illustrates that the author(s) of the Covenant Code created the Israelite legal collection in connection with a version of the Exodus narrative. Wright maintains that the story of Moses' birth and rescue in Exodus 2:1–10 may have appeared in this original narrative as a reflection of the Assyrian Sargon tale, perhaps composed or revised during the reign of Sargon II. If correct, then Wright's theory places the chronological window for the creation of both the Covenant Code and its accompanying narrative from 710–640 BC. This theory opens up the possibility that in contrast to the previous consensus, the E source may have been written

that E actually came before J (exactly when we cannot say) and that P was written as a priestly reaction to these sources some time later toward the beginning of the Judean exile (remember P is earlier than D, and D for the most part is clearly pre-exilic). Dating the sources is like putting together a puzzle in which we have to fit all of the various parts together so that the entire picture makes sense.

The Neo-Assyrian monarchs Tiglath-Pileser III and Shalmaneser V commenced their conquest of the Northern kingdom of Israel beginning in 740 BC. During this era, the Southern kingdom of Judah became an Assyrian vassal state. Scribalization and direct Neo-Assyrian influence that we find in the Pentateuch (discussed in Chapter 5) remained minimal in Judean society until the mid-eighth century. Recent studies have shown that during this later period of Neo-Assyrian occupation, Israelite and Judean scribes began to construct their own literary works in response to their direct exposure to Mesopotamian sources.[28] This is significant for our understanding of the Bible. This reaction to Neo-Assyrian imperialism appears to have provided the original creative spark that led to the development of the written Pentateuchal sources.

Returning therefore to the J source, we find that a comparative analysis with other Near Eastern traditions indicates that the author was familiar

---

prior to the J narrative. J, after all, seems to resolve the difficulty of E's depiction of the revelation of the divine name Yahweh given to Moses in Exodus 3:15 by intentionally pushing the divine name back to the beginning of time. If correct, this theory need not indicate that J's account of prehistory was written decades or even a century following the composition of E's original Exodus account, despite its impact upon J's narrative. In spite of their differences, one could easily imagine a scenario in which these respective Israelite sources developed almost simultaneously to one another. A detailed exploration of these issues, however, extends beyond the scope of the present study and bears little consequence for the present textual exploration. Despite the plausibility of the theory that E was composed prior to J, a historical consideration of J in relationship to the other Pentateuchal sources reveals that J's account of prehistory most certainly *does* reflect one of the earliest historical layers of biblical material.

Suffice it to say that like the Covenant Code and its accompanying narrative, J appears to have been originally composed by its author as a direct response to the view of national history and Assyrian imperialism. This theory would explain J's focus on traditional Mesopotamian themes. See the analysis provided by David P. Wright, *Inventing God's Law: How the Covenant Code of the Bible Used and Revised the Laws of Hammurabi* (Oxford: Oxford University Press, 2013).

28. See the analysis provided in Chapter 5.

with earlier Mesopotamian sources (including Gilgamesh) and that many of these sources' major themes regarding creation and origins occur in Genesis 1–11. A preoccupation with Mesopotamian themes makes sense in an age in which Israelite scribes were being trained by their Assyrian rulers for political service.[29] Though in the past some scholars have traditionally ascribed these connections between the Bible and Mesopotamia to oral or even early scribal traditions from the second millennium BC, in view of the types of evidence we will see in the subsequent chapter, the probability that Pentateuchal sources developed out of direct Israelite scribal contact with Neo-Assyrian literature appears most likely.[30]

Conclusion

As we have seen throughout this study, unraveling the documentary sources in the Pentateuch resolves discrepancies and creates a coherent narrative flow. The highly uniform themes and vocabulary that consistently appear throughout these individual sources provides impressive secondary evidence that these are independent texts that recount the story of Israel. Our ability to historically analyze the Hebrew that appears in these documents provides further support for this perspective. The most likely scenario for the creation of these texts is that they were written by Israelite and Judean authors, who were trained in the arts of Neo-Assyrian scribalism, including the technical skill to read and write some of the most famous Mesopotamian texts.

It's difficult to know precisely when the Pentateuchal sources were written. The Neo-Assyrian Mesopotamian influence responsible for inspiring the initial creative spark behind the sources began in the mid-ninth century BC. However, it remained somewhat negligible until the mid-eighth century. During this time, the Northern kingdom of Israel was more politically powerful than Southern Judah. Given political his-

---

29. Wright observes, "The J portion of the primordial history reflects and develops ideas found in Mesopotamian literature and culture. The J story informs its readers that the nation Israel ultimately derives from a Mesopotamian context. By this description, J acknowledged and conceded the primacy of Mesopotamian civilization. But J simultaneously undermined Mesopotamian power or prestige by characterizing it as having developed in ways opposed to the will of the creator Yahweh." Wright, *Inventing God's Law*, 358.

30. See especially the analysis by David Wright on the the direct links between the Covenant Code and the Laws of Hammurabi in Chapter Five.

TABLE 4.1 SUMMARY OF DATING AND AUTHOR LOCATIONS

	Elohist (E)	Yahwist (J)	Priestly (P)	Deuteronomic (D)
Dating	Mid-8th century BC	Late 8th through 7th centuries BC	6th century BC, yet perhaps not finished until the Exile in 586 BC	Final form written after P, yet core produced at the end of the 7th century BC
Location	Northern scribes	Southern scribes	Southern scribes	Northern scribes exiled in the Southern kingdom.

tory, it is difficult to imagine that a Southern text would have influenced the development of a Northern source.

A good working model is that E was probably written first in the North (although it was possibly a Southern text produced by exiled Northern scribes) during the mid-eighth century BC. The narrative may have been written to provide historical context for the Covenant Collection influenced by Israelite scribal interaction with the Mesopotamian legal collection known as the Code of Hammurabi (discussed in Chapter 5). The J source was probably composed in the South shortly thereafter; however, portions of J cannot be earlier than the seventh century BC. P was probably then composed during the sixth century BC, and perhaps not even finished until the Exile (i.e., after 586 BC).

Like E, Deuteronomy has a strong Northern influence. As a source, Northern scribes may have begun the initial stages of the project prior to the Assyrian conquest in 721 BC, but D was not put together in the form we know it until after P. Assuming that a version of D was connected with King Josiah's reforms, the basic core must have been written towards the end of the seventh century BC around 640–609 BC. This would put J a few years earlier, since P knows J, and D knows P. Dating the sources in this way means that the Pentateuch most likely came together in its current form following the Babylonian exile, perhaps during the Persian era (550–330 BC).

Chapter Five

Mesopotamian Influence on the Pentateuch

Introduction

Today, many Christians (including some Latter-day Saints) tend to assume that scripture, by definition, is literature that transcends cultural boundaries and thereby conveys the unadulterated "word of God." This perspective can be seen, for example, in the "Chicago Statement on Biblical Inerrancy," created in 1978 by more than 200 evangelical leaders at a conference sponsored by the International Council on Biblical Inerrancy. Since its formulation, many people have used this statement as a guide to define the meaning of scripture. In article XVIII of the statement, these leaders expressed their view with the following assertion:

> We deny the legitimacy of any treatment of the text or quest for sources lying behind it that leads to relativizing, dehistoricizing, or discounting its teaching, or rejecting its claims to authorship.

This statement seems to serve as a response to the types of observations made by biblical scholars we have surveyed throughout this study. For many Bible-believing Christians, God is the only source lying behind the text; and therefore, any suggestion that an author may have used a "pagan" (or non-Israelite) Near Eastern document to create scripture must obviously be mistaken.

As we have seen, however, the Chicago Statement on Biblical Inerrancy could not be more at odds with the views that Joseph Smith held. Still, some Latter-day Saints find themselves unwittingly adopting a view of scripture similar to the one articulated by this statement.[1] Because the

---

1. In the book *How Wide the Divide*, BYU Religion professor Stephen Robinson states that both he and his evangelical co-author "agree that the present biblical

Book of Deuteronomy depicts Moses as the literal author of its sermons and legal collections, and Historical Criticism shows that this position cannot be sustained, they may leave thinking that by accepting the theses of source criticism, they can no longer consider the Bible to be inspired.

In addition to uncovering the existence of multiple sources in the Pentateuch, Historical Criticism shows that these documents were directly influenced by non-Israelite texts. This influence occurred as a result of the scribalization process during the Neo-Assyrian period in Judean and Israelite history. While identifying the ways in which non-Israelite material has been adopted and reformulated by biblical authors in the creation of the Pentateuchal sources is an exciting endeavor, this process can prove challenging to some. However, understanding that sacred religious texts are not produced in a cultural vacuum, but are products of their environment can alleviate many of these concerns.

When it comes to non-Israelite sources that have impacted the development of the Pentateuch, nothing can surpass the influence of Mesopotamia. Literally, the term *Mesopotamia* refers to "the land between the two rivers," meaning the Tigris and Euphrates. Historians have called this region of the world, which includes the territory of modern-day Iraq, the "cradle of civilization," since writing and other forms of what we would today consider signs of a civilized state first emerged in this region around 3000 BC.[2]

---

text is the word of God within the common parameters of the Chicago Statement and the eighth Article of Faith." Craig L. Blomberg and Stephen E. Robinson, *How Wide the Divide? A Mormon and an Evangelical in Conversation*, 75. Similar views accepting a traditional evangelical approach to scripture while expressing skepticism in Historical Criticism can be found in a variety of LDS writings. For example, concerning the "motivations" of biblical scholars, BYU Religion Professor Robert Millet writes "Some seek to suggest naturalistic explanations for what in reality came about through divine intervention. . . . We have seen the handiwork of such approaches in regard to the holy scriptures: the Bible has been stripped of its divinity and historicity by many who see only through the lens of secular scholarship. . . . It is frequently the case that when we aspire to the honors of men— adapting our work to make it acceptable in the eyes of prominent men—we offend the Lord. . . . The crying need in our day is for academically competent Latter-day Saint thinkers to make judgments by the proper standards—the Lord's standards." Robert Millet, "How Should Our Story Be Told," 3–4.

2. The literature on this point is vast; for a basic introduction, see George Roux, *Ancient Iraq*, 66–84; for a specific focus upon how the emergence of civilization

For much of its history, Mesopotamia was divided between its northern section controlled by Assyria and its southern region of Babylonia. During the third millennium BC, the southern region itself became politically fragmented into a group of city-states. This lower region gave rise to the culture of the Sumerians. The upper region of northern Mesopotamia was named after the city of Akkad, from which we get the general term "Akkadian" for the Semitic languages of Babylon and Assyria. By 2000 BC, both areas had adopted the same language and pantheon of gods. At the time the Pentateuchal sources were created, Mesopotamia was home to some of the most powerful kingdoms in the world, including the Assyrians and Babylonians. These empires had a tremendous impact upon the history and culture of ancient Israel (not to mention the rest of the Near East). In terms of the creation of the Pentateuch, Historical Criticism has shown that it is really impossible to overstate the significance of Mesopotamian influence.

When we open up the Bible, the first few chapters of Genesis provide a clear "bread-crumb-like" trail documenting this imprint. The story of creation in Genesis 1 reads somewhat like a traditional Mesopotamian creation narrative, similar to the classic Babylonian epic Enūma Elish.[3] The story of Eden shares many motifs in common with the famous Mesopotamian Epic of Gilgamesh, including references to sexuality as a type of pathway to becoming human and a serpent that robs a person of a plant that would provide everlasting life.[4] According to the Genesis account, the garden itself was located to the land "east" of Israel, and the Bible specifically identifies Eden as a land connected with the Tigris and Euphrates rivers (Gen. 2:14). Genesis then features the two flood narratives from P and J. Both of these accounts appear to borrow heavily from a traditional Mesopotamian flood story. Before the Bible enters into what

---

in ancient Mesopotamia relates to the Hebrew Bible see Michael D. Coogan, "In the Beginning: The Earliest History," 3–31.

3. For a recent analysis of conceptual parallelisms between Enūma Elish and a variety of biblical texts, including Job, Psalms, and Genesis 1, see Luciano Zanovello, "Enuma Elish e Bibbia Ebraica," 205–22; for an argument for direct dependence, see Victor Hurowitz, "The Genesis of Genesis: Is the Creation Story Babylonian?" 36–48.

4. For a basic introduction to these parallels see Alexander Heidel, *The Gilgamesh Epic and Old Testament Parallels* (Chicago: University of Chicago Press, 1963); Harold Victor Matthews and Don C. Benjamin, *Old Testament Parallels: Laws and Stories from the Ancient Near East*, 21–32.

its authors would have considered the "historical" era, we encounter the story of Babel, an account regarding the construction of a Mesopotamian ziggurat that directly critiques Babylonian culture and religion. As one scholar has expressed it, "biblical authors were indebted to Mesopotamian models for not only in matters of arrangement but also in some of the subject matter."[5]

After these introductory chapters, readers encounter a type of reversal of the Babylonian exile of the Jewish community, as Abraham, the great biblical patriarch, leaves the city-state of Ur in southern Mesopotamia and enters the promised land of Canaan.[6] And yet, even at this point, as readers continue to make their way through the subsequent books of the Pentateuch, the direct Mesopotamian influence on the Bible has really only just begun.

What is even more striking than the thematic connections between the Bible's opening chapters and Mesopotamian culture is the fact that the later books in the Pentateuch, including Deuteronomy, directly borrowed from Mesopotamian legal collections and vassal treaties for their structure and themes. All of this information suggests that the Pentateuchal sources were shaped by a result of Israelite and Judean scribes interacting with Mesopotamian sources. Indeed, the connections between Mesopotamia and the Pentateuch are so striking that we might say *without Babel there would be no Bible.*

This perspective was once famously articulated by Friedrich Delitzsch, almost sixty years after the death of the Prophet Joseph Smith, when the

---

5. E.A. Speiser, *Genesis: Introduction, Translation, and Notes*, 9.

6. Because of a desire to connect Ur with Egyptian influences suggested in the Book of Abraham, some LDS scholars have tried to argue for a Northern location for Ur, but these problematic arguments have failed to impact the mainstream consensus locating Abraham's Ur in southern Mesopotamia; see for example, Paul Y. Hoskisson, "Where Was Ur of the Chaldees?" 119–136; John Gee and Stephen D. Ricks, "Historical Plausibility: The Historicity of the Book of Abraham as a Case Study," 69–72. The following statement by Jean-Cl. Margueron regarding Ur in the *Anchor Bible Dictionary* illustrates the general academic view: "A very important Sumerian city that played an active role in the 3d millennium and in the beginning of the 2d millennium B.C. It's modern name is Tell Muqqayyar. . . . After Babylon, it is without a doubt the best known Mesopotamian site in the Bible because it is mentioned in connection with Abraham. According to Gen. 11:31 it is from the city of Ur in Chaldea that Terah and his clan left to go to Haran, a great caravan site located in the belt of the Euphrates in n. Syria." Jean-Cl. Margueron, "Ur," 766.

important textual and archeological remains of Mesopotamia were first coming to light. In the first of a series of three famous lectures, Delitzsch made the following statement:

> The conviction has steadily and universally established itself that the results of the Babylonian and Assyrian excavations are destined to inaugurate a new epoch, not only in our intellectual life, but especially in the criticism and comprehension of the Old Testament, and that from now till all futurity the names of Babel and Bible will remain inseparably linked together.[7]

Even though many of Delitzsch's views were based upon ideas of German nationalism and anti-Semitism, his main message has proven almost prescient.[8] Based upon both relative dating (meaning in relationship to one another) and through a critical analysis of the Hebrew, scholars know both approximately when these sources were produced and the Mesopotamian sources they rely on.

Some readers might wonder if it is possible that Israelite texts influenced Mesopotamian sources rather than the other way around. To answer this question, we must first recognize that there is no historical reason for Mesopotamian scribes to have adopted Israelite sources. On the other hand, throughout its history, Israel and Judea were controlled by Mesopotamian empires, and Israelite scribes were trained in Akkadian (the languages in which many of these Mesopotamian sources were written). Also, the way the Bible adapts the Laws of Hammurabi and Assyrian Vassal Treaties indicates that it draws upon Mesopotamian texts rather than the other way around. Moreover, the Mesopotamian texts simply predate the period in which the biblical sources were written. Based on the Bible's own internal chronology, it is impossible for *any* of the Hebrew sources to have existed prior to the mid-second millennium BC when the Hebrew nation originated through Abraham. Thus, if for the sake of argument, Abraham somehow brought with him into the land of Canaan written sources from Ur that subsequent biblical authors drew upon, then these hypothetical sources would have been "Mesopotamian."

In this chapter, we will consider some of the specific non-Israelite sources that appear to have influenced the development of the Pentateuch. While some of these cases are compelling examples of this type of cultural borrowing, others are admittedly a bit more speculative. Readers should

---

7. Friedrich Delitzsch, *Babel and Bible: Two Lectures*, 2.

8. See the summary provided by Mogens Trolle Larsen, "The 'Babel/Bible' Controversy and its Aftermath," 95–106.

remember, however, that even with the examples that only provide a possible hint of cultural borrowings, these cases are made more compelling by the explicit instances that we *can* identify of Mesopotamian influence and the historical circumstances under which the authors of the Pentateuchal sources wrote their narratives.[9]

Genesis 1 and Enūma Elish

We will begin with the Priestly story of creation in Genesis 1 and its apparent connection with the Babylonian myth, Enūma Elish. The Enūma Elish tells the story of Marduk's (the chief god of ancient Babylon) rise to a position of cosmic kingship. A seven-tablet collection, the Enūma Elish appears in various copies or forms from Babylon and Assyria. Though its compositional date has been a source of considerable debate amongst scholars, the most compelling theory is that "the emphases and approach of Enūma Elish would agree with composition in the first millennium at a point when Babylon's ascendency was threatened either by the Aramaeans or the Assyrians."[10] While not consistent with a second-millennium BC perspective, the universalistic worldview in Enūma Elish works well with the concept of world-empire that took shape in Mesopotamian political and religious thought during the first millennium BC. Ultimately, Enūma Elish reflects the Assyrian world model and seeks to elevate the position of Marduk and the city of Babylon when Babylon's position would appear to have been threatened. This would place the creation of Enūma Elish to approximately the same era as Genesis 1, although possibly predating the biblical source by up to one or two centuries.[11]

Named after its opening words "When above," Enūma Elish tells the story of two primeval realities, Apsu, the god of the fresh water, and Tiamat, the goddess of the salt waters. According to the myth, these divinities mixed together, and from their union was born the initial genera-

---

9. This brief survey serves as a basic introduction to these issues. I would suggest that anyone interested in additional information should refer to both the footnotes and suggestions for further reading at the conclusion of this book.

10. Tzvi Abusch, "Marduk," 1023.

11. Although some scholars have dated Enūma Elish as early as the eighteenth to sixteenth century BC (i.e., the time of the famous Babylonian king Hammurabi or perhaps the early Kassite era), even a late compositional date from the rise of the Neo-Assyrian empire suggests that Enūma Elish was written before the Priestly story of creation.

tion of gods. Geographically, southern Mesopotamia was in essence a large floodplain. Historically, the Tigris and Euphrates rivers flowed into the Persian Gulf and their alluvial deposits gradually extended that plain. The image of fresh and salt water mixing together to create the beginnings of life reflects the idea that the land and the sky came into existence where the fresh waters of the Tigris and Euphrates rivers reach the salt water of the Persian Gulf. From this union, land and the horizon emerged, as well as the first generation of deities, including the great storm god Marduk. Enūma Elish is the story of how this local god of Babylon became the chief god of the universe and the creator of human beings.

Archaeologists originally discovered Enūma Elish in the ancient Royal Library of Ashurbanipal (Assyrian king, son of Esarhaddon 668–627 BC) at Nineveh (current day Mosul, Iraq) in 1849. Since its discovery, scholars have noted the various connections between the Bible's first creation story and this important example of Mesopotamian mythology. For example, the two stories actually share the same basic structural pattern:

Enūma Elish	Genesis
1. Divine Spirit and cosmic matter are coexistent and coeternal	1. Divine Spirit creates cosmic matter and exists independently of it
2. Primeval chaos; Ti'amat enveloped in darkness	2. The earth is desolate waste, with darkness covering the deep (*tehom*)
3. Light emanating from the gods	3. Light created
4. The creation of the firmament	4. The creation of the firmament
5. The creation of dry land	5. The creation of dry land
6. The creation of the luminaries	6. The creation of luminaries
7. The creation of man	7. The creation of man
8. The gods rest and celebrate	8. God rests and sanctifies the seventh day

As shown through this outline, the chronological order of events is identical in both texts: the heavens are created and the waters are separated, land is put on top of the water, the sun and the moon are created, animals and plants are created, humans are created, God rests. The only major difference being that Enūma Elish omits the creation of plants and animals.

In addition to the connection between the two accounts in terms of structure, one of the most striking similarities between Enūma Elish and Genesis 1 is the process by which the Earth was created. Genesis 1:2 seems to allude to the great cosmic battle fought between the god Marduk and the sea monster Tiamat:

> And the earth was without form, and void; and darkness was upon the face of the deep. And the Spirit of God moved upon the face of the waters. (Gen. 1:2)

The Hebrew word translated as "deep" (*tehom*) is an exact cognate of the Akkadian word Tiamat. Unlike the King James translation, however, *tehom* appears in the Hebrew text without the definite article ("the" in English, *ha-* in Hebrew). Hence, the word should be translated as the proper rather than common noun, "Deep." The biblical story, therefore, seems to be preparing readers for a retelling of the theomachy (or divine combat) between God and the Deep recounted in Enūma Elish. Instead, however, the God in P's creation narrative simply speaks and the cosmic waters obey.[12] Yet even this motif has a parallel with Enūma Elish in that the god Marduk's words are described as possessing the power to both create and destroy (4.25).

In Genesis, God created a dome called the "firmament" to separate the waters above from the waters below. Similarly, Marduk in Enūma Elish also seals the water off from the heavens. Additionally, the very concept of night and day are introduced in both stories as a means by which to create divine order. God creates lights in the sky to "mark the fixed times, the days and the years," making ultimately two lights, one to govern the day and one to govern the night (Gen. 1:14). In Enūma Elish, Marduk likewise assigns the moon the duty to "guard the night and to mark the month with its phases."

Another connection between the two accounts includes the concluding literary formula within P "these are the generations of heaven and earth" (Gen. 2:4). The Hebrew word translated as "generations" in the KJV is *toldot*. It stems from the root *yld*, which means literally "to give birth."[13] This may reflect the fact that Enūma Elish begins by recounting a series of births, including the subsequent generation of gods and goddesses of the divine council. Even the word pair "heaven and earth" in Genesis 1:1 and 2:4 was used anciently as a type of metonymy or literary allusion to the gods of the council.[14] The council of deities represents the

---

12. P even includes a reference to the cosmic sea monsters in Genesis 1:21 through the Hebrew word *taninim* which the LDS footnote of the Bible correctly notes means "sea monsters." These creatures do appear as God's foes in creation in Psalms 74:13.

13. Ludwig Koehler and Walter Baumgartner, *The Hebrew and Aramaic Lexicon of the Old Testament*, 1:411.

14. Concerning the biblical word pair "heaven and earth," G. Ernest Wright argues that readers should specifically "interpret such passages in the light of the

audience God addresses in his invitation spoken through the plural, "Let us make man in our image after our likeness" (Gen. 1:26).[15]

The two accounts even begin with the same type of expression. In the King James translation, the opening verse of the Bible reads: "In the beginning God created the heaven and the earth," which represents a very literal interpretation of the Hebrew. Originally, however, Genesis 1 was written without any vowels. The vowels were only added to the biblical text at a much later date as points above and below the actual words. It is most likely that the vocalization of the Hebrew used to produce the King James version of Genesis 1:1 is incorrect, instead the verse should be read as a dependent clause: "When in the beginning God created the heavens and the earth . . ."[16] For example, the more recent *Jewish Publication Society* translation of Genesis 1:1 reflects this nuance: "When God began to create heaven and earth . . ."[17] This more precise understanding of the first line of the creation account provides yet another parallel between the two stories, since Enūma Elish begins with a temporal clause:

> When on high no name was given to heaven, nor below was the netherworld called by name, Primeval Apṣu was their progenitor.[18]

Because of the historical dating of these two texts and the strong cultural influence that Mesopotamia had on Israelite and Judean scribal activities, it would seem that Genesis 1 has been influenced by this Babylonian myth. It is even possible, as some scholars have argued, that the creation story in Genesis 1 was written as a type of polemical response to the claims in the Babylonian myth.[19] And yet, as one famous biblical scholar has suggested, we should keep in mind that in using the Babylonian story as a type of conceptual guide, the Priestly author may have intended to simply suggest that on the subject of creation, he aligned his account with the traditional tenets of Babylonian "science."[20]

Divine Assembly, the members of which constitute the host of heaven and of earth." G. E. Wright, *The Old Testament Against Its Environment*, 36.

15. David E. Bokovoy, "Invoking the Council as Witness," 37–51.

16. John J. Collins, *Introduction to the Hebrew Bible*, 76.

17. See Marc Zvi Brettler and Adele Berlin, eds., *The Jewish Study Bible*, 12.

18. As cited in William H. Hallo and Lawson K. Younger, ed. *The Context of Scripture*, 1:390

19. B. Alster, "Tiamat," 1639.

20. Speiser, *Genesis*, 11.

J's Creation Narrative and Mesopotamian Mythology

The Bible's second creation account (J) also appears indebted to Mesopotamian sources. Like P's narrative, J's earlier version begins with a dependent clause, followed by a parenthetical statement (in italics) that explains the situation prior to actual creation:

J

[2:4b] When Yahweh god made earth and the heavens—[5] *there was not yet any plant of the field, and no shrub* had yet sprung up since Yahweh god had not caused *it to rain upon the earth, and since there was no one to till the ground,* [6] *yet a stream would rise from the earth and water the whole face of the ground*— [7] Yahweh god formed the man out of dust of the ground and breathed into his nostrils the breath of life so that the man became a living soul. [8] Then Yahweh god planted a garden in Eden, in the east; and there he placed the man that he formed.

P

[1] When God created heaven and earth— [2] *the earth was unformed and void, with darkness over the surface of the great deep and a wind from God swept over the water*— [3] God said let there be light, and there was light!

The parenthetical statements in both versions show that, like Mesopotamian traditions, the Bible does not teach the later theological idea of creation *ex nihilo* (out of nothing) professed by many Christians today. In the minds of the biblical authors, raw material existed prior to God's initial creative act, and God used this preexisting matter to organize or give structure to the universe.

This perspective reflects Joseph Smith's own views regarding creation:

You ask the learned doctors why they say the world was made out of nothing; and they will answer, "Doesn't the Bible say He created the world?" And they infer, from the word create, that it must have been made out of nothing. Now, the word create came from the word *baurau* which does not mean to create out of nothing; it means to organize; the same as a man would organize materials and build a ship. Hence, we infer that God had materials to organize the world out of chaos—chaotic matter, which is element, and in which dwells all the glory.[21]

The parenthetical clauses in both creation accounts in Genesis provide theological notions that accord with Joseph Smith's own religious views.

---

21. Joseph Smith, *Teachings of the Prophet Joseph Smith*, 350–51.

Both biblical versions follow the literary pattern for creation narratives that appears in the Mesopotamian myth known as Atrahasis and its derivative Enūma Elish:

> When gods were man, they did forced labor, they bore drudgery. (Atrahasis)

> When on high no name was given to heaven, nor below was the netherworld called by name . . . (Enūma Elish)

> When Yahweh God made the earth and the heaven . . . (J Gen. 2:4b)

> When God began to create heaven and earth . . . (P Gen. 1:1)

This comparison demonstrates how each of these ancient creation accounts follows the same literary pattern in opening the story of creation with a dependent clause.

The Mesopotamian myth of Atrahasis, which predates the Enūma Elish, tells the story of a wise man who built an ark and saved humankind from a flood.[22] The myth describes how Atrahasis survives the flood with his wife and is granted immortality by the gods. It also includes a creation narrative that depicts humans as creatures formed by the birth-goddess Belet-ili from a mixture of clay and the blood of a slain deity. A somewhat parallel idea appears in the depiction of human creation featured in Enūma Elish:

> When [Mar]duk heard the speech of the gods,
> He was resolving to make artful things:
> He would tell his idea to Ea,
> What he thought of in his heart he proposes,
> "I shall compact blood, let 'Man' be its name.
> I shall make stand a human being, let 'Man' be his name.
> I shall create humankind,
> They shall bear the gods' burden that those may rest."[23]

This motif parallels the idea in J's creation story that Yahweh created the first man from a mixture of soil and a divine substance, "breath" (Gen. 2:7).

J's creation story begins by stating that "the LORD God planted a garden eastward in Eden" and placed man in the garden as his semi-divine assistant (Gen. 2:8). Yahweh created man to physically resemble him so

---

22. For an analysis of Atra-hasis and its relationship to the opening chapters of Genesis, see Tikva Frymer-Kensky, "The Atrahasis Epic and Its Significance for Our Understanding of Genesis 1–9," 147–55.

23. Tablet VI, lines 1–8 as translated by Benjamin F. Foster in Hallo and Younger, *The Context of Scripture*, 1:400; for the Akkadian transliteration see Philippe Talon, *The Standard Babylonian Creation Myth: Enuma Elish* (Helsinki: The Neo-Assyrian Text Corpus Project, 2005).

that the human could both "dress/work" and "keep/guard" the garden paradise (Gen. 2:15). Thus J presents God as the divine gardener who created the first human to be his servant. Interestingly, the Book of Mormon draws upon this same theological construct in several places, including King Benjamin's sermon on service:

> I say unto you that if ye should serve him who has created you from the beginning, and is preserving you from day to day, by lending you breath, that ye may live and move and do according to your own will, and even supporting you from one moment to another—I say, if ye should serve him with all your whole souls yet ye would be unprofitable servants. (Mosiah 2:1)

The themes of creation, man, and service to God/the gods appear throughout LDS scripture—themes that ultimately derive from Mesopotamia's temple centered, politico-economic system.[24]

All throughout Mesopotamian mythology, we encounter the idea that humans were created to act as agricultural servants of the gods. For example, in the Sumerian myth "Birth of Man," the task of caring for the creator god's productions initially falls upon a group of lesser deities who appear in the myth "shouldering the menial labors . . . dredging the rivers . . . piling up their silt on projecting bends" and "lugging the clay."[25] In response to their complaints over the difficulties of their agricultural assignment, the mother goddess Namma appears in the myth instructing the god Enki to create a "fill-in worker" to assist the lesser gods:

> My son, rise from your bed,
> and when you
> with your ingenuity
> have searched out

---

24. For a consideration of humanity's role as temple servants of deity in Hittite conceptions see Mary R. Bachvarova, "Relations Between God and Man in the Hurro-Hittite 'Song of Release,'" 45–58; concerning Mesopotamian conceptions, one scholar writes, "in the Sumerian city-state, . . . the characteristic and most significant organization was the temple-estate, in which thousands of people cooperated in works of irrigation and agriculture in a politico-economic system centered on the temple, with all these people thought of as the servants of the god. The myth of the creation of man, therefore, was not basically a comment on the nature of man but an explanation of a particular social system, heavily dependent upon communal irrigation and agriculture, for which the gods' estates were primary foci of administration. H. W. F. Saggs, *The Encounter with the Divine in Mesopotamia and Israel*, 168.

25. "The Birth of Man," as cited in Thorkild Jacobsen, *The Harps that Once: Sumerian Poetry in Translation*, 151–66.

> the (required) skill,
> and you have fashioned
> a fill-in worker
> for the gods,
> may they get loose
> of their digging![26]

Similar portrayals of humanity functioning as fill-in agricultural servants of the gods occur throughout Near Eastern literature, including Atrahasis. The account describes the primeval history, a time when "gods were men," complaining to the high deity Ea to ease their agricultural labors. In response to their petition, the myth recounts the decision of Ea:

> Let [Belet-ili], the midwife create a human being,
> Let man assume the drudgery of god.[27]

These examples of Mesopotamian creation myths show that this idea (that the gods created humans to serve as agricultural assistants) appeared as an important notion in the world of the Bible.

In his literary efforts, it would appear that the author of Genesis 2–3 (J) absorbed some of these basic Mesopotamian constructs. J placed the man directly in the role of the lesser gods of the assembly and made him responsible for agricultural efforts. The animals and woman were man's assistant. In other words, man appears in J as a fill-in worker for his god, just as he does in the Mesopotamian sources. J omits the traditional theme of lesser gods, however, and instead, places the man directly into *their* customary position. Thus, instead of the pattern of high god to *lesser god* to man, the Eden story presents the order of creation as high god to *man* to animals/woman.

In terms of its perspective of the first humans as semi-divine beings created to assist God in an agricultural assignment, J's Eden story shares a similar perspective to a brief Sumerian/Babylonian creation tradition in a text known as KAR 4, dating to approximately 800 BC.[28] As Alexander Heidel explained regarding this myth, "on this tablet mention is made for the first time in Babylonian-Assyrian literature of the first two human beings and their names, Ulligarra and Zalgarra; before each one's name is placed the sign for 'deity,' which means that the first ancestors of mankind were regarded as being divine

---

26. Ibid.

27. Atra-hasis 1.130 lines 190–91 as translated by Benjamin F. Foster in Hallo and Younger, *The Context of Scripture*, 1:451.

28. KAR 4 in Benjamin R. Foster, *Before the Muses: An Anthology of Akkadian Literature*. For a transliteration of the text see Giovanni Pettinato, *Das altorientalische Menschenbild und die sumerischen und akkadischen Schopfungsmythen*, 74–81.

at least to some degree."[29] This portrayal of humankind as gods makes sense, in view of the account's description of human creation occurring through the shedding of divine blood (a commonly attested Mesopotamian motif).[30] The text presents the Mesopotamian gods Anu, Enlil, Shamash, and Ea discussing the need for humanity to complete their creative acts:

> Enlil said to them:
> 'O Anunna-gods, great gods,
> What should we do next?
> What should we make now?'
> The great gods who were present,
> And the Anunna-gods, ordainers of destines,
> Both replied to Enlil,
> 'In Uzumua, the linking place of heaven with earth,
> 'Let us slaughter Alla-gods,
> 'Let us create humankind from their blood.
> 'Their labor shall be labor for the gods;
> 'To maintain the boundary ditch for all time,
> 'To set the pickaxe and workbasket in their hands,
> 'To make the great dwelling of the gods,
> 'Worthy to be their sublime sanctuary,
> 'To add field to field!
> 'To maintain the boundary ditch for all time,
> 'To regulate irrigation works for you(?)
> 'To water the four abodes (of the earth),
> 'To make the plant life flourish,
> '[ ] rainfall [ ].'
> 'For maintaining the boundary ditch,
> 'For heaping up plies of harvested grain
> 'For making the fields of the Anunna-gods yield in plenty,
> 'For making great the prosperity of the land,
> 'For celebrating the gods' festivals as they should,
> 'For libating cool water,
> 'For making the great house of the gods worthy
> To be their sublime dwelling.
> 'You shall call their names Ullegarra and Annagarra.'[31]

---

29. Alexander Heidel, *The Babylonian Genesis*, 68.

30. See Tzvi Abusch, "Ghost and God: Some Observations on a Babylonian Understanding of Human Nature," 363–83.

31. KAR 4 lines 14–37; *1'–6'* as translated by Benjamin R. Foster, *Before the Muses*, 492–93. For a critique of Foster's labels for the periodization of Akkadian

Not enough clarity exists to draw a definite conclusion that KAR 4 directly influenced the Bible. However, various themes within the story of Eden, which are also foundational to Mesopotamian creation mythology (like the type that appears in KAR 4) illustrates the kinds of traditions that may have impacted the development of J's account.

Uzumua, for example, identified in KAR 4 as the linking place of heaven with earth, assumed a significant role in traditional Sumerian portrayals of human origins. The Uzumua of Nippur was considered sacred ground into which the Mesopotamian god Enlil drove his pickax in order to create humankind. As Assyriologist Thorkild Jacobsen explained, the "Uzu-mú-a, the '(place where) flesh sprouted forth,'" was the location where "the first men grew up from the earth like plants."[32] This motif is similar to J's description of the man, who like the plants and animals, came up "from the ground."

Additionally, both in P's version of creation and in KAR 4, the decision to create man appears as a declaration of self reflection on the part of the divine council of the Gods. P states: "then God said, 'Let us make man in our image and likeness'" (Gen. 1:26). The comparable Akkadian phrase in KAR 4 directed to the gods of the assembly is "Let us create man" (*i nibnâ amīlūta*).[33] This line parallels the grammatical and perhaps conceptual imagery in Genesis 1:26.[34] These types of first person common plural expressions directed to the council in Near Eastern texts provide evidence that biblical authors and their original audience may have conceived such expressions as addresses to the council of the Gods.

Finally, KAR 4 shares the biblical view that humanity was created to assist with an originally divine agricultural labor. "Their labor shall be labor for the gods," states the account in terms of the purpose of human existence, for they shall "make the plant life flourish" and cause "the fields of the Anunna-gods [to] yield in plenty." These motifs suggest a strong

---

literature, see Joan Goodnick Westenholz, "Review: *In The Shadow of the Muses a View of Akkadian Literature*," 84.

32. Thorkild Jacobsen, "Sumerian Mythology: A Review Article," 136.

33. For a definition of the Akkadian word *banû* and its use in the context of deities creating humans, see A.L. Oppenheim, et al., eds. *Chicago Assyrian Dictionary of the Oriental Institute of the University of Chicago*, 2:87.

34. For an analysis of the cohortative in Hebrew attested in Genesis 1:26, see Joüon and Muraoka, *A Grammar of Biblical Hebrew*, 114; note, however, that the authors refer to the grammatical form as "plural of deliberation with oneself," p. 374.

thematic and perhaps even historical correspondence between KAR 4 and biblical traditions.[35]

As has long been noted, the biblical description of the woman being created from the man's rib likewise reflects an ancient Mesopotamian tradition. The Sumerian word for "rib" is *ti* (pronounced "tee"). The very same Sumerian word also means "to make live." Thus, the name of the Sumerian goddess Nin-ti means both "the lady who makes live," as well as "the lady of the rib" through a play on words.[36] In a famous study of this motif, Samuel Noah Kramer drew attention to the fact that the passage in Genesis where Eve, "the mother of all living" is taken from the man's *rib* may echo this Sumerian pun, since the word play only works in Sumerian, not in Hebrew.[37]

J's opening story concerning the Garden of Eden shares much in common with the famous Epic of Gilgamesh, a classic combination of Mesopotamian myths regarding the great king of the Sumerian city-state of Uruk. The earliest version of the record dates to the eighteenth century BC. The geographical and historical distribution of the Epic uncovered by archaeologists reveal that Gilgamesh was one of the most popular myths in the world of the Bible. J's creation narrative shares many of Gilgamesh's basic themes, a fact that suggests that the biblical author was most likely influenced by some version of the Gilgamesh Epic. Both accounts feature the presence of a snake, a plant that grants a type of immortality, a focus upon human death and morality, and the use of sexuality as a type of rite of passage that transforms people from being animal-like into human beings.

The Epic of Gilgamesh tells the story of a man named Enkidu who lives in harmony with the animals until he is seduced by a woman. By choosing to engage in sexual intercourse with the woman, Enkidu loses his own closeness to the animals in a way that reflects the basic plot in J's Eden account.

J's story of the primordial man is not a "fall" in the traditional Western sense. Instead, it is the story of how man lost his immortality and gained the type of sexual awareness that humans possess but which animals' lack. Rather than falling, the man experienced a type of apotheosis or diviniza-

---

35. For Mesopotamian textual and cultural traditions upon the opening chapters of Genesis, see Stephanie Dalley, "The Influence of Mesopotamia upon Israel and the Bible," 64–68; Jeffrey H. Tigay, "On Evaluating Claims of Literary Borrowing," 250, 252, 255.

36. Samuel Noah Kramer, "Mythology of Sumer and Akkad," 103.

37. Kramer, "Mythology of Sumer and Akkad," 103.

tion, coming "to know" "like the gods."[38] Yahweh makes this clear in his conversation with the other non-specified deities in his council:

> And the LORD God said, Behold, the man is become as one of us, to know good and evil: and now, lest he put forth his hand, and take also of the tree of life, and eat, and live for ever. (Gen. 3:22)

When Yahweh expresses this concern over the man's new divine-like status, J seems to leave open the identity of the other beings who are *like* Yahweh, who confirms the previous observation made by the snake that "knowledge" would make the man and woman "like gods" (Gen. 3:5). Thus, although the story seems to have been influenced by many of the themes and even plot narratives in Gilgamesh, J's creation story offers its own view on the topics of death, immortality, sexuality, and human nature.

In his efforts to maintain the boundary separating humans from the divine, Yahweh's pronouncement concerning the consequences the primordial couple faced for consuming the fruit were made very clear:

> But of the tree of the knowledge of good and evil, thou shalt not eat of it: for in the day that thou eatest thereof thou shalt surely die. (Gen. 2:17)

In order for the separation between gods and humans to remain intact, humans could only endure in one of two states, either as sexually aware and mortal creatures or as non-sexually aware and immortal beings. From a traditional Near Eastern perspective, if the humans were both immortal and sexually aware, they would not only be "like gods," the humans would in fact *be* gods. The gods in Near Eastern mythology, including the Epic of Gilgamesh, often appear depicted as sexual beings.

When reading the Garden story contextually, the "knowledge" that the fruit imparted in J's story, making the primordial couple "like gods," appears specifically linked with sexual awareness. As the myth opens up, the man already possesses the basic attributes of knowledge and discernment. Prior to eating from the fruit, the man holds enough *knowledge* to recognize and name the animals Yahweh creates, and the man shows enough discernment to recognize that the woman proves fit for the role of a "helper." Therefore, the knowledge that the primordial couple obtains in J's myth is not simply intelligence, for the man already possesses this attribute prior to consuming the forbidden fruit. The knowledge the couple gains is specifically sexual awareness.

---

38. Wright noted, "if there is a vertical movement in the story, it is not a 'Fall,' but an 'ascension' toward the rank and species of deity." David P. Wright, "Holiness, Sex and Death in the Garden of Eden," 320.

Appearing as a *leitwort* or "theme word" throughout J's prehistory, the term "to know" (Hebrew *yd'*) is used consistently as a sexual euphemism.[39] Outside of Eden, the term appears in J's prehistory in the context of the man *knowing* his wife Eve (4:1), Cain *knowing* his wife (4:17), and the first man *knowing* his wife, once again (4:25). Throughout the Old Testament, the verbal form of *yd'* typically refers to *intellectual* knowledge, yet more than a dozen times, the verb carries specifically the type of intimate knowledge that occurs during sexual intercourse.[40]

Like all cultures, biblical Israel made use of a variety of euphemisms or evasive expressions for sex and other bodily functions. Examples of biblical euphemisms for sex include the act of eating, the very performance that provides the means for the primordial couple's *knowledge* in the Eden myth, such as in:

> For the way of an adulteress:
> she eats, and wipes her mouth,
> and says, "I have done nothing wrong."[41]

This does not suggest that in the case of Eden, eating the fruit functioned as a euphemism for *having* sex, but only that the physical act itself perhaps highlighted the event as a right of passage, signifying a change in sexual status.

Evidence in support of the reading that the knowledge the primordial couple obtained was specifically a sexual *knowledge* includes the fact that the initial discernment that the man and woman demonstrate after consuming the fruit is a "knowledge" of nakedness, and by extension gender distinction (Gen. 3:7). Additionally, J presents the woman's consequence for eating the fruit directly in the context of sexual "knowledge" (Gen. 3:16). Eating from the fruit leads to not only a change of status, but also a change of name for the woman. In contrast to other LDS versions of the story, this new name, "Eve" (meaning "life giver") is only given to the woman *after* she possesses the knowledge that the fruit produced (Gen. 3:20). Perhaps most significantly, the first time that the man appears using this newly acquired "knowledge" from the fruit, J's account states: "And Adam *knew* Eve his wife; and she conceived, and bare Cain, and

---

39. Ronald S. Hendel, "Leitwort Style and Literary Structure in the J Primeval Narrative," 98.

40. Examples of this nuance include Gen. 4:1; 19:5, 8; Num. 31:17–18; Deut. 21:10–14; Judg. 21:12; 1Kgs. 1:4.

41. Proverbs 30:20, as translated by the author from *Biblia Hebraica Stuttgartensia*.

said, I have gotten a man from the LORD (Gen. 4:1). This proves important in terms of the text's narrative flow. The last thing the man did prior to knowing his wife in this verse is naming her "Eve." Verses 21–24 in chapter three are merely something of an aside. In the narrative, the man names his wife Eve, and subsequently *knows* her.

This analysis illustrates an important point. Although most likely influenced by the famous Epic of Gilgamesh, adopting such themes as the presence of a snake, a plant that grants a type of immortality, a focus upon human death and morality, and the use of sexuality to signify a type of rite of passage that transforms people from being animal-like into human beings, J has its own unique story to tell. Like the author of the Epic of Gilgamesh, J observed that human sexual behavior is different than the types of activities in which animals engage. For J, humans possessed an advanced knowledge of sex unlike the animals, but very much like the gods.

Genesis and the Sumerian King List

In terms of narrative structure, both P and J begin with creation accounts followed by individual stories that depict a mythic time period before the great flood. Each account uses this prehistory (before Abraham) to set up the historical era (Abraham and beyond). In light of the ways in which biblical authors appear to have had access to and were directly influenced by Mesopotamian sources, it is possible that both P and J borrowed this pattern from one of the Sumerian King Lists.

The Sumerian King List is an ancient manuscript originally recorded in the Sumerian language listing kings of the city-state of Sumer (ancient southern Iraq) and its neighboring dynasties. The list provides each king's alleged reign lengths, together with the locations from which these ancient kings ruled. Kingship appears depicted as an institution that was given to humankind by the gods; and as a divine power, it could be transferred from one city to another.

The list evolved into an important political tool. Dating to the Middle Bronze Age, the final version seeks to legitimize the political claims of the Mesopotamian city-state of Isin during a time in which Isin was competing for dominance with the city of Larsa and other areas in southern Mesopotamia.

Since its initial discovery in the early 1900's, at least 18 other examples of the King List have been found, most of them dating from the second half of the Isin dynasty (about 2017–1794 BC). No two of these documents, however, are exactly identical. Significantly, one of these versions actually features the same pattern found in the Old Testament, tracing the origin of Sumerian kingship back to the beginnings of human history and including an account of the great Mesopotamian flood.

In addition to the basic structure for constructing a lengthy narrative of the distant past, a specific connection appears to exist between Genesis 5 and the King List. Beginning with Adam, Genesis 5 features a list of ten patriarchs that bridges the gap between creation and the flood. The ages attributed to all of these men are unusually high. Cainan, for example, lives 910 years (v. 14), Mahalaleel 893 (v. 16), Jared 962 (v. 20), and Methuselah 969 (v. 27). The flood, therefore, signifies the transition into the historical era. From that point, biblical narratives no longer present "mythic" type stories and instead depict human ages as much more reflective of a natural lifespan.

Before the flood, the Sumerian king Alulim is claimed to have ruled for 28,800 years, Alaingar for 36,000, En-men-lu-ana for 43,200, En-men-gal-ana for 28,800 years, etc. The lengthy lifespans that humans enjoyed in both the Sumerian King List and in Genesis reflects a common perspective of a type of idyllic age in the distant past followed by successive generations of increasingly worse and worse eras. This same theme appears as one of the primary points in J's narrative. As God became less pleased with his human creations, human life spans appear reduced. This same theme is then adopted in P in the genealogy list that appears in Genesis 5. Noah is described as having lived 950 years (Gen. 9:29). Then, after Noah and the flood, the number of years quickly becomes more reflective of the human condition. By adopting this motif, P therefore presents the basic substance of J's narrative of an increasing divine displeasure in humankind. The original idea, however, appears in the Sumerian King List.

In an interesting analysis of Genesis 5 and the Sumerian King List, John Walton has shown that the passage of time in each are identical, even though the biblical list of patriarchs relied upon a different numerical system than the Sumerians. If the total of years connected with the names in Genesis 5 are calculated, the list covers a span of 6,695 years. Then, if we convert this number to a sexagesimal number (the form used by the Sumerians), the result is 241,200—the exact total of the Sumerian King List.[42] This provides further evidence that the basic narrative of long last-

---

42. Watson, it should be noted, uses this reading to suggest that the Mesopotamian version relies upon an earlier Semitic decimal system. However, despite his efforts, I see no compelling reason to accept the notion that an Israelite scribe could not have made the same calculations that Watson reproduced. John A. Watson, *Ancient Israelite Literature in its Cultural Context*, 130.

ing life spans occurring before the great flood and the beginning of the historical era is a literary pattern adopted by the biblical authors from this ancient Sumerian text.

Genesis and the Mesopotamian Flood

In 1872, archaeologist George Smith made a startling find. He discovered and translated the Epic of Gilgamesh, which features a Babylonian version of the biblical flood story. Ever since Smith's discovery, scholars have recognized that the Israelite flood stories must be dependent upon an earlier Mesopotamian tradition. The unearthing of the flood story in the Epic of Gilgamesh was soon followed by discoveries of other Mesopotamian versions of this narrative, including the version found in Enūma Elish. Since the initial uncovering of these Mesopotamian flood stories, which dated from the seventh-century BC, additional finds have been made. These discoveries illustrate that the versions found in the Epic of Gilgamesh and Enūma Elish were actually later forms of this story and that these narratives were drawing upon one of the most ancient Mesopotamian traditions: the flood.

In terms of its origin, the story of a devastating flood makes greater sense as a Mesopotamian tradition than it does an Israelite myth, since Mesopotamia was subject to such natural disasters via the Tigris and Euphrates rivers. The shifting tides of the Euphrates River were especially turbulent and prone to severe flooding. It was these types of movements that produced the alluvial plain upon which the city-states of Mesopotamia created their civilization. With very little rain to work with, Mesopotamians were forced to develop a complex system of irrigation ditches and canals in order to sustain agricultural production. In contrast, flooding was never a major issue in Canaan.

And yet, both P and J feature a version of the great flood story. P was clearly aware of and drew upon the earlier Israelite form of the myth that appears in the J narrative. In J, the creation of humankind is presented as a type of "experiment gone awry."[43] Yahweh created the humans to resemble the gods in order to help with agricultural labor in the garden. After Yahweh sees how humans are continually threatening to usurp divinity, the account states:

> And the LORD [Yahweh] saw that the wickedness of man was great in the earth, and that every imagination of the thoughts of his heart was only evil

---

43. Collins, *Introduction to the Hebrew Bible*, 79.

continually. And it repented the LORD that he had made man on the earth, and it grieved him at his heart. (Gen. 6:5–6)

This justification for the flood story in J resembles the Babylonian myth Atrahasis where the gods come to regret the fact that they made humanity. The Babylonian myth indicates that after their creation to serve as agricultural servants to the gods, humans reproduced too rapidly. Humanity's constant noise proved irritating to the god Enlil:

> Twelve hundred years [had gone by].
> [The land had grown numerous], the peoples had increased,
> The [land] was bellowing [like a bull].
> The god was disturbed with [their uproar],
> [Enlil heard] their clamor.
> [He said to] the great gods,
> 'The clamor of humankind [has become burdensome to me],
> "I am losing sleep [to their uproar]."

As a result of this problem, Enlil determined to eradicate this "experiment gone awry" (i.e., the creation of demi-god agricultural servants), and he initiated a series of catastrophes, including disease and starvation, in order to wipe-out humanity. After each attempt, however, another god, Enki, created a plan to overcome Enlil's plot by rescuing humanity. Finally, Enlil decided to send the great flood, and Enki warned Atrahasis (the Babylonian equivalent of Noah) of the coming disaster and the need to build a boat in order to escape. Both biblical accounts skip the earlier attempts to eradicate humanity through sickness and starvation and instead move immediately to the final event, the flood.

Scholars believe that there were originally two separate versions of the flood story in Babylonian literature, making it impossible to know which one was reformulated by the biblical authors. One version presents the hero who escapes the destruction in an ark as Atrahasis, the other as a man named Utnapishtim. Significantly, when we line up the separate accounts, all of the heroes, including Noah, cover their boats with pitch or bitumen. Both Utnapishtim and Noah's ark finally rest on a mountaintop. Like Noah, Utnapishtim sends out birds (a dove, swallow, and a raven) to determine whether or not the waters of the flood have abated. In all three of the accounts (treating P and J as a unit), when the hero emerges from the ark, we read that the hero offers a sacrifice.

After the sacrifice in the story of Atrahasis, the gods come to a compromise and agree to allow humanity to continue living upon the earth.

They devised a plan, however, to reduce human population through less drastic catastrophes, such as wild beasts, famine, unsuccessful births.

This thematically parallels the resolution we find in J's version of the flood story. In J's account, Yahweh reacts to the sacrifice offered by Noah in the following manner:

> And Noah builded an altar unto the LORD; and took of every clean beast, and of every clean fowl, and offered burnt offerings on the altar. And the LORD smelled a sweet savour; and the LORD said in his heart, I will not again curse the ground any more for man's sake; for the imagination of man's heart is evil from his youth; neither will I again smite any more every thing living, as I have done. (Gen. 8:20–21)

The compromise in J is that Yahweh comes to terms with the fact that man's heart is simply evil and Yahweh is going to have to live with this problem.

Both P and J share a focus on human reproduction and food. These same themes are found in the Mesopotamian flood stories. For example, following creation in Atrahasis, the myth states that humanity multiplied too rapidly since the gods did not place limitations on reproduction:

> [Twel]ve hundred years [had not gone by],
> [The land had grown numerous], the peoples had increased,
> The [land] was bellowing [like a bull].[44]

After the flood, the gods come to terms with the fact that they need the food humans provide through sacrifice. The resolution to the problem is that natural disasters, sicknesses, and war will limit population problems.

J borrows these same themes. The reason for the flood is given in Genesis 6:5: "[Yahweh] saw that the wickedness of man was great in the earth, and that every imagination of the thoughts of his heart was only evil continually." Humanity is evil, constantly seeking to usurp the boundary Yahweh sought to maintain between gods and humans. However, following the flood and the sacrifice that "feeds" Yahweh through smell, he changes in the course of the story. Yahweh comes to terms with humanity's nature:

> And the Lord smelled a sweet savour; and the LORD said in his heart, I will not again curse the ground any more for man's sake; for the imagination of man's heart is evil from his youth; neither will I again smite any more every thing living, as I have done. (Gen. 8:21)

P shares the same Mesopotamian themes, however, it invokes them differently. In P, God created humans and commanded them to only eat plants:

---

44. Old Babylonian version of Atrahasis as translated by Benjamin R. Foster in *Before the Muses: An Anthology of Akkadian Literature*, 239.

> And God said, Behold, I have given you every herb bearing seed, which is
> upon the face of all the earth, and every tree, in the which is the fruit of a tree
> yielding seed; to you it shall be for meat. (Gen. 1:29)

However, humanity proves unable to rule and have dominion as the "image" of God; and with overpopulation and not enough food, the earth became filled with "violence" (Gen. 6:11). In P, God sends the flood to eradicate this problem. Without the sacrifice that we find in both J and Mesopotamian tradition, P's resolution to the flood story simply involves God changing his stipulation that humans could not eat meat:

> Every moving thing that liveth shall be meat for you; even as the green herb
> have I given you all things. (Gen. 9:3)

All of the accounts, therefore, focus upon the themes of human reproduction and food.

While it may be impossible to determine precisely which Mesopotamian version of the flood story influenced J (and, therefore P), there is little doubt that the biblical story of Noah is an Israelite reformulation of this very popular Mesopotamian tradition. It is interesting to consider, however, that the biblical flood accounts begin with a story in which humans are acting too much like gods by engaging in sexual activities with a group of divine beings referred to in the text by the title "sons of God" (Gen. 6:1–4). It has been noted that this story (and the theme of humanity encroaching upon divinity within J's prehistory) reverses the idea that appears in Atrahasis. Instead, Atrahasis views prehistory as a time "when Gods *were* men."[45] P represents a type of middle position. Humans are not gods, but they are like them in terms of "image."

Tower of Babel

J's documentary source contains a story regarding a great tower of Babylon that shows a strong interest in Mesopotamian technology. The story depicts the way in which the famous Mesopotamian city got its name by playing upon the Akkadian words *bab-ilu* or "Gate of God."[46] The proper name *Babel* seems to be a mixture of two separate languages: the Akkadian word *bab*, meaning "gate," and the Hebrew word *'el* (a play upon Akkadian *il*), meaning "God." Through this account, the J source

---

45. See the analysis provided by William L. Moran, *The Most Magic Word: Essays on Babylonian and Biblical Literature*, 73.

46. For a definition of the Akkadian word *bab-ilu*, see Oppenheim, *Chicago Assyrian Dictionary*.

provides a Hebrew explanation for the name Babylon (*bbl*) because the LORD "babbled/confounded" (*bll*) human language.[47]

The story of the great tower recounts the ambition of its Mesopotamian builders to construct "a city and a tower, whose top may reach unto heaven" (Gen. 11:4). In this sense, the builders' pride reflects the boasting of the Babylonian king in the Book of Isaiah who declares:

> For thou hast said in thine heart, I will ascend into heaven, I will exalt my throne above the stars of God: I will sit also upon the mount of the congregation, in the sides of the north: I will ascend above the heights of the clouds; I will be like the most High. (Isa. 14:13–14)

The thematic connection between these two texts suggests a type of taunt regarding Babylonian arrogance. As one scholar has written, "one senses both astonishment at the advanced technological level of Babylonian culture and a keen sense that technology poses grave dangers when it is not accompanied by reverence for God."[48]

In recent years, some scholars reading this biblical story have interpreted the city and the tower as symbols of foreign dominion and oppression.[49] This reading makes sense in light of the political relationship between Babylon and Israel, and the way in which the story pokes fun at the ziggurat by playing with the name "Babel." Interpreted from this angle, rather than a punishment *per se*, the confusion of languages represents a political liberation from Babylonian oppression. Following a short political allegiance with Egypt, the kingdom of Judah and its capital city Jerusalem came under Babylonian control around 605 BC. Judah's capital city, however, never fully accepted this vassal relationship. Together with other communities in the Levant, Jerusalem led an unsuccessful revolt against Babylon. A second Babylonian siege took place around 586 BC, which led to the destruction of Jerusalem and the beginning of the Jewish exile. The polemical account concerning Babylonian arrogance told through the Tower of Babel story may reflect a Judean desire to see individual nations free to express their own unique ethnic identity or "language," independent from Babylonian oppression.

---

47. Richard Elliott Friedman, *Commentary on the Torah*, 46.

48. Jon D. Levenson, "Genesis: Introduction," 29.

49. This interpretation of the story has been drawn out especially well by those writing from a third-world perspective; see José Miquez Bonino, Solomon Avotri, and Choan-Seng Song, "Genesis 11:1–9: A Latin-American Perspective," 13–33; Danna Nolan Fewell, "Building Babel," 1–15; John J. Collins, *The Bible After Babel: Historical Criticism in a Post-Modern Age*, 2.

As Latter-day Saints, we find a similar religious view regarding cultural diversification and language in what has become known as the revealed preface to the Doctrine and Covenants. In reference to the way in which God speaks to people, we read:

> Behold, I am God and have spoken it; these commandments are of me, and were given unto my servants in their weakness, after the manner of their language, that they might come to understanding. (D&C 1:24)

The idea that God speaks to all people in their own language provides an important justification for a revelation Joseph Smith received on spreading the Gospel message:

> For it shall come to pass in that day, that every man shall hear the fulness of the gospel in his own tongue, and in his own language, through those who are ordained unto this power, by the administration of the Comforter, shed forth upon them for the revelation of Jesus Christ. (D&C 90:11)

These passages indicate that communities have a right to hear divinity in their own language. This theme may reflect ideas held by the author of the biblical story of Babel in his reaction to Babylonian oppression.

The Covenant Code and the Laws of Hammurabi

As was discussed in Chapter 1, we find three distinct blocks of legal collections in the Pentateuch: Exodus 20–23 (the Covenant Code), Leviticus, and Numbers (the Priestly code), and Deuteronomy 12–26 (the deuteronomic code). All three collections feature repetitions. The laws themselves appear in two different literary forms that scholars refer to as casuistic and apodictic.

The adjective "casuistic" derives from the term "casuistry," which simply means "case-based reasoning." We might think of it as "applied law." Casuistic laws are structured according to an if-then formula. For instance, an example of a casuistic law in the Bible is Exodus 21:20: "If a man smite his servant, or his maid, with a rod, and he die under his hand [then] he shall be surely punished." The second type of legal formulation, "apodictic," is an adjective that derives from the Greek term "apodicticity," meaning "capable of demonstration." It refers to an absolute command such as "thou shalt not kill" (Ex. 20:13), or "thou shalt not commit adultery" (v. 14).

These legal patterns are ancient and appear in other Near Eastern legal collections outside of the Bible. The oldest complete law collection in the world is the famous Code of Hammurabi dating from approximately 1772

BC. This over seven-foot-high statue, engraven with Babylonian laws, was discovered at the beginning of the twentieth century by a French archaeological expedition in what is today modern Iran. Many of the Babylonian laws are similar to those that appear in the Covenant Code. The clearest example of these connections is the goring ox laws:

Exodus 21:28–32

[28] If an ox gore a man or a woman, that they die: then the ox shall be surely stoned, and his flesh shall not be eaten; but the owner of the ox shall be quit. [29] But if the ox were wont to push with his horn in time past, and it hath been testified to his owner, and he hath not kept him in, but that he hath killed a man or a woman; the ox shall be stoned, and his owner also shall be put to death. [30] If there be laid on him a sum of money, then he shall give for the ransom of his life whatsoever is laid upon him. [31] Whether he have gored a son, or have gored a daughter, according to this judgment shall it be done unto him. [32] If the ox shall push a manservant or a maidservant; he shall give unto their master thirty shekels of silver, and the ox shall be stoned.

Laws of Hammurabi 250–52:

[250] If an ox gores a man while passing through the street and kills (him), that case has no claim. [251] If a man's ox were want to push with his horn in time past, and his district informed him that it is a habitual gorer, but he did not file its horns and did not control his ox, and that ox gores a man and kills (him), he shall pay one-half mina (thirty shekels) of silver. [252] If it is the slave of a free person, he shall pay one-third mina (twenty shekels) of silver.

Though these laws exhibit differences, they are remarkably similar in content (goring oxen), formulation, and even sequence. Over the years, scholars have debated why these connections between the laws in Exodus and Hammurabi exist. Many have assumed that rather than a direct influence, the similarities were simply a result of oral tradition reaching back from the second millennium BC, which Israelite authors drew upon. This view, however, has been challenged recently. In his book, *Inventing God's Law: How the Covenant Code of the Bible Used and Revised the Laws of Hammurabi*, David P. Wright provides strong evidence that the author of the biblical Covenant Code revised the Laws of Hammurabi to create his own Israelite version of the Babylonian collection.

The Covenant Collection in Exodus can be divided into three sections of apodictic and casuistic laws. The casuistics (if-then) laws appear in the center of the block, and the apodictic (command forms) laws appear as bookends:

- Apodictic Laws: Ex. 20:23–26
- Casuistic Laws: Ex. 21:2–22:19
- Apodictic Laws: Ex. 22:20–23:19

Wright's study illustrated that the casuistic laws in the center of the block have very close connections with the casuistic laws that appear in the Code of Hammurabi and that the outer apodictic laws feature close thematic connections with the outer sections of Hammurabi's laws.

This study shows that whoever created the casuistic laws in Exodus 21:2–22:19 used the Code of Hammurabi as a type of topical guide. The laws in Exodus follow almost the exact same topical sequence as the last half of Hammurabi's collection. They discuss the exact same fourteen themes in almost the exact same order: (1) male debt servitude; (2) female (daughter) debt servitude; (3) murder; (4) child rebellion and kidnapping; (5) injury and murder; (6) miscarriage and talion (eye for eye/tooth for tooth); (7) ox goring a human; (8) negligence; (9) ox goring an ox; (10) animal theft and burglary; (11) grazing and fire in a field; (12) deposit of goods for safekeeping; (13) injury and death of animals; and (14) animal rentals. Wright also shows that the apodictic laws in Exodus feature an equally tight set of connections with the Code of Hammurabi. The final apodictic laws follow the exact same sequence of themes in the "exhortatory block" of the conclusion to the Code of Hammurabi.

Further, in Exodus, the apodictic laws replace Hammurabi and Mesopotamian gods with Yahweh. Instead of the Babylonian king, Yahweh is now the author and revealer of law. As the symbol of his worship, Yahweh's altar replaces Hammurabi's temple statue. Thus, in the same way that the exhortatory block has Hammurabi's name memorialized at a sacred place, "May my name [Hammurabi] be recalled in the Esagil temple favorably forever," the Covenant Code presents Yahweh's name memorialized at a sacred place, "in every place where I [Yahweh] cause my name to be recalled."

The connections are really astounding and convincingly illustrate that this legal collection in Exodus was produced by an Israelite scribe who had direct access to the Code of Hammurabi and used these Mesopotamian laws to create the Covenant Code. There's really no other way to account for the connections. Biblical scholar David Carr, for example, previously wrote extensively on the importance of oral tradition in the formation of biblical texts. At one point, he was a strong proponent of the view that connections between the Covenant Code and the Laws of Hammurabi derived from oral tradition. He has since endorsed Wright's analysis that "the Covenant Code stands as another biblical example of creative adaptation of a prominent non-biblical precursor text."[50]

Deuteronomy as Assyrian Vassal Treaty

The Book of Deuteronomy is another example of a biblical text that was influenced by Mesopotamian sources. The structure of Deuteronomy is unlike any other book in the Bible. Despite its emphasis upon laws, the primary legal block doesn't begin until chapter 12. Formally, Deuteronomy commences with an Introduction (chapters 1–11), then moves to a Legal Core (12–26), and finally a Conclusion (27–34). The structure parallels the format for the Code of Hammurabi, which features a prologue, a legal block, and an epilogue. Yet despite this basic structural connection, Deuteronomy is quite different from both the Covenant Code in Exodus and the Code of Hammurabi.

In the early 1950s, a biblical scholar by the name of George Mendenhall made an interesting connection between the structure of Deuteronomy and second-millennium BC Hittite treaties. The Hittites were an ancient people from Anatolia (modern-day Turkey), that established a powerful empire during the mid-fourteenth century BC. In building their empire, the Hittites entered into treaties with subjugated Near Eastern states. These treaties declared the Hittite king to be the overlord (or "suzerain") and the conquered lesser ruler to be his vassal. Mendenhall noted that these ancient treaties feature the same basic structure as Deuteronomy including a preamble, historical prologue, treaty stipulations, provisions for deposit in the temple and periodic readings, witnesses, curses, and blessings. Since both Deuteronomy and the Hittite Vassal Treaties feature the same elements, Mendenhall made the logical deduction that the Book of Deuteronomy was influenced by these Hittite documents.

From this angle, Deuteronomy does precisely what Exodus does in terms of the apodictic laws. It replaces the Hittite monarch with the God of Israel and interprets the relationship between God and Israel as that of suzerain to vassal. Thus, the Hebrew word for "covenant" (*berit*) that appears in the Bible as a technical description of the "treaty" between

---

50. David Carr, *The Formation of the Hebrew Bible: A New Reconstruction*, 470.

Israel and other foreign nations is also used in Deuteronomy to depict the "covenant" Israel makes with God.

Since Mendenhall's original article appeared in print, a variety of first-millennium Mesopotamian vassal treaties have been published. These treaties formulated between Assyrians and their vassals reveal even stronger, more direct parallels with Deuteronomy than the earlier Hittite formulas. This is especially true for the Esarhaddon treaties of the early seventh-century BC. Esarhaddon was an Assyrian monarch who reigned over the Assyrian empire (including Judea) from approximately 681–669 BC. The curses that appear at the conclusion of Deuteronomy are similar to those used in the Vassal Treaties of Esarhaddon. For instance, Deuteronomy 28:23–24 states:

> And thy heaven that is over thy head shall be brass, and the earth that is under thee shall be iron. The LORD shall make the rain of thy land powder and dust: from heaven shall it come down upon thee, until thou be.

And the Vassal Treaty of Esharddon (VTE) features the curse:

> May they [the gods] make your ground like iron so that no one can plough it. Just as rain does not fall from a brazen heaven, so may rain and dew not come upon your fields and pastures. (VTE 528–31)

An even more remarkable connection with the Mesopotamian Vassal Treaties occurs in Deuteronomy 28:26–33. Both the Esarhaddon treaty and Deuteronomy list the same curses in almost an identical sequential order:

- Carcasses carrion for animals (v. 26; VTE 41)
- Skin inflammations (v. 27; VTE 39)
- Madness, "blindness," and dismay (v. 28–29; VTE 40)
- Fiancée raped, loss of house, vineyard (v. 30; VTE 42A)
- Possessions and children plundered (vv. 31–33; VTE 42B)

One might argue, although not convincingly, that all of this is simply a mere coincidence. But the order for these curses is actually intentional. The curses in Deuteronomy and the VTE are set up in accordance with traditional groupings of the gods in Mesopotamian texts.[51] While this may not be enough evidence to suggest that the authors of Deuteronomy copied the VTE (in the same way that we see Israelite scribes literally reworking the Code of Hammurabi), the connections provide more evidence that the first five books of the Bible have been heavily influenced by Mesopotamia.

---

51. See Jeffrey H. Tigay, *Deuteronomy; JPS Torah Commentary*, 497.

One of the most interesting issues raised in connecting Deuteronomy with the Assyrian Vassal Treaties is the commandment to love God. The Assyrian Vassal Treaties were designed to create a political contract between the high king over the Assyrian empire (known technically as a suzerain) and a lesser king that governed his own home territory (known technically as a vassal king). In Deuteronomy, this relationship between suzerain and vassal appears reconceptualized to describe the relationship between Yahweh and Israel. Biblical scholar Norman Gottwald explains the matter: "Israel conceived of its relation to Yahweh as that of subject peoples to a world king and . . . they expressed this relationship in the concepts and formulas of the suzerainty treaty."[52] In the Assyrian treaties, vassals were specifically required to love their superiors: "If you do not love the crown prince designate Ashurbanipal," warns the Assyrian treaty of Esarhaddon, "[then] may Ashur, king of the gods, who determines the fates, decree for you an evil, unpropitious fate."[53] In this ancient context, "loving the king with one's entire heart signified the severance of all contact with other political powers."[54]

In recent decades, scholars have shown that in the biblical world the word "love" often represented a covenantal devotion to one's superior, while its opposite, "hate," at times signified the status of an individual outside of this affiliation.[55] While the connotation of these words for Westerners usually signifies an intense emotional charge, in the ancient Near East, love and hate often carried the aforementioned unique covenantal connotation.[56] Hence, Israel's command to "love the Lord thy God with all thine heart, and with all thy soul, and with all thy might," presented in the Book of Deuteronomy, seems to refer to a political commitment rather than an emotional attachment (Deut. 6:5).[57]

Thus, when Hosea proclaims, "All their [the Ephraimites'] wickedness is in Gilgal: for there I hated them: for the wickedness of their doings I will drive them out of mine house" (Hosea 9:15), he is saying that the

52. Norman K. Gottwald, *The Hebrew Bible: A Socio-Literary Introduction*, 205.

53. As cited in James B. Pritchard, ed., *Ancient Near Eastern Texts Relating to the Old Testament*, 537, 538.

54. Moshe Weinfeld, *Deuteronomy and the Deuteronomic School*, 81.

55. N. Lohfink, "Hate and Love in Osee 9, 15," 417.

56. This would explain why the Lord says that he loves Jacob (Israel) but hates his brother Esau (Malachi 1:2–3; Romans 9:13).

57. William L. Moran, "The Ancient Near Eastern Background of the Love of God in Deuteronomy," 77–87.

Ephraimites' wickedness resulted in their loss of the blessing associated with having the God of Israel serve as their sovereign. God hated the Ephraimites "for the wickedness of their doings" because, in the context of Assyrian treaties, these acts were tantamount to a political insurrection. As a result, the Ephraimites were removed from God's covenantal house or family. "I will love them no more," declared Yahweh: "all their princes are revolters" (v. 15).

With this observation in mind, the Book of Mormon passage in Helaman 15, where Samuel the Lamanite describes God's love and hatred, seems to convey a specific nuance derived from the world of antiquity. When Samuel presents his message to the people of Nephi, he declares, "They [the Nephites] have been a chosen people of the Lord; yea, the people of Nephi hath he loved" (v. 3). With these words, Samuel attempts to remind the Nephites that they have traditionally served as God's covenant people. In this relationship, the Lord has acted as the Nephite suzerain from whom the people of Nephi have received reciprocal "love." In contrast, Samuel presents his own people, the Lamanites, as those whom God "hath hated because their deeds have been evil continually" (v. 4). Significantly, Samuel uses the verb hate in the same context in which it appears in the book of Hosea. God hated the Lamanites in a parallel manner to the way he hated the Ephraimites: their evil acts had placed them outside the boundary of his covenantal relationship.

While some readers have expressed concern regarding this apparently harsh statement preserved in the Book of Mormon, Samuel's message relates perfectly to the context of "love" and "hate" in the ancient sense of alliance, as witnessed in Deuteronomy and the Assyrian Vassal Treaties.

Sargon of Akkad and Moses

The beginnings of Moses's life are recounted in Exodus 1:22–2:10, where Moses has a secret birth to a Levite (and therefore priestly) mother (2:1–2), his life is saved by placing him in the Nile River in a reed basket sealed with pitch (v. 3), and he is found and adopted by the daughter of Pharaoh and raised as her son (vv. 5–10). These stories of Moses, however, may have been influenced by the Mesopotamian legend of Sargon, the founder of the Dynasty of Akkad (also translated as Agade), which appears listed in the biblical "Table of Nations" in Genesis 10 and is connected with Nimrod, the mighty hunter (whose name may reflect the Mesopotamian king Naram-Sin, the grandson of Sargon).[58]

Sargon was a famous figure in Mesopotamia that created the first world empire in the Near East around 2300 BC. Though an historical figure, his life became legend. The Akkadian story of his birth reads:

> I am Sargon the great king, the king of Agade.
> My mother was a high priestess, I did not know my father . . .
> My mother, the high priestess, conceived me, she bore me in secret.
> She placed me in a reed basket, she sealed my hatch with pitch.
> She left me to the river, whence I could not come up.
> The river carried me off, it brought me to Aqqi, drawer of water.
> Aqqi, drawer of water, brought me up as he dipped his bucket.
> Aqqi, drawer of water, raised me as his adopted son.[59]

The parallels to Moses should be obvious. Both were born to "priestly" mothers who bore her son in secret, both were placed in a river in a reed basket sealed with pitch, and both were then discovered and raised as adopted sons.

As the namesake of the earlier Akkadian king, the Assyrian king Sargon II (721–705 BC) took special interest in the legend of Sargon of Akkad, which may have even been written during the reign of Sargon II in order to provide support for his own royal claims.[60] Israelites and Judeans would have been familiar with Sargon II, as he appears to have responded to their rebellions after Shalmaneser V's conquest of Israel.[61] Moreover,

---

58. See Eckart Otto, "Political Theology in Judah and Assyria: The Beginning of the Hebrew Bible as Literature," 72–75.

59. As translated by Benjamin F. Foster in Hallo and Younger, *The Context of Scripture*, 1:461.

60. See David P. Wright, *Inventing God's Law*, 243.

61. Unfortunately, no historical texts exist from the Assyrian king Shalmaneser V who was ruler when Hoshea, the last king of Israel, rebelled against Assyria. Shalmaneser V died in 722 BC during his campaign against Israel. His "brother" Sargon II succeeded him in power (though the actual relationship to Shalmaneser's family cannot be confirmed). Sargon II was the father of Sennacherib, the king who laid siege to Jerusalem. The story of the Assyrian siege is told in the Old Testament books of Isaiah, 2 Kings, and Chronicles. An Assyrian version of these events appears as part of the official annals, including the famous Sennacherib Prism. Sennacherib was succeeded by his son Esharhaddon whose Vassal Treaties inspired the development of the Book of Deuteronomy. For a survey of this history, including citations of the Sennacherib Prism, see Collins, *Introduction to the Hebrew Bible*, 270–78.

Sargon II was the grandfather of Esharhaddon, whose Vassal Treaties influenced Deuteronomy.

Conclusion

Scripture is never produced in a cultural vacuum. For example, to be properly understood, Joseph Smith's revelations in the Doctrine and Covenants must be read and interpreted in accordance with the historical events and circumstances that originally inspired the revelation. According to the preface to the Doctrine and Covenants, when God reveals his word to humanity, he does so within the context of their own culture (D&C 1:24). This is certainly no different for the authors of the Hebrew Bible, for the Pentateuchal sources were produced by Israelite and Judean scribes interacting with the Mesopotamian culture that impacted their world and provided a framework for recording their own religious histories. Like creation itself, these scriptural texts were not created *ex nihilo*. For those who produced the documentary sources in the Pentateuch, their language and understanding was dictated by a direct interaction with Mesopotamian texts.

While these observations may prove concerning to some readers, the adaptation and reformulation of earlier traditions is often times an important part of the production of scriptural texts. For Joseph Smith, God did not create the word out of nothing. He took pre-existent matter and gave divine structure to what already existed. The Bible, therefore, can be interpreted by Latter-day Saints as a reflection of the way God himself creates. In the case of the Pentateuch, through Historical Criticism we learn that without Babel there really *would* be no Bible.

Chapter Six

Reading the Pentateuch Critically as a Latter-day Saint

Introduction

In this study, we have taken an approach to the first five books of the Bible similar to the one Joseph Smith used. Instead of interpreting the Bible as a privileged text, we have examined the texts using Historical Criticism, paying close attention to the internal contradictions and historical context of the Pentateuch. While no doubt exciting, the insights gained from this approach can prove challenging for some readers. A critical analysis, however, need not be interpreted as antithetical to religiosity. It only presents problems for certain religious paradigms that run against such an approach.

Higher Criticism, an effort to explain textual inconsistencies by identifying original sources, is an essential part of Historical Criticism. It challenges traditional assumptions. However, as Elder John A. Widtsoe recognized, this type of analysis does not conflict with Mormonism:

> In the field of modern thought the so-called higher criticism of the Bible has played an important part. The careful examination of the Bible in the light of our best knowledge of history, languages and literary form, has brought to light many facts not sensed by the ordinary reader of the Scriptures. Based upon the facts thus gathered, scholars have in the usual manner of science proceeded to make inferences, some of considerable, others of low probability of truth . . . To Latter-day Saints there can be no objection to the careful and critical study of the scriptures, ancient or modern, provided only that it be an honest study—a search for truth . . . Whether under a special call of God, or impelled by personal desire, there can be no objection to the critical study of the Bible.[1]

---

1. John A. Widtsoe, *In Search of Truth: Comments on the Gospel and Modern Thought*, 81–82.

Historical Criticism can run counter to traditional perspectives of the Bible that are commonly held by Latter-day Saints.[2] This is certainly the case with suggestions that some of the stories in the Bible's opening chapters, from Eden to the flood narrative, are ancient Israelite myths composed by scribes who were interacting with earlier, oftentimes Mesopotamian, myths and legal collections.

These insights are from scholars of the Bible who have devoted years of careful analysis to uncover the historical background of the text. In our *own* quest for truth, we as Latter-day Saints need not feel afraid to lay aside incorrect traditional beliefs regarding scripture. The Prophet Joseph Smith made this point clear in his letter written from Liberty Jail. "We should waste and wear out our lives in bringing to light *all* the hidden things," wrote the Prophet (D&C 123:13; cf. Morm. 8:16, D&C 1:30). The question concerning who wrote the Bible's first five books is a quest to bring to light that which for many centuries has been hidden.

An Intellectual/Spiritual Reading of the Text

The insights into the question "who wrote the Pentateuch?" presented in this study derive from what might be referred to as an *intellectual* reading of the text. They are independent from any specific theological agenda, including Mormonism. However, Joseph Smith taught that, "one of the grand fundamental principles of Mormonism is to receive truth let it come from where it may."[3] This process of accepting truth from whatever source it stems was important to him. On another occasion, the Prophet similarly taught:

> The first and fundamental principle of our holy religion is, that we have the right to embrace all, and every item of the truth, without limitation or without being circumscribed or prohibited by the creeds and superstitious notions of men.[4]

For Joseph, truth could be uncovered from a variety of sources. When a Latter-day Saint encounters truth, Joseph taught that he or she should be willing to set aside traditional paradigms and embrace a new perspective.

---

2. Over the years, LDS leaders have generally expressed serious concerns about Higher Criticism. (See the survey provided in Barlow, *Mormons and the Bible*, 112-61.) However, with enhanced data, the arguments raised through Higher Criticism have evolved with greater sophistication in recent decades.

3. Andrew F. Ehat and Lyndon W. Cook, *The Words of Joseph Smith*, 229.

4. Joseph Smith to Isaac Galland, in *The Personal Writings of Joseph Smith*, ed. Dean C. Jessee, 420.

The School of the Prophets

Joseph Smith was constantly seeking to uncover truth. We find an illustration from Church history of the manner in which Joseph Smith demonstrated his belief that a person could gain significant insights through biblical scholarship and that these ideas could then be used to accentuate spiritual truths. Over the course of a three-day period (December 27, 28, 1832, and January 3, 1833) Joseph Smith received a revelation concerning a school for Church leaders that should be organized to teach from the "best books words of wisdom. . . by study and also by faith" (D&C 88:118). Known as the "School of the Prophets," this select group of early Church leaders began meeting under the direction of Joseph Smith shortly after the revelation was given (January 23, 1833). Courses were taught on both secular and theological topics until April of 1833 when spring weather allowed for an increase in missionary work. Courses then later resumed in Kirtland, Ohio from late fall to early spring in 1834–1835 and 1835–1836.

As part of this project, William E. McLellin and Orson Hyde were sent to Hudson, Ohio, in January of 1836 to find an instructor who could teach biblical Hebrew. Two days later, McLellin returned from the Hudson Seminary with news that he had hired an instructor Joshua Seixas, who would teach a seven-week course for $320.[5] Seixas was a respected biblical scholar who had taught Hebrew at New York and Charlestown, Massachusetts. He even wrote a textbook in 1833 used by Joseph Smith entitled *A Manual Hebrew Grammar for the Use of Beginners.*

Joseph Smith was clearly excited at the prospect of studying with such an accomplished biblical scholar. Concerning Seixas, Joseph wrote: "He is highly celebrated as a Hebrew scholar, and proposes to give us a sufficient knowledge during the above term to start us reading and translating the language."[6] After their lessons Joseph recorded that Seixas said that they "were the most forward of any class he ever instructed for the same length of time."[7]

The evidence suggests that Joseph applied himself to his Hebrew studies. His journal entries diligently report the time spent studying with Seixas in class. Regarding his student Joseph Smith, Seixas eventually wrote the following certificate:

---

5. For a history and analysis of Joshua Seixas' role as Joseph's Hebrew instructor, see Louis C. Zucker, "Joseph Smith as a Student of Hebrew," 41–55.

6. Joseph Smith, *History of the Church*, 2:356.

7. Smith, *History of the Church*, 2:396. The class had been studying Hebrew for some time on their own prior to Seixas' arrival.

Mr Joseph Smith Jun has attended a full course of Hebrew lessons under my tuition; & has been indefatigable in acquiring the principles of the sacred language of the Old Testament Scriptures in their original tongue. He has so far accomplished a knowledge of it, that he is able to translate to my entire satisfaction; & by prosecuting the study he will be able to become a proficient in Hebrew. I take this opportunity of thanking him for his industry, & his marked kindness towards me.[8]

Joseph's own words regarding the experience paint a picture of a man profoundly influenced by studying biblical Hebrew. On February 17th, 1836, the Prophet wrote in his journal:

My soul delights in reading the word of the Lord in the original, and I am determined to pursue the study of the languages, until I shall be come master of them, if I am permitted to live long enough. At any rate, so long as I do live, I am determined to make this my object; and with the blessing of God, I shall succeed to my satisfaction.

For Joseph, a detailed study of the Bible was a moving experience. This fascinating episode in Church history illustrates that the Prophet recognized the importance of understanding the language and context of the Bible. The fact that Joseph Smith went to scholars to gain knowledge concerning the scriptures shows that he believed that revelation was not the only way to read scripture.

From a historical perspective, studying Hebrew had a tremendous effect upon the development of Joseph's theology. It's surely no coincidence that at the same time Joseph was learning Hebrew, the Prophet was simultaneously working with the Egyptian documents that would lead to the Book of Abraham.[9] Learning Hebrew from a biblical scholar caused the Prophet to set aside some of his traditional views concerning the Old Testament. From Seixas, Joseph learned that the Hebrew noun *elohim* can mean either God or gods (plural). Most of the Christian world in Joseph's day did not accept the idea of the existence of multiple deities beyond the biblical God. Learning the dual meaning of this Hebrew noun clearly inspired the Prophet to abandon these traditional beliefs. Later in his ministry, Joseph drew upon this idea in Nauvoo sermons:

In the very beginning the Bible shows there is a plurality of Gods beyond the power of refutation. It is a great subject I am dwelling on. The word *Eloheim*

---

8. Certificate from Joshua Seixas, 30 March 1836.

9. For an analysis on the impact Joseph Smith's study of Hebrew had on the Book of Abraham, see Michael T. Walton, "Professor Seixas, the Hebrew Bible and the Book of Abraham," 41–43 .

ought to be in the plural all the way through—Gods. The heads of the Gods appointed one God for us; and when you take [that] view of the subject, it sets one free to see all the beauty, holiness, and perfection of the Gods. All I want is to get the simply, naked truth, and the whole truth.[10]

A second illustration of the way in which studying Hebrew with a biblical scholar appears to have affected the development of Joseph's theology is the Prophet's rejection of the traditional Christian doctrine of Creation *ex nihilo*, meaning "out of nothing." Though this was the traditional paradigm that Joseph Smith inherited, the Prophet abandoned this view and adopted an alternative perspective as a result of his studies. Joseph articulated this position in his King Follett Sermon:

> You ask the learned doctors why they say the world was made out of nothing; and they will answer, 'Doesn't the Bible say He *created* the world?' And they infer, from the word create, that it must have been made out of nothing. Now, the word create came from the word *baurau* which does not mean to create out of nothing: it means to organize; the same as a man would organize materials and build a ship. Hence we infer that God had materials to organize the world out of chaos—chaotic matter, which is element, and in which dwells all the glory.[11]

Joseph's use of Hebrew in the formulation of his theology shows how he was willing to abandon traditional paradigms as he gained new insights through a combination of revelation and an advanced personal study of the Bible.

Joseph Smith as Guide

Using Joseph Smith's full revelatory approach to Mormonism as a guide, Latter-day Saints need not feel beholden to the tradition that Moses himself wrote the Pentateuch, nor should we feel obligated to maintain a type of *creedal* allegiance to assumptions regarding the Bible when a historical analysis directly counters those claims. To do so runs opposite to the way Joseph Smith understood Mormonism.

Undoubtedly, these insights challenge some commonly held perspectives on scripture. However, simply because Higher Criticism reveals that Moses did not write the Pentateuch and that the Bible adopts and reformulates non-Israelite mythology, it does not mean that the Old Testament is somehow devoid of inspiration or that it is not truly scripture. The Old

---

10. Joseph Smith, *Teachings of the Prophet Joseph Smith*, 372; see Kevin L. Barney, "Joseph Smith's Emendation of Hebrew Genesis 1:1," 103–35.

11. Joseph Smith, *Teachings of the Prophet Joseph Smith*, 350.

Testament is an ancient record of human beings striving to respond to the divine by which they had been touched.[12] It has much to offer. Anthony Campbell and Mark O'Brien write

> The biblical text bears witness both to the struggles of many generations in coming to grips with their experience of God in their lives and to the attempt to give that experience adequate articulation. . . . Views are expressed and traditions told, modifications are made, contradictory positions are proposed, composite texts are compiled, prophetic texts are updated, and so on—and all the while, faith is eternally questing for understanding.[13]

Evolution and contradiction occurs in this process.

The sources that appear in the Pentateuch were written by Israelite authors trying to explain their history through theological constructs and ancient traditions. This procedure can be a bit *messy*. Yet given our own history, we as Latter-day Saints should allow room for *messiness* in the production of scripture. Even the Book of Mormon, the scripture that Latter-day Saints define as the "most correct book," allows for the possibilities of human error and contradiction when Moroni points out that "if there be faults they be the faults of man" (Moro. 8:17).

If we again turn to Joseph Smith as an example, we find that he often struggled to cast his own spiritual experiences into words. Throughout his life, the Prophet frequently reinterpreted and even corrected accounts of his earlier experiences with divinity as he gained an enhanced perspective. This process occurred, for example, in the separate accounts of the First Vision.[14] Also, contradictions and textual growth can be witnessed in several of Joseph's revelations in the Doctrine and Covenants. These changes appear well documented in the Church's Joseph Smith Papers Project.

One of the most famous examples of the dynamic nature of Joseph's revelations appears in a revelation the Prophet received for Oliver Cowdery in April 1829.[15] Joseph's original revelation appeared in the Book of Commandments (now Doctrine and Covenants 8) and referred to Oliver's ability to use a divining rod:

> Now this is not all, for you have another gift, which is the gift of working with the rod: behold it has told you things: behold there is no other power

12. Adopting the expression from Philip L. Barlow, "The Uniquely True Church," 239.

13. Anthony F. Campbell and Mark A. O'Brien, *Sources of the Pentateuch: Texts, Introductions, Annotations*, xiv.

14. See Dean C. Jessee, "Early Accounts of Joseph Smith's First Vision," 275–94.

15. In addition to the Papers project, these changes appear documented in H. Michael Marquardt, *The Joseph Smith Revelations Text and Commentary*, 36.

save God, that can cause this rod of nature, to work in you hands, for it is the work of God.

Later, however, the Prophet felt a need to significantly revise this earlier revelation. He eradicated references to the rod so that when published in the 1835 edition of the Doctrine and Covenants, the text read:

> Now this is not all *thy gift*, for you have another gift, which is the gift of *Aaron*: Behold it has told you *many* things: behold, there is no other power save *the power of* God that can cause this *gift of Aaron* to *be with you; therefore, doubt not, for it is the gift of God, and you shall hold it* in your hands, *and do marvelous works; and no power shall be able to take it away out of your hands*; for it is the work of God.

There is evolution in Joseph's efforts to cast his revelations into words that effectively captured relationships to divinity.

Another illustration of this process at work occurs in Joseph's United Firm revelations (D&C 78, 82, 92, 96). These revelations show signs of significant revisionary efforts. Part of this growth occurred as a result of the Prophet's desire to keep hidden from outsiders the identities of the men who's names appear in the revelations. The original revelations referred openly to men who were participating in Joseph's United Firm, an organization that supervised the management of the Church's financial enterprises and distribution of properties from 1832–1834. The Prophet changed his own name to Enoch and Gazelam in the texts, and he gave ancient-sounding names to his cohorts: Newel K. Whitney was changed to Ahashdah, Edward Partridge to Alam, John Whitmer to Horah, A. Sidney Gilbert to Mahalaleel, Martin Harris to Mahemson, Oliver Cowdery to Olihah, Sidney Rigdon to Pelagoram, W. W. Phelps to Shalemanasseh, Frederick G. Williams to Shederlaomach, and John Johnson to Zombre.

The changes made to these financial revelations concerning the United Firm included more than simply a substitution of ancient code names. The revelations were intentionally revised in order to sound like ancient texts.[16] Anachronistic Bible references that originally appeared in the texts were substituted for terms connected with an even more ancient setting. The word "Israel" appears changed to a more archaic "Zion." John Johnson's lineage through Joseph of Egypt is changed to that of Seth, and even the name Jesus

---

16. In the words of historian Christopher Smith, "Significant additions and deletions were made in order to give these revelations an authentically ancient veneer." Christopher C. Smith, "The Inspired Fictionalization of the 1835 United Firm Revelations," 16.

Christ was switched to describe its Adamic form, "Son of Ahman."[17] These changes allowed the revelations to appear as ancient rather than modern.

The objective behind these changes is made clear in the way Joseph revised the revelation that eventually became Doctrine and Covenants 78. In the 1835 version of this text, the Prophet added the clause, "the Lord spoke unto Enoch, saying . . ." to the beginning. This effectively transformed the *Sitz im Leben* or "Setting in Life" for this nineteenth-century economic revelation concerning the United Firm to read as if it had been given to the ancient prophet Enoch:

> Hearken unto me saith the Lord your God O ye who are ordained unto the high priests hood of my church, who have assembled [yourselves together]. (Original manuscript version)[18]

> The Lord spake unto Enoch, saying, Hearken unto me saith the Lord your God, who are ordained unto the high priesthood of my church, who have assembled yourselves together. (D&C 75:1; 1835 edition)

> The Lord spake unto Joseph Smith, Jun., saying: Hearken unto me, saith the Lord your God, who are ordained unto the high priesthood of my church, who have assembled yourselves together. (D&C 78:1; current edition)

Moreover, the 1835 edition of the revelation Joseph published was given the title, "The Order of the Lord to Enoch, for the purpose of establishing the poor."[19]

These changes to Joseph's revelations are significant. They illustrate that the Prophet viewed his efforts to express the word of God as a malleable endeavor. The 2013 Introduction to the Doctrine and Covenants takes note of this process: "Joseph and the early Saints viewed the revelations as they did the Church: living, dynamic, and subject to refinement with additional revelation."[20] If Joseph was therefore subject to this struggle in gaining religious truth "line upon line precept upon precept," we should expect the same in the Old Testament.

---

17. Ibid., 25.

18. Revelation Book 1, p. 196, as published in Robin Scott Jensen, Robert J. Woodford, and Steven C. Harper, *Revelations and Translations, Volume 1: Manuscript Revelation Books*, 368–69.

19. Marquardt, *The Joseph Smith Revelations*, 30.

20. Available on the wesbite for the Church of Jesus Christ of Latter-day Saints at http://www.lds.org/scriptures/dc-testament/introduction (accessed October 22, 2013).

LDS Scripture

When it comes to scripture, we can be both religiously and critically minded. Concerning the activity of interpreting ancient scriptural records, a revelation received by Joseph Smith in 1829 integrates both viewpoints: "But, behold, I say unto you, that you must study it out in your own mind; then you must ask me if it be right" (D&C 9:8). This assertion unites the practice of critical thought with divine inspiration and helps us see why Joseph Smith desired to learn Hebrew and other sciences to help him better understand scripture. All of this directly challenges the notion that a Latter-day Saint cannot be both critically minded and religious at the same time with regards to scripture.

Joseph Smith was not alone among our prophets in trying to understand scripture more critically. President Gordon B. Hinckley appears to have been quite open to the possibility that the Bible is composed of separate sources and yet still inspired. Speaking in General Conference, he declared:

> The Christian world accepts the Bible as the word of God. Most have no idea of how it came to us. I have just completed reading a newly published book by a renowned scholar. It is apparent from information which he gives that the various books of the Bible were brought together in what appears to have been an unsystematic fashion. In some cases, the writings were not produced until long after the events they describe. One is led to ask, 'Is the Bible true? Is it really the word of God?' We reply that it is, insofar as it is translated correctly. The hand of the Lord was in its making.[21]

As President Hinckley acknowledged, even if the Bible was not produced in the exact manner we have traditionally assumed, this does not preclude the possibility that God directed the over-all development of the book in order to raise the spirituality of humankind.

When all is said and done, ancient theologians, *not* historians, authored the sources in the Pentateuch that recount the creation of the world and the rise of the House of Israel. As opposed to a scientific retelling of the past, these authors were fundamentally interested in religious matters pertaining to both their own time period and the future. This observation has been especially well-articulated by Israeli scholar Yosef Havim Yerushalmi when he said that in the scriptures "Israel is told that it must be a kingdom of priests and a holy people; nowhere is it suggested that it become a nation of historians."[22]

---

21. Gordon B. Hinckley, "The Great Things Which God Has Revealed," 81.
22. Yosef Hayim Yerushalmi, *Zakhor: Jewish History and Jewish Memory*, 10.

This does not mean, however, that in its literary accounts, the Old Testament *never* presents an accurate reflection of the past. It simply indicates that the authors of the Pentateuch had something much more important to tell their readers than a mere recitation of past events. These authors sought to explain God's relationship with humankind. The manner in which they presented this interaction with divinity can be interpreted both critically and religiously.

Studying a religious text independent from any specific theological lens can present some challenges to certain religious traditions regarding the text, and a believer on occasion may need to shift his or her paradigm of faith in order to account for new historical insights. Upon reflection, we can see that this is something we have already been doing continually throughout our lives since our first nursery and Primary school lessons. For example, while we may not have all fully embraced evolution, few of us have discounted scientific claims about the age of the Earth and still hold to traditional beliefs that the Earth was created six thousand or thirteen thousand years ago. Even though we know that the Earth is billions of years old, we still see value in Genesis's seven-day creation.

In his introduction to reading the Hebrew Bible from a critical perspective, Dr. Marc Brettler concludes his book with a chapter explaining how he is able to exist in both the academic realm of critical scholarship and in the religious world of an observant Jew. Brettler writes:

> In a nutshell, here is my view of the Bible as a Jew: The Bible is a sourcebook that I—within my community—make into a textbook. I do so by selecting, revaluing, and interpreting the texts that I call sacred.[23]

A textbook, according to Brettler, adopts a singular point of view; in contrast, a sourcebook presents multiple perspectives. Because the Bible has been authored by different groups, at different times, and in different circumstances, it should be expected to share different narratives attempting to both understand and explain our relationship with God. Thus, it contains more than one opinion on almost any single item of importance, from the nature of God to intergenerational punishment to the relationship between men and women.

While Brettler approaches this issue from the perspective of an observing Jew, this same basic tactic can be adopted by Latter-day Saints. In many ways, reading and seeing the various sources for the Pentateuch can be very similar to our experiences in our own wards—especially during fast and testimony

---

23. Marc Zvi Brettler, *How to Read the Bible*, 280.

meetings. In our worship services and Sunday meetings we listen to fellow members who all experience God in different and varying ways. And while we may not always fully agree with them, we are still able to appreciate and even learn from their testimonies. Rather than being persons who we completely depend on for worship, they are persons whom we worship *with*. Such can be the case for those who do not read the Bible as the direct inerrant word of God but as a real book with real testimonies by real and different people.

Conclusion

In the remaining chapters, we will explore the implications that Higher Criticism and other observations made by biblical scholars have for our modern scripture texts, including the books of Moses and Abraham, as well as the Book of Mormon. If we accept the observations identified thus far regarding the Bible, there are two basic ways we might reconcile this approach with the revelations of the Restoration concerning these biblical figures who hold prominent roles in our theology and scripture: (1) we can assume that these were historical figures whose stories, as told in the Hebrew Bible, reflect early Israelite and Near Eastern oral traditions incorporated into the documentary sources; or (2) we can assume that some of these men were *not* historical figures of the material past, and that rather than having the purpose of providing a chronological record of the past, with scripture God uses ideas, assumptions, mythology, and even foreign texts to help us establish a relationship with Him and others. We find hints for this perspective in the preface to the Doctrine and Covenants: "these [revelations] are of me and were given unto my servants in their weakness, after the manner of their language, that they might come to understanding" (D&C 1:24). We will now turn our attention to Latter-day scripture directly affected by the scholarly insights of Historical Criticism.

Chapter Seven

Higher Criticism and the Book of Moses

Introduction

A revelation given to Joseph Smith in 1841 depicts God's perspective concerning the prophet: "I give unto you my servant Joseph to be a presiding elder over all my church, to be a translator, a revelator, a seer, and prophet" (D&C 124:125). As prophet of God, Joseph did indeed translate religious texts that Latter-day Saints define as scripture comparable to the Bible. However, that translation process was in every instance non-traditional; most of Joseph's translation projects did not involve literally working with foreign language texts. In nineteenth-century American English, the verb "translate" carried a variety of nuances (much as it does today). In addition to its meaning of "the act of turning into another language," *translation* could also signify "interpretation," or a "version" in addition to its primary meaning of "the act of removing or conveying from one place to another."[1] Each of these 1828 definitions works well as a characterization of the Joseph Smith Translation, a revelatory work that created a new interpretation or new version of the Bible. This chapter explores the Book of Moses (an important part of the Joseph Smith Translation) in light of the findings of Historical Criticism.

Joseph Smith was a translator of religious texts, but he was not a translator in the traditional sense. "We can save ourselves much rumination," argues Karl Sandberg, "if we accept at the outset that Joseph Smith never did document-to-document translation based on a knowledge of two lan-

---

1. Noah Webster, *American Dictionary of the English Language* (Anaheim: Foundation for American Christian Education, 1967).

guages, except as an exercise in his Hebrew class in the winter of 1835–36."[2] In his study of the way Joseph understood the religious concept of "translation," Sandberg focused on illustrations of inspired translators in the Book of Mormon, including Ammon's comments to king Limhi concerning the Jaredite record:

> Now Ammon said unto him: I can assuredly tell thee, O king, of a man that can translate the records; for he has wherewith that he can look, and translate all records that are of ancient date; and it is a gift from God. And the things are called interpreters, and no man can look in them except he be commanded, lest he should look for that he ought not and he should perish. And whosoever is commanded to look in them, the same is called seer. (Mosiah 8:13)[3]

As Sandberg recognized, the Book of Mormon provides a window into Joseph Smith's views concerning the spiritual gift of translation. It reveals the way Joseph himself produced scriptural texts as a seer and how the process of translation was in every way non-traditional. For Joseph, a translator was a seer who made known that which was hidden from the world.

In his efforts to combine his revelatory work with past dispensations, Joseph had the ability to create new scriptural texts. However, these texts were never traditional translations that resulted from directly working with another language.[4] In the case of the Book of Mormon, the Prophet does not seem to have directly used the plates while producing his translation.[5] That access to an actual copy of an ancient source was unnecessary

---

2. Karl C. Sandberg, "Knowing Brother Joseph Again: The Book of Abraham and Joseph Smith as Translator," 19.

3. Summarizing his findings, Sandberg writes, "Translation, as understood in the Book of Mormon, is the gift of seeing hidden things, both good and evil, and making unknown things known. It is carried out or made possible through the use of physical objects—stones which enable the user to see what is hidden and thus to describe it and bring it to light. Translator is synonymous with seer. The capacity of revelator and the status of prophet derive from seership." Ibid., 21.

4. See Richard van Wagoner and Steven Walker, "Joseph Smith: 'The Gift of Seeing,'" 48–68.

5. On the translation process, Richard Bushman writes: "By the time Cowdery arrived, translator and scribe were no longer separated. Emma said she sat at the same table with Joseph, writing as he dictated, with nothing between them, and the plates wrapped in a linen cloth on the table. When Cowdery took up the job of scribe, he and Joseph translated in the same room where Emma was working. Joseph looked in the seerstone, and the plates lay covered on the table. Neither Joseph nor Oliver explained how translation worked, but Joseph did not pretend

for his translations is evidenced by both his inspired translation of the Bible and the revealed text "translated from parchment written and hid up by [John the beloved disciple] himself," found in Doctrine and Covenants 7. In Joseph's work, a translator (or seer), did not depend entirely upon an original document to produce a translation of an inspired text; instead, the seer depended primarily upon God, or in other words, the original source of the inspired word.

Since the time that Joseph Smith produced his translation of the Bible, scholars have uncovered many significant insights into the texts and history of ancient Israel. The previous chapters illustrated how Genesis is a compilation of Judean sources originally written several centuries after Moses. Yet Joseph Smith's Inspired Translation presents a revised version of the opening chapters of Genesis as words written by the biblical prophet himself. If Moses did not literally write the Pentateuch, how might a Latter day Saint reader who accepts the conclusions of Higher Criticism retain a view of the Book of Moses, an essential part of Joseph Smith's Inspired Translation, as inspired scripture?

The Book of Moses

Shortly after organizing a church and publishing his Book of Mormon, the Prophet Joseph Smith began a subsequent scriptural project, adding to and correcting the Bible. "It is hard to imagine now how this twenty-four-year-old came to believe that he could revise the Bible," writes historian Richard Bushman, "it was a striking demonstration of his outrageous confidence; to take on this hallowed book, he had to think of himself as a prophet among prophets."[6]

Bushman is certainly correct in his assessment. Joseph's project was both shocking and bold. And yet, Joseph's confidence that he could "correct" the Bible was no doubt influenced by the general sentiments of his age, which were a product of European rationalism. From this perspective, Joseph was very much a comparable figure to students of the Bible like Hobbes, Paine, and Wellhausen—men who recognized that when read critically, the Bible contains a variety of internal inconsistencies that re-

---

to look at the 'reformed Egyptian' words, the language on the plates, according to the book's own description. The plates lay covered on the table, while Joseph's head was in a hat looking at the seerstone, which by this time had replaced the interpreters." Richard L. Bushman, *Joseph Smith: Rough Stone Rolling*, 71–72.

6. Ibid., 132.

quire explanation. Like many of his day, Joseph rejected the traditional religious view that the Bible was a "privileged" text.[7]

The Bible that the Prophet used for his project was a King James Version purchased on October 8, 1829, at the E.B. Grandin bookstore in Palmyra, New York, where the Book of Mormon was being typeset. This process of translating the Bible differed from both traditional means of translation and that of the Book of Mormon, as Joseph was not basing this work off of another language nor using the Urim and Thummim or seer stones. Instead, Joseph and his scribe would sit at a table while the Prophet verbally dictated his revisions.[8]

In June of 1830, Joseph's scribe Oliver Cowdery began writing these changes. The original editorial introduction read: "A Revelation given to Joseph the Revelator June 1830." Unlike subsequent portions of the JST, this revelation was not dependent upon any text that appears in the King James Bible. The revelation set the stage for Joseph's subsequent revisionary efforts to the Old Testament.

Known today as Moses 1, this revelation provides a new introduction to the Bible. Identified as the "words of Moses," the text creates a new *Sitz im Leben* or "Setting in Life" for the opening chapters of Genesis.[9] Here the Bible's stories of human prehistory, including creation, the Fall, and

---

7. For an analysis on this approach see Chapter 1.

8. "The original documents behind this publication are an 1828 KJV Bible (with Apocrypha) having various markings in pencil and ink, purchased by Smith and Oliver Cowdery in October 1829, and hundreds of sheets of paper with writing on both sides by various scribes. These documents reveal that Smith's revision progressed in stages; many passages contain not only revisions of the KJV but revisions of revisions of still earlier revisions. Other passages show evidence of revisions that were later discarded in favor of the original KJV reading. Some show later revisions of biblical chapters previously marked 'correct.' Joseph Smith clearly experimented with the Bible as he sought to bring its text in line with the insights of his revelations and understanding." Philip Barlow, *Mormons and the Bible: The Place of Latter-day Saints in American Religion*, 50.

9. The term *Sitz im Leben* is a German phrase used in biblical scholarship typically translated as "Setting in Life." It originated with German scholar Hermann Gunkel. The expression describes the classification or contextualization of a scriptural passage. It is linked with the process of defining literary genres in the Bible by exploring such issues as who the speaker of a passage was, what was his status or position, and what is the nature of his audience. Answering these questions directly affects how an interpreter reads and understands a passage. In other words, is it a parody, a sermon, a ritual, etc.? What is its "setting in life"?

the flood are identified as narratives written by the Prophet Moses himself. They were words given to Moses as part of a visionary experience on an "exceedingly high mountain."

From a literary perspective, Joseph's revelation features a biblical-like *inclusio* bracketing the text through a repetition of key words in its introduction and conclusion. It begins with the superscription:

> The Words of God, which he spake unto Moses at a time when Moses was caught up into an exceedingly high mountain. (Moses 1:1)

The revelation then concludes forty-one verses later with an editorial colophon (or conclusion) that repeats key thematic elements from the beginning of the text:

> These words were spoken unto Moses in the mount, the name of which shall not be known among the children of men. And now they are spoken unto you. Show them not unto any except them that believe, Even so. Amen. (Moses 1:42)

This editorial technique parallels the envelope structure that brackets P's opening story of creation as a distinct literary unit:

> In the beginning God created the heaven and the earth. (Gen. 1:1)

> These are the generations of the heavens and of the earth when they were created. (Gen. 2:4a)

Appearing both in Moses 1 and in Genesis 1–2:4a, an *inclusio* serves as a textual marker identifying a segment of literature as an independent literary unit.

As discussed in previous chapters, Genesis's prehistory is a compilation of two originally separate documentary sources created by Judean scribes (P and J) rather than the writings of Moses. From this perspective, Moses could not have literally written Joseph Smith's Book of Moses (since Moses 1 introduces Genesis as a book written by the biblical prophet).

Even without the perspective of Higher Criticism, this assertion should be apparent to all careful readers of Joseph's revelation. Moses 1 constantly invokes the voice of an omniscient narrator speaking about Moses in the third person. Statements such as, "and *he* saw God face to face, and *he* talked with him, and the glory of God was upon *Moses*; therefore *Moses* could endure his presence. And God spake unto *Moses* . . ." (vv. 2–3), appear throughout the revelation. This pattern stands in stark contrast to the first-person biographical formulation of Joseph's subsequent scriptural text, the Book of Abraham. Hence, when read critically, the text itself does not view Moses as its author.

Moreover, later in his ministry, Joseph delivered a sermon in which he described the original form of Genesis 1:1 (as written by the original author) that appears in Moses 2:1. According to Joseph, prior to scribal tampering, the original version of the biblical passage read: "'In the beginning the head of the Gods brought forth the Gods,' or, as others have translated it, 'The head of the Gods called the Gods together.'"[10] Thus, putting the three scriptural texts together (i.e., Genesis 1:1, Moses 2:1 and Joseph Smith Urtext) we witness that the Book of Moses was not even the original form of the Priestly creation narrative from Joseph's perspective:

> In the beginning God created the heaven and the earth. (Gen. 1:1 KJV)

> In the beginning I created the heaven, and the earth upon which thou standest. (Moses 2:1–2)

> In the beginning the head of the Gods brought forth the Gods. (Joseph Smith Urtext)

Still, Moses 1 sets the stage for interpreting the opening chapters of Genesis as words originally written down by Moses himself. The conclusion to Joseph's revelation presents God giving Moses the following command:

> And now, Moses, my son, I will speak unto thee concerning this earth upon which thou standest; and thou shalt write the things which I shall speak. And in a day when the children of men shall esteem my words as naught and take many of them from the book which thou shalt write, behold, I will raise up another like unto thee; and they shall be had again among the children of men—among as many as shall believe. (Moses 1:40–41)

As we have discussed, not only do the first three books of the Bible never present themselves as the words written by Moses, they do not envision a time in Israelite history when prophets wrote inspired scripture. Instead, the texts focus upon orality rather than textually. Deuteronomy, however, as a later Judean source, begins the process of depicting Moses as an author of scriptural material.

This observation reflects the historical reality of the lack of literacy in ancient Israel. As literacy gradually became more important in Judean society, the authors of later biblical and non-canonical sources (like the Book of Jubilees), began to depict Moses as author. The Book of Moses, therefore, parallels the trend in later Judean sources that depict Moses as more than simply the mouth of God, but as the author of God's words. Because of this, the Book of Moses cannot be linked with early Israelite

---

10. Joseph Smith, *History of the Church*, 6:475.

history and instead reflects a later view that emphasized textuality instead of orality.

In fact, the Book of Moses goes so far as to push the historical concept of textuality and authorship of scriptural records back to the beginning of human history:

> And a book of remembrance was kept, in the which was recorded, in the language of Adam, for it was given unto as many as called upon God to write by the spirit of inspiration. (Moses 6:5)

The Book of Moses, therefore, does not follow the ancient Israelite trend of textual anonymity; the scribal authors of J, P, E, and D never identify themselves as authors of the text. Historically, the concept of identifying an author of a text (such as Moses, Enoch, Abraham, etc.) was a tradition that entered into Judaism through the influence of Greek culture during the later Hellenistic era.[11]

Thus, not only does the Book of Moses follow the later historical trend concerning authorship and textuality, it revises sources that were originally produced by Judean scribes interacting with Mesopotamian texts hundreds of years after Moses would have lived. Moses simply could not have written the Book of Moses.

If Joseph's Book of Moses does not, therefore, recreate what the ancient prophet himself actually wrote, how might a believing Latter-day Saint who encounters these academic perspectives interpret this important component of the LDS canon? If the Book of Moses is not literally what it seems to purport to be, can the text still be considered inspired scripture?

The Book of Moses as Pseudepigraphy

In presenting itself as words once literally written by the prophet Moses himself, the Book of Moses follows an ancient literary pattern for revelatory text. This same type of genre is seen in later Jewish pseudepigraha and Rabbinic midrash, as well as within the Bible itself. Throughout Israelite and Judean history, pseudonymous authors from antiquity often appear identified as the authors of ancient texts. Jewish books (held as "scripture" by various communities) appear attributed to Adam, Enoch, Noah, Melchizedek, Abraham, Jacob, Moses, Elijah, and Ezekiel (just to name a few).

---

11. J.D.G. Dunn, "Pseudepigraphy," in *Dictionary of the Later New Testament and its Development.*

One of the ancient Jewish texts that parallels the type of structure in the Book of Moses is 1 Enoch. A second-temple Jewish text with literary layers that existed at least as early as the third century BC, 1 Enoch was originally composed in Aramaic long after the time associated with the biblical Enoch. The book contains five separate segments in a way that reflects the traditional Jewish notion of the Torah consisting of five books.[12] These have been preserved in translation and remain part of the scriptural canon of the Ethiopian Christian church.

1 Enoch features revised segments of the opening chapters of Genesis (including the story of the "Sons of God" in Genesis 6:1–4). These revisions are presented as a vision received by the biblical patriarch Enoch and begin with an editorial superscription or introduction that speaks about Enoch in third person:

> The blessing of Enoch: with which he blessed the elect and the righteous who would be present on the day of tribulation at (the time of) the removal of all the ungodly ones. And Enoch, the blessed and righteous man of the Lord, took up (his parable) while his eyes were open and he saw, and said . . . (1 Enoch 1:1–2a)[13]

The account then presents a depiction of Enoch's own words:

> [This is] a holy vision from the heavens which the angels showed me: and I heard from them everything and I understood. I look not for this generation but for the distant one that is coming. (1 Enoch 1:2b)

Following an introduction that runs through 1 Enoch 5, the text transitions to a revised version of J's story of the Sons of God in Genesis 6:1–4.

1 Enoch, therefore, directly parallels the structure for the Book of Moses. The Book of Moses begins with an editorial introduction that speaks about Moses in third person and then transitions to Moses using direct first person speech followed by a revised version of material found in the Book of Genesis. In so doing, both texts present a revised version of Judean documentary sources as revelations dictated by earlier prophetic figures. Known as pseudepigrapha (meaning "false superscriptions or titles"), this type of literature is a very common feature in ancient Jewish scriptural texts.

---

12. For the various elements in 1 Enoch and an analysis of their historical development, see George W. E. Nickelsburg, *1 Enoch 1: A Commentary of the Book of Enoch Chapters 1–36, 81–108*, 7–8, 21–26.

13. As translated by E. Isaac in James Charlesworth, ed., *Old Testament Pseudepigrapha*, 1:13.

Even many of the books in the New Testament are pseudepigraphic works attributed to early Christian leaders. The New Testament, for instance, contains an epistle depicted as a letter written by Paul to his missionary companion Titus. Titus is one of a series of epistles attributed to Paul that biblical scholars almost universally believe were not written by the Apostle, including the epistles to Timothy and the Ephesians. Colossians and 2 Thessalonians are also held by many critical scholars as pseudepigraphic texts. As Bart Ehrman explains,

> Letters allegedly written by Paul continued to be produced in the second and later centuries [i.e., long after his death]; among those that still survive are a third letter to the Corinthians, a letter addressed to the church in the town of Laodicea, and an exchange of correspondence between Paul and the famous Greek philosopher Seneca.[14]

These later texts illustrate how the pseudepigraphically attributed letters of Paul in the New Testament follow a common pattern in early Christian writings. Indeed, the same holds true for other scriptural sources from the New Testament. Most New Testament scholars, for instance, do not believe that Peter was the author of the two epistles ascribed to him in the Bible, or that the Epistle of Jude was a book truly written by the brother of Jesus and James.[15]

Other pseudepigraphic texts not included in the traditional New Testament canon include such works as the Gospel of Peter and the Gospel of Judas. In fact, a critical survey of early Christian literature, including the books that appear in the New Testament, illustrates that creating a religious text as the words of a famous Christian leader was not simply a pervasive tradition, it was the norm. The authors of many of these ancient religious texts were in many cases not who they claimed to be.

Attributing a literary work to another person who held an important religious role, such as a prophet or apostle, elevated the religious status of the document as sacred literature.[16] In his recent work focusing upon early Christian writings that follow this trend, Ehrman explains:

---

14. Bart Ehrman, *New Testament: An Historical Introduction to the Early Christian Writings*, 292–93.

15. Historically, Jesus' brother Jude would have been a lower class, Aramaic-speaking Jew. The author of "Jude," however, was highly educated in Jewish apocryphal writings and he possessed an ability to write in Greek. The author, for example, cites the book of 1 Enoch as scripture in v. 14.

16. James C. VanderKam, *From Revelation to Canon: Studies in the Hebrew Bible and Second Temple Literature*, 23–25; G.W.E. Nickelsburg, "Revealed

The single most important motivation for authors to claim they were some-one else in antiquity . . . was to get a hearing for their views. If you were an unknown person, but had something really important to say and wanted people to hear you—not so they could praise you, but so they could learn the truth—one way to make that happen was to pretend you were someone else, a well-known author, a famous figure, an authority.[17]

In other words, claiming that your revelation was actually given to Enoch, Isaiah, Abraham, or Paul gave the work a type of religious credence.

This interpretation of the purpose of pseudepigraphy works well for many of the early Christian examples Ehrman's study focuses upon. However, imposing the same idea upon the Book of Moses is problematic. Joseph did not need to attribute his revelation (Moses 1) to the biblical Moses in order to provide his revelation with greater validity. As prophet of God, in addition to translating the Book of Mormon, Joseph was al-ready dictating his own personal revelations as scripture in 1830. There was no need for Joseph to bolster his religious views by claiming that they were Moses's. Instead, Moses 1 presents the opening chapters of Genesis as a revelation given to Moses on a mountaintop. It therefore elevates the religious authenticity of the Bible, not Joseph's revelations.

From this perspective, the Book of Moses reflects a different pseude-pigraphic perspective. Ancient authors who produced a religious source as the words of an earlier prophet or sage did not always seek to identify the text as a document that ultimately derived from that authoritative figure (though such an attempt was common). Instead, ancient authors occasionally sought to produce a text wherein one who communicated with God could serve as a type of conduit for the disclosure of divine knowledge. This is one of the ways Moses can be understood in Joseph's revelation. For those who accept Joseph's Book of Moses as inspired text, Israel's great lawgiver serves as an instrument or conduit for the disclosure of the divine knowledge that appears in Genesis. The text, therefore, ac-cords with Joseph's role as a Restorer, bridging the spiritual and scriptural gaps between the ancient and modern worlds.

Pseudonymous authors legitimize the scriptural authority of the text. In this sense, the pseudonymous writer is "not so much creator or author

---

Wisdom as a Criterion for Inclusion and Exclusion: From Jewish Sectarianism to Early Christianity," 73–91. Ibid., "The Nature and Function of Revelation in 1 Enoch, Jubilees, and Some Qumranic Documents," 91–120.

17. Bart D. Ehrman, *Forged: Writing in the Name of God—Why the Bible's Authors Are Not Who We Think They Are*, 31.

as he is tradent and guarantor."[18] Hence, the ancient art of pseudepigraphy should not be viewed through modern notions of fraud or forgeries. This point is well-articulated by Annette Yoshiko Reed:

> When grappling with the presence of Pauline pseudepigrapha in the New Testament . . . scholars . . . have cautioned against assuming that this ancient literary practice was necessarily motivated by any radical intent to replace an earlier text or tradition. Like the prophetic pseudepigraphy that formed second and third Isaiah, for instance, the Pauline pseudepigraphy of the Pastoral Epistles may be better understood in terms of a claim to faithful oral reception and written transmission of Pauline teachings and/or as a claim to the inspired interpretation and faithful continuation of Pauline tradition. Rather than a rebellion against the textual authority of Paul's own writings, this literary choice may reflect a conservativism vis-à-vis received tradition, forged in settings in which its preservation seemed, to some, to be endangered by competing readings of the meanings of Paul's written words.[19]

A Latter-day Saint who accepts the arguments of Higher Criticism could adopt Reed's perspective of pseudepigrapha as a reflection for what the Book of Moses does for Genesis. The Book of Moses, therefore, can be seen to conceptually parallel Joseph's reworking of his United Firm revelations discussed in Chapter 6. In both instances, we find the Prophet Joseph Smith reworking previous religious texts into the prophetic vision of biblical figures. In the Book of Moses, Genesis is placed into the context of Moses' revelation; in Joseph's United Firm texts, the Prophet's economic revelations were reworked into the vision(s) of Enoch. From a theological perspective, these revised revelations illustrate the Prophet's understanding of dispensationalism (that history, in types and shadows, repeats itself from dispensation to dispensation).[20] This unique perspective gave Joseph precedence to rewrite scriptural texts (including his own) into the words of ancient prophets.

A religious text that attributes the scriptural account to an ancient figure does not necessarily recreate words he or she once literally wrote. Instead, as one scholar has observed regarding this ancient venerable tradition,

> Attribution (attaching names to Biblical books) belongs to the realm of literary scholarship, and has little to do with the intentions of the composers of

---

18. Annette Yoshiko Reed, "Pseudepigraphy, Authorship and the Reception of the 'the Bible' in Late Antiquity," 477.

19. Reed, "Pseudepigraphy, Authorship and the Reception," 475–76.

20. This thesis is argued by Christopher Smith, "The Inspired Fictionalization of the 1835 United Firm Revelations," 30.

works. It isn't so much about what an author did write, but rather it is about what he would have written (or; from the perspective of ancient literary interpreters, what he must have written).[21]

The Book of Moses therefore can be seen from this angle as an account of what Moses, Israel's great lawgiver, would have written; or, from the perspective of Joseph's revelatory text, what Moses must have written.

Like Wellhausen and other nineteenth-century critical thinkers, Joseph Smith recognized that the Bible was a product of human hands. Its problems needed to be addressed. Joseph identified some of these issues, and then attempted to correct the errors (as he perceived them) via his new translation. However, unlike Wellhausen whose critical approach to the Bible humanized the work, Joseph's critical assessment represents a type of religious conservatism that seeks to elevate the inspired authenticity of the Bible by providing Genesis' prehistory with a new interpretive lens.

The second-century BC Book of Jubilees reports that during the first year of the Exodus, Moses experienced a forty-day epiphany on a sacred mountain. On this occasion, God shared with his prophet a panoramic vision concerning the history of the world (see Jubilees 1:1–4). According to the account, God intended this vision and the subsequent testimony Moses would record to provide a witness to the descendants of Israel concerning the covenants of the Lord. The account presents God's words to Moses:

> Set your mind on every thing which I shall tell you on this mountain, and write it in a book so that [Israel's] descendants might see that I have not abandoned them on account of all of the evil which they have done to instigate transgression of the covenant which I am establishing between me and you today on Mount Sinai for their descendants. (Jubilees 1:5–6)

This account shows that Joseph Smith's Book of Moses follows a later historical trend in ancient Jewish traditions. The Book of Moses not only defends the inspired nature of Genesis's prehistory, it elevates the text to a revelatory status by using the biblical prophet Moses as a conduit for Joseph's own revelations that corrected the Bible.

Like the Book of Jubilees, Joseph's revelation follows a pattern first witnessed in ancient Judean history as a response to Hellenistic concerns. Greek philosophical traditions that influenced later Jewish thought held a text like Genesis with suspicion because it features accounts that many Greek philosophers would associate with the category of myth rather than history.

---

21. Jed Wyrick, *The Ascension of Authorship: Attribution and Canon Formation in Jewish, Hellenistic, and Christian Traditions*, 80.

Early Jewish efforts to identify the Pentateuch with a historical author such as Moses derived in part from an effort to respond to Greek criticism. The idea of a prophet writing scripture such as the Book of Genesis emerged as a late Judean concept, long after the time period of Moses.

The Book of Moses as Temple Text

While from the perspective of Historical Criticism the Book of Moses cannot be attributed to Moses himself, the text can be interpreted as accomplishing a profound religious purpose. In fact, one might argue that this rationale is more meaningful than simply recreating words once written by a biblical figure. The Book of Moses provides a new *Sitz im Leben* for the opening chapters of Genesis as a mountain, and therefore "temple," revelation.

In ancient Near Eastern thought, mountains were often seen as sites connected with the gods. In the Bible, Ezekiel 28:13–15 depicts Yahweh's home in the Garden of Eden as a mountain; Abraham shows his faithfulness to deity by his willingness to sacrifice his son on a mountain (Gen. 22:1–14); God appears to Moses and speaks from the burning bush on a mountain in the Book of Exodus; and later, Mount Zion was the sacred site of the Jerusalem temple. Concerning this temple mount, Isaiah's famous prophecy declares:

> And it shall come to pass in the last days, that the mountain of the LORD's house shall be established in the top of the mountains, and shall be exalted above the hills; and all nations shall flow unto it. And many people shall go and say, Come ye, and let us go up to the mountain of the LORD, to the house of the God of Jacob; and he will teach us of his ways, and we will walk in his paths: for out of Zion shall go forth the law, and the word of the LORD from Jerusalem. (Isa. 2:2–3)

Thus, by placing the opening chapters of Genesis into the context of a revelation Moses received on a mountain, the Book of Moses can be understood as a revelation that transforms the opening chapters of the Bible into a temple text. Significantly, not only does Joseph's revelation refer to the mountain where Moses received God's word as "high," it goes so far as to stress that like a temple, this mountain linked heaven and earth. The place of Moses' theophany was, after all, "exceedingly high" (Moses 1:1).

There is some evidence that the Prophet Joseph Smith recognized this perspective. In 1842, the same year Joseph revealed the Nauvoo endowment ceremony, the Prophet stated:

I preached in the grove on the keys of the Kingdom, Charity &c The keys are certain signs and words by which false spirits and personages may be detected from true, which cannot be revealed to the Elders till the Temple is completed—The rich can only get them in the Temple, the poor may get them on the mountain top as did Moses. . . . No one can truly say he knows God until he has handled something, and this can only be in the holiest of holies.[22]

Joseph believed that Moses received the sacred temple endowment on a mountain and that through this process, the biblical prophet truly came to know God. Through the Book of Moses, readers are invited to recreate a similar spiritual encounter with deity by approaching the opening chapters of the Bible as revelatory temple literature.

As a revelation prefiguring the Nauvoo endowment, the Book of Moses features the following biblical and temple motifs:

- Withdrawal of God leaving Man (Moses) to himself, followed by lessons on confronting and dismissing Satan by the name of the Only Begotten (Moses 1:10–21)
- Story of Creation (Moses 2)
- Story of the Fall (Moses 3–4)
- Creation of sacred clothing (Moses 4:27–28)
- Adam and Eve call upon the name of the Lord in prayer (Moses 5:4)
- Law of Obedience (Moses 5:4)
- Law of Sacrifice taught and explained including a command to "do all that thou doest in the name of the Son" (Moses 5:7)
- False secret ritual worship sworn by the throat in order to get gain (Moses 5:29–30)
- Gospel preached unto Adam by holy angels (Moses 5:58)
- Building of Zion, the Kingdom of God on Earth (Moses 7)

When interpreted from this perspective, the Book of Moses allows readers to approach the opening chapters of Genesis from the perspective of temple worship, covenants, and rituals.

In ancient Jewish and Christian traditions, Moses was the great lawgiver and traditionally assumed author of the Pentateuch. He served as a mediator between God and his covenant people (Ex. 32:11–12; Num. 14:15–16; Deut. 9:26–29). Therefore, in Joseph's revelation, the temple perspective on Genesis is presented through Moses as a reflection of what Israel's great prophet *would* have written if given the chance. Moses and his authority serves as the instrumentality for this temple-based approach to the Bible's opening chapters.

---

22. Joseph Smith, "Journal, December 1841–December 1842."

From this perspective, Latter-day Saints who have experienced the Temple Endowment can interpret the opening chapters of Genesis in a highly personal way. Ultimately, the Book of Moses allows its readers to place themselves and their families directly into the context of creation, the Fall, the development of human culture, and the doctrine of Atonement. It does so by using Adam and Eve to define its readers' very own personal relationship to deity.

Near Eastern Connections

Despite its nineteenth-century origin, the Book of Moses contains an impressive variety of thematic and religious connections with Near Eastern traditions. Often times these links are very subtle. They suggest a highly sophisticated relationship between the Book of Moses and the ideas that influenced the Hebrew Bible. The Book of Moses, therefore, can be understood by a Latter-day Saint as an inspired text that not only restores ancient theological insights concerning divinity, but that builds upon and advances these earlier perspectives. In this study, we will consider four such concepts.

Controlling Water as God

One of the important theological concepts that appears throughout the Bible is the notion of *imatio dei*, or "imitation of God," referring to a religious concept in which humans achieve a state of virtue by acting like divinity. It appears in biblical texts such as Jesus's statement, "Be ye therefore perfect as your Father in Heaven is perfect" (Matt. 5:48), and within H's depiction of God's commandment given to Israel, "ye shall be holy unto me: for I the LORD am holy" (Lev. 20:26). From this perspective, man should strive to be like God.

One of the ways in which the Book of Moses captures this theological notion is through the account's use of water, where it presents a promise to the biblical prophet that he will be like God exercising dominion over water:

> Blessed art thou, Moses, for I, the Almighty, have chosen thee, and thou shalt be made stronger than many waters; for they shall obey thy command as if thou wert God. (Moses 1:25)

When read from an ancient Near Eastern perspective, this statement regarding Moses's spiritual gift to command water as if he were God proves meaningful. In recent decades, the discovery of cuneiform tablets from

Mesopotamia and Canaan has provided biblical scholars with vital clues regarding the literary and mythological motifs from the world of the Bible. For example, the Canaanite deity El, "the father of the gods," appears in the Ugaritic tablets discovered at modern-day Ras Shamra as the deity "situated at the fountain of the two Rivers, in the middle of the bedding of the two floods."[23] This idea suggests that El's divinity is directly associated with his power over water.

We find a similar view in P's creation story. In Genesis 1, the creation narrative states that the Spirit of God moved upon the face of the "waters" (v. 2); God separated the "water from the water" (v. 6); God commanded the water below the sky to gather in one place (v. 9); God named the collective waters "Sea" (v. 10); God created living creatures from the water including the *tannīm* or "sea monsters"[24] (vv. 20–21); God filled the water with living creatures (v. 22); and finally, God created man to rule the fish of the water (v. 26). With this emphasis, the account clearly stresses the central role of water in God's creation. P, therefore, uses the motif as a way of demonstrating the ultimate power of deity.

Often in Near Eastern mythology, the gods demonstrated their divinity by controlling the water through theomachy or divine combat. Enūma Elish, for instance, depicts the Babylonian deity Marduk overcoming Tiamat, the personified primeval ocean.[25] In the Ugaritic tablets, the Canaanite deity Baal appears in conflict with his anthropomorphically shaped enemy Yam, meaning "Sea." One of the interesting biblical passages that features this same motif is Psalms 74:

> For God is my King of old, working salvation in the midst of the earth. Thou didst divide the sea by thy strength: thou brakest the heads of the dragons in the waters. Thou brakest the heads of leviathan in pieces, and gavest him to be meat to the people inhabiting the wilderness. Thou didst cleave the fountain and the flood: thou driedst up mighty rivers. (vv. 12–15)

This passage differs from the creation narrative in Genesis 1, which depicts God's power over the sea manifested simply through divine speech rather than combat.

---

23. F. Stolz, "Sea," 1395.

24. The KJV renders the Hebrew word *tannīm* as "great whales"; however, the LDS Bible footnote correctly notes the term's true meaning as "sea monsters." The same word is used in Psalms 74 (cited above) and translated in the KJV as "dragons in the water."

25. See the analysis of Enūma Elish in Chapter 5.

Thus the notion of God controlling the sea (oftentimes in the form of theomachy), and by extension, granting this authority to Moses as if *he* were God, provides evidence for Joseph's ability to capture in his revelation key theological concepts in the Bible. These concepts make greater sense to scholars today than they did in the nineteenth century. Though a mortal man, the Book of Moses tells us that Moses was to act like God himself and demonstrate from an ancient Near Eastern perspective an extraordinarily divine power.

Man of Council

Another intriguing link between the Book of Moses and traditional Near Eastern ideas appears in Moses 7. The text depicts a very intimate conversation between God and the biblical patriarch Enoch concerning the extreme wickedness of humanity during Genesis's period of prehistory. In the midst of this discussion, the account depicts God interjecting the names that personify his divinity:

> Behold, I am God; Man of Holiness is my name; Man of Counsel is my name; and Endless and Eternal is my name, also. (Moses 7:35)

This passage which identifies God's name as "man," parallels a biblical notion featured in the Book of Exodus concerning Yahweh: "the LORD is a man of war: the LORD is his name" (15:3). God is a man, according to such conceptions, and His name(s) prove meaningful in defining His divinity.

Moreover, the statement in Moses 7:35 that one of God's sacred names is "Man of Counsel" suggests another profound connection between traditional Israelite theology and Joseph's revelation. In previous chapters, we have discussed how the scholarly consensus holds that when God speaks to a non-specified group of others in Genesis, this refers to God speaking to a divine council of deities.

Joseph Smith's views concerning a plurality of Gods shocked many contemporary nineteenth-century Christians. Today, scholars recognize that the council of God provides "a fundamental symbol for the Old Testament understanding of how the government of human society by the divine world is carried out."[26] Recent textual and archaeological discoveries have convinced scholars of the fundamental position held by the divine council within Israelite theology. As prominent Near Eastern archaeolo-

---

26. Patrick D. Miller, "Cosmology and World Order in the Old Testament," 432.

gist William Dever has explained, this view has affected the scholarly consensus concerning the development of Israelite monotheism:

> A generation ago, when I was a graduate student, biblical scholars were nearly unanimous in thinking that monotheism had been predominant in ancient Israelite religion from the beginning—not just as an "ideal," but as the reality. Today all that has changed. Virtually all mainstream scholars (and even a few conservatives) acknowledge that true monotheism emerged only in the period of the exile in Babylon in the 6th century B.C.E., as the canon of the Hebrew Bible was taking shape. . . . I have suggested, along with most scholars, that the emergence of monotheism—of exclusive Yahwism—was largely a response to the tragic experience of the exile.[27]

This understanding has had an impact upon recent translations of the Bible. The *New Revised Standard Version*, for example, translates the Hebrew in Psalm 82:1 as "God has taken his place in the divine council; in the midst of the gods he holds judgment." This translation accords with theological perspectives taught by Joseph Smith during his Nauvoo ministry.

In light of this perspective, it is interesting to consider that in Joseph Smith's original version of Moses 1, God refers to himself by the designation "Man of *Council* is my name."[28] The form "Man of Counsel," in the sense of "advice" rather than assembly, was first inserted into the text by Orson Pratt in 1878. Prior to that time, the original manuscript versions of Moses 7 use "Council"—as in assembly—alluding to the primary governing body controlled by God and used for making decisions in biblical and general Near Eastern traditions.

The Cursed Earth

Another way in which the Book of Moses shows a profound connection between Joseph's revelatory revision of Genesis and subtle Israelite ideas appears in a revelatory experience given to the patriarchal figure Enoch. Through this revelation, Enoch learns of the great wickedness that would exist upon the earth up until the time of his descendent Noah. The account reads:

> And it came to pass that Enoch looked upon the earth; and he heard a voice from the bowels thereof, saying: Wo, wo is me, the mother of men; I am pained, I am weary, because of the wickedness of my children. When shall I rest, and be cleansed from the filthiness which is gone forth out of me? When

---

27. William Dever, *Did God Have a Wife? Archaeology and Folk Religion in Ancient Israel*, 294–95, 297.

28. See Kent P. Jackson, *The Book of Moses and the Joseph Smith Translation Manuscripts*.

will my Creator sanctify me, that I may rest, and righteousness for a season abide upon my face? (Moses 7:48)

The idea found in the Earth's lament—that anything that comes forth from out of the earth qualifies as "filthiness"—provides the theological justification for why God rejected Cain's offering in J's story.

J's story of Cain and Abel presents a tale that depicts the first ever offerings presented to Yahweh. In the biblical account, God accepts the offering that Abel presents yet rejects the offering given by Cain. The reason why Yahweh rejected Cain's offering has historically generated much confusion. Although the account derives from J, the P source shows that offerings from the ground (such as grain or fruit) were acceptable ritual performances in at least some Israelite traditions:

> When anyone presents a grain[29] offering to the Lord, the offering shall be of choice flour; the worshiper shall pour oil on it, and put frankincense on it, and bring it to Aaron's sons the priests. After taking from it a handful of the choice flour and oil, with all its frankincense, the priest shall turn this token portion into smoke on the altar, an offering by fire of pleasing odor to the Lord. (Lev. 2:1–2; NRSV)

Why then did God reject Cain's offering that came from the ground?

Though often asked, this question derives from a failure to link the story of Cain with previous motifs in J's primordial history. Regarding this issue, biblical scholar Gary Herion has shown that Yahweh rejected Cain's offering since Cain presented produce from the ground, which in the preceding chapter Yahweh had pronounced cursed.[30]

> And unto Adam [Yahweh] said, Because thou hast hearkened unto the voice of thy wife, and hast eaten of the tree, of which I commanded thee, saying, Thou shalt not eat of it: cursed is the ground for thy sake; in sorrow shalt thou eat of it all the days of thy life. (Gen. 3:17)

---

29. The Hebrew word translated as "grain" in the NRSV is *qārbān*. As defined by Ludwig Koehler and Walter Baumgartner, *The Hebrew and Aramaic Lexicon of the Old Testament*, the word *qārbān* means "a gift or fruit, flour, bread," 2:1136–37.

30. Herion notes, "for us, the curse has become primarily an etiology for the hard work of raising crops. In viewing the curse in this way, we have glossed over the effect that the curse had on the character who pronounced it—God. But once we are made aware of this dimension of a curse, we are immediately reminded that what is accursed is, by definition, considered abhorrent to God—and so, by extension, are its fruits." Gary A. Herion, "Why God Rejected Cain's Offering: The Obvious Answer," 54.

Readers relying on the King James translation often understand this passage to be stating that God cursed the ground for man's benefit (a misreading of "sake") and that working for his daily food by "the sweat of his brow" is a positive rather than a negative consequence. The statement, however, is explicitly a curse rather than a blessing; and God's statement literally means that the ground will be cursed because of what the man did. The *Jewish Publication Society* translation clarifies this issue translating Yahweh's statement as "cursed be the ground because of you."

Though throughout J's creation narrative man, animals, and fowl all appear originally formed from the "ground," the status and quality of the ground changes throughout the story. According to Herion, in its original pristine condition, the ground was "lifeless" and was not yet capable of producing any vegetation prior to the creation of man. By the time Yahweh created the beasts and birds in Genesis 2:9, the life producing soil was no longer "inert."[31] This was the first change the ground experienced. The ground underwent a second change in status when Yahweh pronounced it "cursed" in connection with the man's decision to eat the forbidden fruit (Gen. 3:14–19).

It is only at this point that the man would till the primordial ground separate from Eden. Yahweh originally created man as a "tiller," yet as a result of eating the forbidden fruit, the man could no longer till the pristine soil in Eden, but instead took his gardening skills outside of Eden and for the first time began to work the cursed, primordial ground (3:18). Therefore, Yahweh rejected Cain's offering from the ground since from the Lord's perspective, the ground, and by extension, everything that came forth out of it was technically "cursed."

The material that the Book of Moses adds to J's story of Cain suggests that Cain's decision to present God with a blasphemous sacrifice was a direct response to a Satanic command:

> And Cain loved Satan more than God. And Satan commanded him, saying: Make an offering unto the Lord. And in process of time it came to pass that Cain brought of the fruit of the ground an offering unto the Lord. And Abel, he also brought of the firstlings of his flock, and of the fat thereof. And the Lord had respect unto Abel, and to his offering. (Moses 5:18–20)

The Book of Moses shows a sensitivity toward this reading of Cain's sacrifice and the cursed earth by presenting a personified mother earth lamenting: "when shall I rest, and be cleansed from the filthiness which is gone

---

31. Herion, "Why God Rejected Cain's Offering," 54.

forth out of me?" (Moses 7:48). The Bible answers this question through J's resolution to the flood story:

> And Noah builded an altar unto the LORD; and took of every clean beast, and of every clean fowl, and offered burnt offerings on the altar. And the LORD smelled a sweet savour; and the LORD said in his heart, I will not again curse the ground any more for man's sake; for the imagination of man's heart is evil from his youth; neither will I again smite any more every thing living, as I have done. (Gen. 8:20–21)

In this account, Yahweh comes to terms with the fact that his creation is evil. At the same time, Yahweh enjoys the offerings man can present. He therefore removes the curse he originally placed upon the earth and determines never to try and eradicate his creations again, despite their wickedness. This reading works well with the notion of the flood as a symbolic representation of baptism.

Continuing this theme, the Book of Moses contrasts the "filthiness" which comes forth out of the earth with the eventual "truth" God will send from out of the earth: "Truth will I send forth out of the earth, to bear testimony of mine Only Begotten; his resurrection from the dead; yea, and also the resurrection of all men" (Moses 7:62). This statement has a possible allusion to the Book of Mormon coming forth "from out of the earth" to testify of Christ. The concept of cleansing the earth from iniquity continues in the text's subsequent line:

> And righteousness and truth will I cause to sweep the earth as with a flood, to gather out mine elect from the four quarters of the earth, unto a place which I shall prepare, an Holy City, that my people may gird up their loins, and be looking forth for the time of my coming; for there shall be my tabernacle, and it shall be called Zion, a New Jerusalem Zion. (Moses 7:62)

The concept of righteousness and truth sweeping the earth clean in a way comparable to the flood waters in the Genesis story provides a poignant metaphor for the work God's children will perform in gathering the elect to His kingdom. This imagery is enhanced by a technical understanding of the curse motif connected with the earth in the Genesis material the Book of Moses revises.

The Nature Of God

The Book of Moses continues this trend through its depiction of deity. Joseph's revelation presents a view of God that draws and then builds upon ancient biblical conceptions. Throughout the Old Testament, we regularly encounter the theological assertion that humans should fear God. One of the classic illustrations of this motif appears in Genesis 22:12. Following Abraham's response to God's command to offer Isaac as a sacrifice, an angel appears with the following statement:

> Lay not thine hand upon the lad, neither do thou any thing unto him: for now I know that thou fearest God, seeing thou hast not withheld thy son, thine only son from me.

It is essential for modern readers of the Bible to remember that its authors lived in a different time and culture than we do. This means that they often conceptualized deity and their relationship to him in ways that seem odd or even incorrect from our perspective.

One of the wonderful aspects of Joseph Smith's work is that the Prophet not only restored ancient truth (in the sense that he brought back that which was lost), but from a Latter-day Saint perspective, Joseph's revelations build upon and enhance earlier historical constructs. Joseph Smith's understanding of this process appears in one of his Liberty Jail letters. Concerning the Restoration Joseph wrote:

> God shall give unto you knowledge by his Holy Spirit, yea, by the unspeakable gift of the Holy Ghost, that has not been revealed since the world was until now; Which our forefathers have awaited with anxious expectation to be revealed in the last times, which their minds were pointed to by the angels, as held in reserve for the fulness of their glory; A time to come in the which nothing shall be withheld, whether there be one God or many gods, they shall be manifest. (D&C 121:26–28)

Joseph viewed his prophetic commission as more than simply restoring ancient knowledge. For the Prophet, his revelations took that foundation and then built upon it concepts that he believed ancient people looked forward to someday understand at a deeper level. Joseph's work, therefore, was to bridge previous dispensations together into a spiritual synthetic whole with the new light and knowledge given in the Restoration.

Returning to the biblical concept of deity, the Hebrew word often rendered "fear" (*yāre'*) literally *does* mean to be "afraid." Yet *yāre'* also can carry the nuance of "to honor."[32] Behind this is the idea that God is a deity filled with intense emotion. He is powerful, but he is also vulnerable. He desires human love and respect. God can admittedly come across a bit frightening in some of the Old Testament stories because he appears so emotional and prone to violence.

---

32. Koehler and Baumgartner, *Hebrew and Aramaic Lexicon*, 1:433.

A great illustration of this perspective appears in the stories of Israel's journey in the wilderness. We read in the book of Numbers that as a result of his people's wickedness, God determined to destroy Israel. Moses was therefore forced to assume the traditional role of a prophetic mediator. With the following argument, Moses attempted to convince God to spare his people's lives:

> Now if thou shalt kill all this people as one man, then the nations which have heard the fame of thee will speak, saying, Because the LORD was not able to bring this people into the land which he sware unto them, therefore he hath slain them in the wilderness. (Num. 14:15–16)

In other words, Moses sought to change God's mind by arguing, "if you destroy Israel after setting them free from Egypt through mighty miracles, what will people say about you?!" And it worked—God determined not to destroy Israel. This exchange reflects the Israelite idea that God is so vulnerable and sensitive that He cares what people say about Him.

The same theological perspective appears in Psalms where the Israelites would use God's longing for human love and praise as a motivation for divine assistance:

> O LORD, rebuke me not in thine anger, neither chasten me in thy hot displeasure. Have mercy upon me, O LORD; for I am weak: O LORD, heal me; for my bones are vexed. My soul is also sore vexed: but thou, O LORD, how long? Return, O LORD, deliver my soul: oh save me for thy mercies' sake. For in death there is no remembrance of thee: in the grave who shall give thee thanks? (Ps. 6:4–5)

The motivation presented by the Psalmist trying to convince God to intervene and heal the person is that if she dies, there will be one less human to praise God on earth.

Today we do not typically conceptualize God in these terms. Yet the idea of the emotional, vulnerable God affected by human action appears as one of the primary themes in the Book of Moses.[33] The account presents the biblical Enoch's surprise after witnessing God's intense, human-like emotion:

> And it came to pass that the God of heaven looked upon the residue of the people, and he wept; and Enoch bore record of it, saying: How is it that the heavens weep, and shed forth their tears as the rain upon the mountains?

---

33. See the recent analysis provided by Terryl and Fiona Givens, *The God Who Weeps: How Mormonism Makes Sense of Life* (Salt Lake City: Ensign Peak, 2012).

> And Enoch said unto the Lord: How is it that thou canst weep, seeing thou art holy, and from all eternity to all eternity? (Moses 7:28–29)

In the Book of Moses, God appears as He does in the Hebrew Bible as a deity possessing immense power. But He is also a God who loves to the extent that human sinfulness causes Him to experience intense sadness, to the point of shedding tears. He is a God who cares so passionately about His work and glory to bring to pass human immorality and eternal life (Moses 1:39) that He experiences human emotion when His creations sin. However, in the Book of Moses, God is not simply a kind sympathetic deity. His Old Testament-like propensity toward emotion combined with immense power appears in the Book of Moses through his tearful decision to annihilate almost all creation:

> And the fire of mine indignation is kindled against them; and in my hot displeasure will I send in the floods upon them, for my fierce anger is kindled against them. (Moses 7:34)

Reading the opening chapters of Genesis through the lens offered via the Book of Moses allows readers to capture what Joseph believed represented key theological concepts concerning deity: a powerful, emotional Man of Council that the forefathers awaited with anxious expectation to be revealed in the last times.

Conclusion

The modern advancements in biblical studies carry significant ramifications for a critical assessment of the Book of Moses. While these insights suggest that some traditional assumptions regarding the nature of Joseph's revelatory texts may be incorrect, the inspired validity of the Prophet's scriptural work is an issue beyond scientific analysis. For Latter-day Saints convinced by the answers that Historical Criticism provides for the question of Pentateuchal authorship, the Book of Moses can be seen as a revelation that not only sustains, but enhances the Bible's divine authenticity. It does so while embracing its contradictions and diversified perspectives. The Book of Moses takes advantage of, and builds upon ancient theological motifs. These include the ability to control water as a sign of divinity, the central cosmological role of the divine council governed by God, the idea of an earth left cursed by the sin in Eden, yet cleansed by flood, and perspectives regarding an emotional God.

The Book of Moses brings the Book of Genesis into harmony with Joseph Smith's revelatory experiences. As a text, it provides readers with a new way of considering the opening chapters of Genesis as revelatory material connected with LDS notions concerning temple worship. From this perspective, the issue of the Book of Moses' status as inspired scripture can be seen as independent from the question of its historicity as the literal words of Moses once attached to the Bible. To quote LDS scholar Phillip Barlow, "If certain truths were not originally included in the Bible, they are truths nonetheless and readers will be edified by studying them; it is not the text of the Bible as such, but rather the truths of God that are sacred."[34] To this might be added, if ancient prophets did not originally write certain truths within scripture, they are truths nonetheless, and studying them will edify readers. Though the attributed author may serve as a conduit by conceptually bridging dispensations together, it is not the author of the text but rather the truths of God that are sacred.

---

34. Phillip L. Barlow, *Mormons and the Bible: The Place of the Latter-day Saints in American Religion*, 57.

Chapter Eight

Higher Criticism and the Book of Abraham

Introduction

The Book of Moses is not the only scriptural text produced by Joseph Smith that reformulates the opening chapters of the Bible. Latter-day Saints also have the Book of Abraham, a scriptural work begun in Kirtland, Ohio. Joseph produced this text as a "translation" of some Egyptian papyri rolls purchased from collector Michael Chandler for $2400. Since its publication, the Book of Abraham has been one of the most passionately debated topics in Mormonism by both critics and apologists alike. After analyzing the evidence, many have come to the conclusion that the Book of Abraham calls into question Joseph's prophetic ability to produce inspired scriptural works. Continuing the ideas from the previous chapter, the present chapter illustrates why it is not necessary for a Latter-day Saint to reject the Book of Abraham, despite the challenges an academic approach to the work presents.

In a revelation given to Joseph Smith on the day the Church was organized, the Prophet was informed that "through the will of God the Father, and the grace of [the] Lord Jesus Christ," Joseph would serve as a seer, an elder, a prophet, an apostle, and a translator (D&C 21:1). By 1835, the Prophet had already demonstrated this final spiritual gift through the production of the Book of Mormon and the Book of Moses. After purchasing the Egyptian papyri from Chandler, Joseph set out to use his calling for a new project. His history reads:

> With W.W. Phelps and Oliver Cowdery as scribes, I commenced the translation of some of the characters or hieroglyphics, and much to our joy found that one of the rolls contained the writings of Abraham, another the writings

of Joseph of Egypt, etc. — a more full account of which will appear in its place, as I proceed to examine or unfold them.[1]

While the Prophet never published the writings of Joseph of Egypt, his translation efforts did lead to the production of one of Mormonism's most famous scriptural texts.

Pagan Connection to Scripture

In the early 1990s, many Latter-day Saints opened up their mailboxes and found an unsolicited book offering a critique of the Book of Abraham. Among the arguments raised against its scriptural authenticity was the following assertion:

> Since the Joseph Smith Papyri have been identified with absolute certainly as prayers to pagan Egyptian gods that, by biblical definition are ripe with occultism, it is inconceivable, given the holy character of God, that He would associate Himself or His revelation in any way with these pagan religious documents. This fact alone is ample grounds for totally rejecting the Book of Abraham as a revelation from the one True and Living God.[2]

It is true that an Egyptian papyrus roll filled with references to "pagan" Egyptian religious practices and beliefs was used by Joseph Smith to produce the text. Not only do we have fragments of this roll in our position today, even the Facsimiles in the Book of Abraham show that Joseph created the work through non-Israelite sources. The Facsimiles contain pictographic representations of Egyptian gods and goddesses that have been reinterpreted to reflect principles and doctrines in the restored Gospel.[3] The criticism that the Book of Abraham cannot be defined as true scripture because God would never directly associate himself or his revelations with pagan (meaning non-Israelite) religious material only holds true for a particular view of what constitutes scripture.

While it is true that a dependency on an Egyptian text automatically delegitimizes the Book of Abraham from some religious perspectives, such as the "Chicago Statement on Biblical Inerrancy,"[4] this view reflects

---

1. Joseph Smith, *History of the Church*, 2:236.

2. Charles M. Larson, *By His Own Hand Upon Papyrus: A New Look at the Joseph Smith Papyri*, 120; for an LDS critique of this book, see John Gee, "A Tragedy of Errors," 93–119.

3. On the adaptation of Egyptian imagery, see Kevin L. Barney, "The Facsimiles and Semitic Adaptation of Existing Sources," 107–30.

4. See the discussion in Chapter 5.

only one possible way of defining scripture. Further, this definition is not consistent with the actual production of biblical texts, particularly those that appear in the Bible's first five books. And even though we would be hard pressed to find any biblical source that was not influenced to some extent by "pagan occultism," we need not assume that the Bible is therefore uninspired.

In terms of Egyptian influence upon the Bible, Jesus's parable of Lazarus and the rich man appears to have been influenced by the Egyptian tale of Setne-Kamwas.[5] The Old Testament has drawn upon Egyptian texts as well. This is especially true of the adaptation of the Instruction of Amenemope by the author of Proverbs. In addition to the way in which Proverbs 22–23 parallels the thought and expression of this Egyptian text, Proverbs 22:20 takes its meaning from an awareness of the thirty chapters of Amenempoe: "Have I not written for you thirty sayings of admonition and knowledge."[6] In later years, the *Apocalypse of Abraham* and *Testament of Abraham* illustrate that this tradition of Jewish adaptation of Egyptian religious traditions continued well into the Christian era.

Moreover, while there exists a direct connection between the Book of Abraham and Egyptian paganism, as we witnessed in Chapter 5, nothing can surpass the influence of Mesopotamia when it comes to non-Israelite sources that have impacted the development of the Pentateuch. If the Bible can be interpreted as scripture despite its reliance upon non-Israelite sources from the ancient Near East, so can the Book of Abraham. Scriptural texts are neither produced in a cultural vacuum nor created *ex nihilo*.

The Joseph Smith Papyri

The Egyptian papyri Joseph used to produce the Book of Abraham were thought to have been destroyed in the 1871 Great Chicago Fire. However, in 1966, officials at the Metropolitan Museum of Art in New York contacted Dr. Aziz Atiyah from the University of Utah regarding eleven papyri fragments held within their archives they believed were con-

---

5. See Kerry Muhlestein, "Egyptian Papyri and the Book of Abraham: Some Questions and Answers," 91–108; and Jared W. Ludlow, "Reinterpretation of the Judgment Scene in the Testament of Abraham," 99–104; Jared W. Ludlow, *Abraham Meets Death: Narrative Humor in the Testament of Abraham* (New York: Sheffield Academic Press, 2002).

6. The KJV misses the allusion to thirty sayings. For this translation and an interpretation, see Miriam Lichtheim, "Instruction of Amenemope (1.47)," 1:115.

nected with Joseph Smith.[7] When these fragments were compared to the papyrus illustrations used in the woodcuts in the Pearl of Great Price, it was confirmed that they were the documents owned by the Prophet and used in the production of the Book of Abraham.[8]

Both LDS and non-LDS scholars have translated these texts and found them to be common Egyptian funerary texts dating to around the first century BC.[9] The fragments stem from three separate papyri rolls. Joseph Smith Papyri I, X, and XI are from the Egyptian Book of Breathings belonging to a Theban priest named Hor, the son of Usirwer. II, IV, V, VI, VII, VIII, and IX all derive from a Book of the Dead that belonged to a woman named Tshemmin, the daughter of Eskhons. Papyri III is part of chapter 125 of the Book of Dead belonging to an individual named Neferirtnub.

In Joseph Smith's published translations, the Book of Abraham features three facsimiles of vignettes from the papyri together with Joseph's interpretations. These, however, do not reflect the way in which modern Egyptologists understand these representations.[10]

In light of the challenge that the Egyptian papyri presents for the Book of Abraham as a literal translation, some LDS scholars have suggested that

---

7. The historical evidence suggests that Museum officials knew that these documents were connected with Joseph Smith when they acquired the papyri in 1918. Earlier accounts that the documents had been discovered by Atiyah are incorrect. See John Gee, "New Light on the Joseph Smith Papyri," 247–49.

8. One of the vignettes on the scrolls, for example, appears in an altered form as Facsimile 1 in the Book of Abraham.

9. For example, concerning Facsimile 1 from the Book of Abraham, LDS Egyptologist Kerry Muhlestein writes: "When the text that accompanied the vignette was translated, it turned out to be a common late Egyptian funerary text known as the Book of Breathings. It bore no resemblance to the Book of Abraham that Joseph Smith had translated from his papyri. Furthermore, Egyptological studies of the facsimiles drew conclusions about their meanings that were different than those Joseph Smith had presented." Muhlestein, "Egyptian Papyri and the Book of Abraham," 91.

10. Concerning the facsimiles, Egyptologist Robert Ritner explains:

"The three woodcut illustrations purport to depict: (1) the 'sacrifice' on an 'altar' (wrongly restored from a scene of Anubis tending Osiris on the funerary bier), (2) an astronomical scene of planets (actually a hypocephalus), and (3) enthroned Abraham lecturing the male Pharaoh (actually enthroned Osiris with the female Isis. In the last image alone, Smith's interpretation turns the goddess Maat into a male prince, the papyrus owner into a 'waiter,' and the black jackal Anubis into a 'slave.'" Robert Ritner, *The Joseph Smith Egyptian Papyri*, 5.

Abraham's writings do not actually appear on the scrolls Joseph possessed. Instead they propose that the papyri acted as a catalyst by which God inspired the Prophet to recreate a long lost text once written by Abraham. Often referred to as the "catalyst theory," this perspective would answer many of the issues raised by critics based on examinations of the rediscovered papyri.[11]

In its 2013 update to the standard works, the Church altered the introduction to the Pearl of Great Price in a way that seems to allow for this possibility. The previous description of the Book of Abraham read:

> A translation from some Egyptian papyri that came into the hands of Joseph Smith in 1835, containing writings of the patriarch Abraham.

The updated description is more ambiguous about the nature of the text:

> An inspired translation of the writings of Abraham. Joseph Smith began the translation in 1835 after obtaining some Egyptian papyri.

This shift illustrates the Church's openness as a "living church" (D&C 1:30), to new understandings of its own scriptures.

P and J in the Book of Abraham

Besides the new understandings of the Book of Abraham brought on by modern Egyptology, the conclusions of Historical Criticism and the Documentary Hypothesis pose challenges for traditional perspectives on this book of scripture. Chief among these is the Book of Abraham's textual dependency on late Judean sources that came into being over a millennium *after* the time of Abraham, making it impossible to directly connect the book of scripture with the ancient Patriarch.

Abraham 4 is a revision of the Priestly creation story in Genesis 1. For example, the first two verses of the two accounts read:

> And then the Lord said: Let us go down. And they went down at the beginning, and they, that is the Gods, organized and formed the heavens and the earth. And the earth, after it was formed, was empty and desolate, because they had not formed anything but the earth; and darkness reigned upon the face of the deep, and the Spirit of the Gods was brooding upon the face of the waters. And they (the Gods) said: Let there be light; and there was light. (Abr. 4:1–3)

---

11. For a summary of the traditional theories used by LDS scholars to defend the Book of Abraham, see John Gee, *A Guide to the Joseph Smith Papyri*, 19–30.

> In the beginning God created the heaven and the earth. And the earth was without form, and void; and darkness was upon the face of the deep. And the Spirit of God moved upon the face of the waters. And God said, Let there be light: and there was light. (Gen. 1:1–3)

Abraham 4 then continues citing and revising the Priestly account's description of the creation of humanity:

> And the Gods took counsel among themselves and said: Let us go down and form man in our image, after our likeness; and we will give them dominion over the fish of the sea, and over the fowl of the air, and over the cattle, and over all the earth, and over every creeping thing that creepeth upon the earth. So the Gods went down to organize man in their own image, in the image of the Gods to form they him, male and female to form they them. And the Gods said: We will bless them. And the Gods said: We will cause them to be fruitful and multiply, and replenish the earth, and subdue it, and to have dominion over the fish of the sea, and over the fowl of the air, and over every living thing that moveth upon the earth. (Abr. 4:26–28)

> And God said, Let us make man in our image, after our likeness: and let them have dominion over the fish of the sea, and over the fowl of the air, and over the cattle, and over all the earth, and over every creeping thing that creepeth upon the earth. So God created man in his own image, in the image of God created he him; male and female created he them. And God blessed them, and God said unto them, Be fruitful, and multiply, and replenish the earth, and subdue it: and have dominion over the fish of the sea, and over the fowl of the air, and over every living thing that moveth upon the earth. (Gen. 1:26–28)

The creation narrative continues in the Book of Abraham into Chapter 5, which adopts P's emphasis upon the Sabbath day as holy time:

> And thus we will finish the heavens and the earth, and all the hosts of them. And the Gods said among themselves: On the seventh time we will end our work, which we have counseled; and we will rest on the seventh time from all our work which we have counseled. And the Gods concluded upon the seventh time, because that on the seventh time they would rest from all their works which they (the Gods) counseled among themselves to form; and sanctified it. And thus were their decisions at the time that they counseled among themselves to form the heavens and the earth. (Abr. 5:1–3)

> Thus the heavens and the earth were finished, and all the host of them. And on the seventh day God ended his work which he had made; and he rested on the seventh day from all his work which he had made. And God blessed the seventh day, and sanctified it: because that in it he had rested from all his

work which God created and made. These are the generations of the heavens and of the earth when they were created. (Gen. 2:1–4)

These citations illustrate how the former are indeed dependent upon the latter.

Some may speculate that perhaps it is P that is dependent upon the Book of Abraham rather than the other way around. However, as we explored in Chapter 3, the creation drama in Genesis 1 that appears in Abraham 4 was composed to specifically reflect the theology of the Priestly author in terms of its portrayal of God, holy time, and creation as a reflection of the tabernacle. Furthermore, there is no internal reason to believe that the story in Genesis 1 was originally written in a language other than Hebrew; and Hebrew was not a written language until at least the tenth (or probably even ninth) century BC.[12] This dates the text found in Genesis 1 and Abraham 4 to at least a thousand years after the time of Abraham (according to the Bible's internal chronology). Moreover, as we discussed in Chapter 5, the literary structure of P seems to have been created as a reflection of the Priestly author's exposure to the creation story in the Enūma Elish, which was also written long after the time of Abraham.[13] And finally, the notion of an ancient prophetic figure or patriarch writing scripture is historically anachronistic. Though traces of Moses as author exist in the Book of Deuteronomy, this view of scripture did not develop fully in Judean thought until the Hellenistic era (321–31 BC).

---

12. David Carr is an example of a scholar who sees Hebrew as a written scribal system attested for the first time in the tenth century BC. Using the tenth century Tel Zayit abecedary, Carr has speculated that the inscription possibly reveals the emergence of alphabetic scribalism in early Israel; David McLain Carr, "The Tel Zayit Abecedary in (Social) Context," 124. Carr's theory supposes that tenth-century Israel featured "an emergent state structure" that included "borrowing or adaptation of the Phoenician alphabetic scribal system in some administrative centers and the learning of this system by a limited number of officials." Carr's thesis has been rightfully criticized. J. Whisenant writes:

> "It is not merely the lack of intermediate training texts that poses an obstacle to Carr's thesis (although he addresses this problem in part on pp. 116–17), it is the near absence of texts dated securely to the tenth century with an inland Canaanite provenance. The likelier explanation for the presence of the abecedary is that it reflects the presence of a lone (and not very experienced) scribe educated in the Phoenician tradition, who scratched out the letters of the alphabet at this site in a border region between the hill country entity and the coastal cities." J. Whisenant, "Review—Literate Culture and Tenth-Century Canaan: The Tel Zayit Abecedary in Context," 551.

13. See the discussion on dating Enūma Elish in Chapter 5.

Perhaps the greatest proof, though, that the Book of Abraham draws upon P rather than the other way around is that following the reformation of P, the Book of Abraham cites J's creation story in Genesis 2. In the Book of Abraham, the two separate Judean sources appear combined as a single story. According to Higher Criticism, it would have been impossible for Abraham to have created these two separate sources that present such distinct visions of God and creation. As discussed in Chapter 4, J's story in Genesis 2 actually predates the account in Genesis 1, and P's version seems to be on some level a reaction to and even correction of J's motifs that the Priestly author rejected. And yet, the Book of Abraham transitions from a revision of P directly into the J account:

> And the Gods came down and formed these the generations of the heavens and of the earth, when they were formed in the day that the Gods formed the earth and the heavens. (5:4)

When read carefully, this passage presents some challenges. The text states that the Gods descended and formed "these the generations of the heavens and the earth." It then presents an awkward dependent clause, "when they were formed in the day that the Gods formed." This cumbersome transition is a result of the fact that the passage treats the two separate documentary sources as if they were a single narrative.

The first line in the Book of Abraham is from P: "these are the generations of the heavens and of the earth when they were created" (Gen. 2:4a). As we discussed in Chapter 1, this was the original conclusion to the Priestly narrative. This portion of the verse links with Genesis 1:1 to create the *inclusio* that marks the text's definitive boundary. The awkward dependent clause in the Book of Abraham 5:4 "when they were formed in the day that the Gods formed the earth and the heavens" derives from the concluding words in P and the subsequent introduction to J.

> P: "These are the generations of the heavens and of the earth when they were created."
>
> J: "In the day that the Lord God made the earth and the heavens."
>
> Gen. 2:4: "These are the generations of the heavens and of the earth when they were created, in the day that the Lord God made the earth and the heavens."
>
> Book of Abraham 5:4: "And the Gods came down and formed these the generations of the heavens and of the earth, when they were formed in the day that the Gods formed the earth and the heavens."

The combination of J and P in the Book of Abraham results in the awkward transition, "when they were formed in the day that the Gods formed the earth and heavens." It shows that the Book of Abraham relies on the Judean documentary sources rather than the other way around.

Abraham 5 also revises J's account of Eden, including the motifs and images central to the theology and literary techniques unique to the Yahwist's tradition (e.g., a focus upon etiology of institutions and practices) yet foreign to the Priestly account in Genesis 1:

> And Adam said: This was bone of my bones, and flesh of my flesh; now she shall be called Woman, because she was taken out of man; Therefore shall a man leave his father and his mother, and shall cleave unto his wife, and they shall be one flesh. And they were both naked, the man and his wife, and were not ashamed. And out of the ground the Gods formed every beast of the field, and every fowl of the air, and brought them unto Adam to see what he would call them; and whatsoever Adam called every living creature, that should be the name thereof. And Adam gave names to all cattle, to the fowl of the air, to every beast of the field; and for Adam, there was found an help meet for him. (Abr. 5:17–21)

The Book of Abraham, therefore, is reliant upon two different documentary traditions that it treats as a unified whole, contrary to the scholarly consensus of over 150 years of them being separate Judean sources.

The dating of biblical Hebrew as a written language, the anachronistic view of prophets writing scripture, and the inclusion of two Judean sources written several centuries after Abraham make it difficult to connect the Book of Abraham with the biblical patriarch. Combined with the Prophet's use of Egyptian funerary texts from the Ptolemaic era as the basis for his "translation" of Abraham's writings, these observations challenge our traditional understandings of this volume of scripture. However, as we have seen with the Book of Moses, the Prophet Joseph can be understood as accomplishing something much more important than simply reproducing ancient texts: he revealed new scripture.

The Book of Abraham as Inspired Pseudepigraphon

As noted in Chapter 7, many ancient books adhere to the literary pattern of pseudepigraphy. For example, numerous Jewish books were attributed to a variety of biblical figures such as Adam, Enoch, Noah, Melchizedek, Abraham, Jacob, Moses, Elijah, and Ezekiel. Additionally, Christian texts were falsely attributed to Peter, Paul, and Jude. Attributing a scriptural work to a prophet or apostle, elevated the authoritative status of the document. Just as a Latter-day Saint who accepts the views of Higher Criticism could adopt the position that the Book of Moses follows this scriptural pattern by elevating the status of Genesis to sacred revelatory literature, a similar view could be adopted for the Book of Abraham.

Until 1878, the Book of Abraham was published with the following introduction: "some records that have fallen into our hands, from the Catecombs of Egypt, *purporting to be* the writings of Abraham."[14] This left open the possibility of the Book of Abraham being a translation of a pseudepigraphic source only purporting to be the writings of Abraham, which, like biblical pseudepigraphic texts, would not immediately disqualify it from being scripture.

Because of the dating of the two separate Judean sources that the Book of Abraham is dependent on, and the even later dating of the papyri Joseph used for his translation, some Latter-day Saint scholars have argued that the Book of Abraham possibly constitutes a late pseudepigraphic text. Either an Egyptian or Jewish scribe of the fourth century BC wrote the text and syncretized biblical and Egyptian religious traditions into the ancient Book of Abraham. In other words, rather than being the translation of a text written by the patriarch Abraham, this view contends that this book of scripture is the translation of a text actually written seventeen centuries later by a (possibly inspired) author pseudepigraphically using Abraham's identity.[15] Of course, despite the biblical inclusion of pseudepigraphic texts, if such a work were simply discovered in the catacombs of Egypt by an archaeologist, many Latter-day Saints would no doubt struggle to view the text as scripture comparable to the works in the Bible. As is the case for the dozens of apocryphal and Christian pseudepigraphic texts discovered in the last couple centuries.[16]

Historicity is never the construct that defines scripture as scripture—afterall, there are thousands of ancient historical texts that we do no consider scripture. Though the issue of historicity is important to consider, theological connections to a text can be completely independent from

---

14. Brian M. Hauglid, *A Textual History of the Book of Abraham: Manuscripts and Editions*, 25; emphasis added.

15. In his defense of this view, Kerry Muhlestein has drawn attention to supposed links between late Egyptian mysticism in the Ptolemaic and early Christian eras and biblical Abraham; see Kerry Muhlestein, "Abraham, Isaac, and Osiris-Michael: The Use of Biblical Figures in Egyptian Religion, a Survey," 246–59.

16. For an analysis of this material in relationship to Mormonism, see C. Wilfred Griggs, *Apocryphal Writings and the Latter-day Saints* (Salt Lake City, Kofford Books, 2007).

such issues. Joseph's work was a type of *imitatio dei*. The Prophet took theological constructs that were in chaos and provided them with an inspired structure. From this angle, Joseph's work can be understood to parallel the divine creative process. It was not *ex nihilo*. It was providing order to pre-existent material. The Prophet's vocation was not simply that of a restorer of truth that was once known. His revelations provide order to biblical chaos, as he adds to and develops earlier religious constructs. Joseph's own pseudepigraphic books of Abraham and Moses can be seen as a crucial part of this process, despite their lack of ancient historicity.

Identifying genre in the sense of categorizing literature is an essential part of textual analysis. Classifying a literary work as parody, for example, leads a reader to interpret the text differently than she would a newspaper editorial, science fiction novel, or a college history text. Despite the fact that the Book of Abraham cannot be identified with Abraham himself, to impose our modern label of "fiction" upon the book would certainly misidentify its genre. Instead of being read as simply fiction or even fraudulent, the text can be understood as inspired modern pseudepigraphy.

As discussed in the previous chapter, pseudepigraphy can be a complicated genre for modern people to understand. In reference to this type of literature in antiquity, Bart Ehrman wrote:

> The single most important motivation for authors to claim they were someone else in antiquity . . . was to get a hearing for their views. If you were an unknown person, but had something really important to say and wanted people to hear you—not so they could praise you, but so they could learn the truth—one way to make that happen was to pretend you were someone else, a well-known author, a famous figure, an authority.[17]

This assessment illustrates how different the Book of Abraham is from what scholars such as Ehrman have labeled "forgery" in the Bible.[18] The

---

17. Bart Ehrman, *Forged: Writing in the Name of God—Why the Bible's Authors Are Not Who We Think They Are*, 31.

18. Some scholars have even questioned the term "forgery" as an appropriate description of ancient pseudepigraphic literature. For instance, Jed Wyrick writes, "I would also caution against the use of the terms 'forgery' or 'plagiarism' to describe the complex motivations in the Jewish world's composition of texts in the name of a prototypical individual. They derive from a Greek understanding of the inviolable connection between a work's composer and the text to which his or her name is affixed, and are out of place in describing Jewish textual production." Jed Wyrick, *The Ascension of Authorship: Attribution and Canon Formation in Jewish, Hellenistic, and Christian Traditions*, 18–19.

Prophet Joseph Smith did not need to pretend his revelation and the theological constructs presented in the Book of Abraham were written by Abraham in order to obtain a hearing for his religious views. For over five years before his work on the Book of Abraham, the Prophet had been giving revelations from his own mouth that believers accepted as the word of God. He did not need to produce a biblical-like forgery in order to claim that a revelation was inspired. He was dictating his own revelations all the time. Certainly producing a lost book of Abraham would have legitimized Joseph's own revelations, but even this perspective illustrates how different the Book of Abraham is from what Ehrman calls forgeries.

A superior genre label for the Book of Abraham that takes into consideration the observations of Higher Criticism would be "scriptural attribution." With this view the 2013 introduction to the Book of Abraham as "an inspired translation of the writings of Abraham" could be understood, not as a description of what Abraham literally wrote, but instead as a description of what Abraham *would* have written if given the chance. In producing this inspired pseudepigraphon Joseph Smith was the revelatory conduit for this scriptural text. In terms of genre, this, in some ways, places the Book of Abraham among the many other pseudepigraphal sources in the biblical canon.

It seems clear that Joseph believed he was producing a literal translation of the papyri he possessed. We should not assume, however, that the Prophet fully understood the revelatory process in which he was engaged. When read as a revealed document, the Book of Abraham can be viewed as another important piece to the theological structure Joseph Smith was revealing. A Latter-day Saint who accepts the views of Historical Criticism need not believe that the Book of Abraham is a supernatural, though traditional, translation of an ancient text written by the patriarch Abraham, nor the translation of a Hellenized pseudepigraphic book of Abraham originally written in the first century BC; instead, it can make even more sense that by engaging the ancient papyri, the Prophet Joseph was inspired to produce this book of scripture as author, or in his vernacular, "seer/translator."

Rather than diminishing the inspired nature of the work, approaching the Book of Abraham from this perspective could provide an even greater authoritative stamp upon the scriptural text. If one accepts the Documentary Hypothesis and the inspired nature of the Book of Abraham, then it must be either (1) a pseudepigraphic work of scripture written by an unknown (though possibly inspired) author in the fourth through first century BC, which was later lost and then restored by the Prophet Joseph Smith; or (2) an inspired pseudepigraphic work written by the Prophet Joseph Smith. The simple application of Occam's Razor would require us to cut out the unnecessary excess and accept the latter option. Not only is this approach more simplified and reflective of the papyri evidence, cutting out the unknown author leaves Latter-day Saints with a directly inspired scriptural text that adopts and transforms biblical concepts by linking images from the past to the framework of a highly sophisticated theological scheme.

Theological Connections with Ancient Israel

The Book of Abraham presents an autobiographical segment of Abraham's life. The account includes a depiction of his near sacrifice upon an altar and his subsequent journey to Canaan and Egypt. It also reveals a vision Abraham received concerning the universe, premortal human existence, and the creation of the world. Throughout its five chapters, the Book of Abraham presents theological constructs central to the way Latter-day Saints understand their relationship to divinity. A careful reading of this material reveals the impressive ways in which Joseph Smith's work both restores forgotten biblical constructs and adds upon their foundation to reveal further religious truth. This study will provide three examples of this process: (1) the altar as a place of deliverance; (2) Joseph Smith's interpretation of Facsimile 3 as ancient temple drama; and (3) the divine council of gods. This will illustrate how the Book of Abraham presents a variety of profound religious and cultural links with ancient Near Eastern tradition, including the Hebrew Bible. It supports the view that in the production of scriptural texts, Joseph Smith created an inspired system that links our present dispensation with the past.

The Altar as a Place of Deliverance

The Book of Abraham begins with a stirring scene in which Abraham escapes being sacrificed upon an altar. According to the account, human sacrifice had become a regular occurrence in Abraham's land of Ur:

> Now, at this time it was the custom of the priest of Pharaoh, the king of Egypt, to offer up upon the altar which was built in the land of Chaldea, for the offering unto these strange gods, men, women, and children. (Abr. 1:8)[19]

19. In an effort to support the historicity of the Book of Abraham, some LDS scholars have argued that the biblical designation for Abraham's birthplace Ur of the Chaldees (Gen. 11:28, 11:31, and 15:7) refers to a northern city in Syria. This would allow for the possibility of the type of Egyptian cultic influence

According to the story, Egyptian priests sought to take away Abraham's life via such a ritual. Abraham recounts the story, referencing the altar scene in Facsimile 1 taken from the Hor Book of Breathings:

> And it came to pass that the priests laid violence upon me, that they might slay me also, as they did those virgins upon this altar; and that you may have a knowledge of this altar, I will refer you to the representation at the commencement of this record. It was made after the form of a bedstead, such as was had among the Chaldeans, and it stood before the gods of Elkenah, Libnah, Mahmackrah, Korash, and also a god like unto that of Pharaoh, king of Egypt. That you may have an understanding of these gods, I have given you the fashion of them in the figures at the beginning, which manner of figures is called by the Chaldeans Rahleenos, which signifies hieroglyphics. And as they lifted up their hands upon me, that they might offer me up and take away my life, behold, I lifted up my voice unto the Lord my God, and the Lord hearkened and heard, and he filled me with the vision of the Almighty, and the angel of his presence stood by me, and immediately unloosed my bands. (Abr. 1:13–15)

The story of Abraham's escape from a sacrificial death upon an altar is thematically linked with the most dramatic event in his life: the Akedah

---

depicted in the Book of Abraham. The Biblical designation Ur Kaśdim, however, is almost universally recognized as a reference to the Babylonian city of Ur (Tell el-Muqayyar), which flourished in the third millennium and first centuries of the second millennium BC. Christopher Woods, Associate Professor in Sumerology at the University of Chicago explains:

> "The Hebrew qualification Kaśdim—Chaldeans—identifies Ur with southern Mesopotamia. The passages of Genesis that contain the term derive from the Priestly source of the Pentateuch written at a time when the designation was in widespread usage, during the period of the Neo-Babylonian—that is the Chaldean—kings (626–539 BC). . . . As such, the designation represents a specification contemporaneous with the writing of the text that the Ur in question is Babylonian Ur. The objection that Babylonian Ur is too far from Haran, entailing a journey approximately one thousand miles, is countered by the fact that cuneiform documents of Old Babylonian date (ca. 2000–1600 BC) detailing merchant activities describe journeys of precisely this route and length. Further, it should not be overlooked that Ur and Haran share important religious, cultural, and historical bonds as major centers for the worship of the Mesopotamian moon god Sin, a fact conspicuously evident for the reign of Nabonidus (556–539 BC)." Christopher Woods, "The Practice of Egyptian Religion at 'Ur of the Chaldees'?" 72.

or "binding" of Isaac (Gen. 22).[20] The two accounts are clearly related. Both stories depict human sacrifice followed by deity's promise to grant Abraham blessings. Moreover, in both altar stories, a heavenly being calls Abraham's name twice at the moment of salvation:

> And the angel of the LORD [Yahweh/Jehovah] called unto him out of heaven, and said, Abraham, Abraham: and he said, Here am I. And he said, Lay not thine hand upon the lad, neither do thou any thing unto him: for now I know that thou fearest God, seeing thou hast not withheld thy son, thine only son from me. (Gen. 22:11–12)

> And his voice was unto me: Abraham, Abraham, behold, my name is Jehovah, and I have heard thee, and have come down to deliver thee, and to take thee away from thy father's house, and from all thy kinsfolk, into a strange land which thou knowest not of. (Abr. 1:16)

In Genesis 22, the dual repetition of Abraham's name makes sense. It stands in contrast to the first time the voice of God is heard at the beginning of the account.

When the deity initially gives Abraham the command to sacrifice Isaac, God only needs to call Abraham's name a single time: "And it came to pass after these things, that God did tempt Abraham, and said unto him, Abraham: and he said, Behold, here I am" (Gen. 22:1). This dual repetition of Abraham's name during the sacrificial act emphasizes the urgency of the angel's words. Abraham's arm had been raised; the knife was in his hand; to stop him at the very last moment, the angel was forced to call his name twice, "Abraham, Abraham STOP!!!"

In contrast, when God calls Abraham's name twice at the altar in the Book of Abraham, there is no need for the urgency. The dramatic moment has already past. The angel had already unloosed Abraham's bands; the moment of terror had subsided. This suggests that the story in the Book of Abraham draws upon its biblical counterpart both in terms of an Abrahamic narrative concerning human sacrifice and for the moment of divine intervention.

When read through the lens of the Book of Abraham, Abraham's obedience to God's command to sacrifice his son increases the emotional drama of the famous biblical event. Abraham is presented as a person who knows what it is like to face death in such a horrific manner and detests

---

20. The term "Akedah" often used for the story derives from the Hebrew verb "to bind" that appears in Genesis 22:9.

the ritual performance of child sacrifice. This makes his biblical sacrifice of his beloved son Isaac all the more intense.

When Jehovah speaks to Abraham at the moment of his deliverance in the Book of Abraham, He promises to bless Abraham because of his obedience. In terms of narrative flow, it is after Abraham is delivered from death at the altar that Jehovah covenants to be his personal deity:

> Behold, I will lead thee by my hand, and I will take thee, to put upon thee my name, even the Priesthood of thy father, and my power shall be over thee. As it was with Noah so shall it be with thee; but through thy ministry my name shall be known in the earth forever, for I am thy God. (Abr. 1:18–19)

This theme from the Book of Abraham reflects the traditional biblical view of the altar as a place where God and man come together to make sacred covenants. This view, for instance, appears in the altar law featured in the Covenant Code:

> An altar of earth thou shalt make unto me, and shalt sacrifice thereon thy burnt offerings, and thy peace offerings, thy sheep, and thine oxen: in all places where I record my name I will come unto thee, and I will bless thee. (Ex. 20:24)

Moreover, God's altar-based promise in the Book of Abraham to be Abraham's personal deity ("I am thy God") and bless him with power reflects the events in J's version of Noah's flood story. While J's account neither reveals a personal relationship between Noah and Yahweh, nor depicts God granting Noah "power" (in the way Abr. 1:18–19 depicts), J's story thematically parallels the Abraham narrative in so far as God makes a sacred promise to a biblical patriarch at an altar:

> And Noah builded an altar unto the LORD; and took of every clean beast, and of every clean fowl, and offered burnt offerings on the altar. And the LORD smelled a sweet savour; and the LORD said in his heart, I will not again curse the ground any more for man's sake; for the imagination of man's heart is evil from his youth; neither will I again smite any more every thing living, as I have done. (Gen. 8:20–21)

In the Book of Abraham God identifies his name as Jehovah in 1:16, and then declares in verse 19, "I am thy God." This view concerning Abraham's familiarity with the divine name is directly opposed to the one given in P, where God states, "and I appeared unto Abraham, unto

Isaac, and unto Jacob, by the name of God Almighty, but by my name JEHOVAH was I not known to them" (Ex. 6:1).[21]

While the Book of Abraham presents an alternative version to P's, it seems to reflect E's word play between the name "Jehovah" and "I Am" in Exodus 3:14–15:

> And God said unto Moses, I AM THAT I AM: and he said, Thus shalt thou say unto the children of Israel, I AM hath sent me unto you. And God said moreover unto Moses, Thus shalt thou say unto the children of Israel, The LORD God [Yahweh Elohim] of your fathers, the God of Abraham, the God of Isaac, and the God of Jacob, hath sent me unto you: this is my name for ever, and this is my memorial unto all generations.

God's response to Moses' question plays upon the possible interpretation of *Yahweh* as a finite verb, meaning "He is" or even "He causes to be"—from the Hebraic root *hyh* meaning "to be." In this passage, God tells Moses the meaning of "Yahweh" is *Ehyeh–Asher–Ehyeh*, a challenging grammatical expression probably best translated as "I Will Be What I Will Be." This has been interpreted as signifying, "My nature will become evident from My actions."[22] E's explanation for the name Yahweh is derived from the verb "*hvh*," a variant form of "*hyh*." Since Yahweh is the speaker, He uses the first–person form of the verb. Thus, God's statement in the Book of Abraham, "Behold, my name is Jehovah. . . . I AM thy God," provides a thematic parallel with this passage in E.[23]

Yet another connection between the altar story in the Book of Abraham and biblical constructs is the way in which the altar appears thematically linked with an escape from death. In addition to their role in sacrifice and covenant making, altars also served as places of asylum. Traditionally, an Israelite accused of committing a serious offense could flee to an altar to escape death. The Old Testament refers to this custom in the Covenant Code:

> He that smiteth a man, so that he die, shall be surely put to death. And if a man lie not in wait, but God deliver him into his hand; then I will appoint thee a place whither he shall flee. But if a man come presumptuously upon his neighbor, to slay him with guile; thou shalt take him from mine altar, that he may die. (Ex. 21:12–14)

---

21. See the analysis of Exodus 6:3 in Chapter 3.

22. Jeffrey H. Tigay, "Exodus," 111, note 14.

23. Of course E shows no indication that Abraham would have known God by the title Yahweh since the revelation is first given to Moses.

As we have discussed, later revisions of this statute amend the practice of altar asylum into cities of refuge (compare Deuteronomy 19:1–7; Numbers 35:9–28; Joshua 20).[24] However, in ancient Israel, the original place of asylum was the altar of God. The Exodus passage quoted above supports this view, as do the accounts in 1 Kings 1:50–51 and 2:28, which tell of Solomon's enemies Adonijah and Joab fleeing to the tabernacle and catching "hold on the horns of the altar" in hopes of deliverance, albeit with different results.

The account, therefore, can be spiritualized as a theological principle: God will intervene in human life, preparing a way to escape from death. Furthermore, the covenants made with deity at the altar are binding, providing not only power, but also deliverance.

Facsimile 3 as Presentation Scene

The Book of Abraham appears with three Egyptian Facsimiles, or vignettes. The first Facsimile comes from the beginning of the Hor Book of Breathings. It appears in the Book of Abraham reinterpreted as an illustration of Abraham's escape from death at the sacrificial altar. The second Facsimile is a copy of a damaged hypocephalus. Shaped like a solar disk, these were amulets placed under the head of deceased Egyptians in order to restore bodily warmth.[25] The Book of Abraham hypocephalus is identified as belonging to an individual named Sheshonq. The third Facsimile in the Book of Abraham would have originally appeared at the end of the scroll containing the Hor Book of Breathings. Translations of the accompanying hieroglyphs indicate that Facsimile 3 is a depiction of Hor, the deceased owner of the scroll, being introduced to Osiris, an Egyptian deity connected with the afterlife. The vignette illustrates that Hor had been proven worthy in the Hall of Two Truths to enter the presence of Osiris. This dramatic scene represents the culmination of what Egyptians hoped for in terms of the afterlife.[26] Clearly, the Prophet's interpretations of these vignettes do not reflect the manner in which Egyptologists understand them today.[27]

---

24. See the analysis on altar laws in Chapter 1.

25. Ritner, *The Joseph Smith Egyptian Papyri*, 215.

26. Michael Rhodes, *The Hor Book of Breathings: A Translation and Commentary* (Provo, Utah: FARMS, 2002).

27. Facsimiles 1 and 3 appear interpreted and translated by Michael Rhodes in the Brigham Young University publication *The Hor Book of Breathings: A Translation and Commentary.*

This fact, however, need not lead to the conclusion that the inter-pretations Joseph Smith offered are not inspired. Rather than a correct Egyptological interpretation of these images, Joseph's explanations can be seen as a religious adaptation of ancient images that reflects newly revealed teachings—perhaps in a way analogous to the manner Joseph revised the Bible and other revelatory texts.

This perspective is especially true for Facsimile 3. With its depiction of the deceased owner of the papyrus scroll proving himself worthy to enter the presence of deity, it portrays a temple-like drama attested com-monly throughout Near Eastern iconography.[28] We find conceptual cor-respondences between the type of Egyptian presentation scene depicted in Facsimile 3 and ancient Mesopotamian cylinder seals. The most common theme displayed is a portrayal of a throne room in which a worshiper (often the owner of the seal and thus equivalent to Hor) enters the presence of a god with the help of a divine spiritual guide who clasps the worshiper's hand. Concerning the depiction, Harvard University Professor Irene Winter writes: "The approaching individual usually wears a simple fringed garment draped over one shoulder, and one arm at least is bent at the elbow, the hand raised almost to the lips in what seems to be a gesture of greeting."[29]

In the presentation scene featured in the Book of Abraham, Hor ap-pears clasping hands with Ma'at, the goddess of truth who together with the deity Anubis, leads Hor into the presence of Osiris seated upon the throne. Such imagery is not foreign to the biblical sphere. The concept of deity clasping hands with a Davidic king appears, for example, in the Psalms. "Nevertheless I am continually with thee," states the Psalmist con-cerning his relationship with deity, "thou hast holden me by my right hand" (Psalms 73:23). Concerning this biblical motif, biblical scholar Hans Joachim Kraus has suggested that the clasping of the right hand

> points to a royal (might we even say, messianic?) procedure. The formula, 'God grasps one by the hand,' when the king ascends the throne and is inducted into royal office, denotes the conferring of privilege and charisma on the king (Isa. 45:1; 42:1).[30]

---

28. For connections between the Joseph Smith papyri and ancient temple motifs, see Hugh Nibley, *Message of the Joseph Smith Papyri: An Egyptian Endowment*, edited by John Gee and Michael D. Rhodes (Salt Lake City: Deseret Book, 2005).

29. Irene J. Winter, "The King and the Cup: Iconography of the Royal Presentation Scene on Ur III Seals," 254.

30. Hans-Joachim Kraus, *Theology of the Psalms*, 173.

Though each Near Eastern source must be analyzed in terms of it specific context, similar ideas of humans clasping hands with deities are conceptually linked with Mesopotamian cylinder seals and Egyptian presentation scenes (including Facsimile 3).

In his adaptation of this vignette, which also features conceptual links with the LDS temple endowment, the Prophet described Facsimile 3 as a depiction of the biblical patriarch Abraham seated upon a throne. In ancient Near Eastern thought, placing an individual upon a throne has been linked with apotheosis or deification. Nicholas Wyatt writes:

> The rituals which transform status of the earthly king, removing him from 'merely human' status to that of a sacral figure, to be couched in a narrative about a god, carries with it the hint that the king himself is to be seen as transformed into a god . . . the enthronement of the king, is thus his apotheosis.[31]

In his exploration of biblical deification, Wyatt refers to Psalm 19:8–10 as a possible ritual text transforming the enthroned king into a divine being. He translates the passage in this manner:

> The teaching of Yahweh is perfect,
>   restoring the breast.
> The testimony of Yahweh is certain,
>   making wise the head,
> The precepts of Yahweh are upright,
>   rejoicing the heart.
> The commandment of Yahweh is pure,
>   making bright the eyes.
> The speech of Yahweh is ritually pure,
>   standing forever.
> The judgments of Yahweh are truth,
>   they are righteous all together,
> More desirable than gold,
>   than much pure gold,
> More sweet than honey,
>   or the refined comb
> Your servant is indeed illumined by them,
>   and in their observance is there great gain.

Concerning this possible reference to ritual anointing, Wyatt argues:

> It is true that there is no narrative statement about unction here: oil is not even mentioned. But only thus can the successive blessings on various parts

---

31. Nicholas Wyatt, "Degrees of Divinity: Some Mythical and Ritual Aspects of West Semitic Kingship," 857.

of the king's body be explained. For comparison we should consider the unction of priests, in Exod. 29:4–9, 19–22, 40:12–15 and Lev. 8:10–12, 22–24, where various parts of the priest's body are anointed with oil and blood, undoubtedly with some liturgical commentary on the action, such is now narrated in these passages, providing a suitable performative utterance.[32]

This suggests that when read through the lens of ancient Israelite and general Near Eastern traditions, the Prophet Joseph revealed a profound theological idea by placing Abraham into the enthroned image of a god.

Taking Joseph Smith's interpretation seriously, this scene prefigures the state Abraham now occupies according to Doctrine and Covenants 132 (and which, by extension, can be given to all humanity):

> Abraham received all things, whatsoever he received, by revelation and commandment, by my word, saith the Lord, and hath entered into his exaltation and sitteth upon his throne. (v. 29)

By approaching the Prophet Joseph's explanation of Facsimile 3 as a revelation concerning important theological principles, we can recognize the actual ancient meaning of the vignette as an Egyptian presentation scene while seeing the revelatory significance of the Prophet's adaption in regards to LDS theology and temple worship. By doing so we can see that Joseph was producing something much more significant for Latter-day Saints than a correct translation of Egyptian papyri. The prophet was creating a visual and almost tangible theology that paralleled and advanced ancient religious motifs.

Divine Council of Deities

In terms of the text itself, one of the most intriguing features of the Book of Abraham is the way in which it revises the opening chapters of Genesis into a single account of creation. The beginning of the text reads:

> And then the Lord said: Let us go down. And they went down at the beginning, and they, that is the Gods, organized and formed the heavens and the earth. (Abr. 4:1)

From that point in the narrative, each of the creative acts appears to be depicted as the Gods working together to organize the world.

This view stands in stark contrast to the revision of the creation stories featured in the Book of Moses, which present God (in the singular) telling the creation story in first person. There, P's reference to God speaking

---

32. Wyatt, "Degrees of Divinity," 875.

in the plural in Genesis 1:26 appears reinterpreted as a speech given to the Only Begotten Son (Moses 2:26). God still performs the creative acts by himself. From a historical perspective, this observation suggests that Joseph's study of biblical Hebrew likely influenced his subsequent revisioning of the creation story in the Book of Abraham, as the Hebrew noun "*elohim*" (which appears in P's creation narrative) can refer to either the singular "God" or the plural "gods" depending on the context.[33]

Though these Gods appear non-specified in the Book of Abraham, Joseph later provided an interpretive key concerning the identity of these deities:

> [An] everlasting covenant was made between three personages before the organization of this earth, and relates to their dispensation of things to men on the earth; these personages, according to Abraham's record, are called God the first, the Creator; God the second, the Redeemer; and God the third, the witness or Testator.[34]

Here, Joseph views at least some of the unnamed Gods to be those of the Godhead.

Toward the end of his ministry, the Prophet Joseph appears to have devoted considerable attention to the theological notion of a divine council of deities. During the April conference of the Church in 1844, the Prophet testified concerning the importance of a heavenly council organized before the creation of the earth. Concerning "the beginning," Joseph declared that "the head of the Gods called a council of the Gods; and they came together and concocted a plan to create the world and people it."[35] In his journal entry for June 11, 1843, Franklin D. Richards wrote that the Prophet taught that "the order and ordinances of the kingdom were instituted by the priesthood in the council of heaven before the world was."[36] Richards later records Joseph's testimony that "all blessings that were ordained for man by the council of heaven were on conditions of obedience to the law there of."[37]

Joseph Smith's view of the divine council suggests that this assembly of deities served a vital administrative role in God's plan of happiness. A

---

33. Michael T. Walton, "Professor Seixas, the Hebrew Bible, and the Book of Abraham," 41–43; and Louis C. Zucker, "Joseph Smith as a Student of Hebrew," 50–52.

34. Joseph Smith, *Teachings of Joseph Smith*, 190.

35. Ibid., 349.

36. Joseph Smith, *The Words of Joseph Smith: The Contemporary Accounts of the Nauvoo Discourses of the Prophet Joseph*, 215, capitalization and spelling somewhat standardized in such quotations.

37. Smith, *The Words of Joseph Smith*, 232.

year after the Prophet's martyrdom, William Clayton recorded his recollection of the Prophet's teachings regarding this doctrine:

> It has been a doctrine taught by this church that we were in the Grand Council amongst the Gods when the organization of this world was contemplated and that the laws of government were all made and sanctioned by all present and all the ordinances and ceremonies decreed upon.[38]

In a discussion concerning this assembly, the Prophet went so far as to suggest that when Latter-day Saints "begin to learn this way, we begin to learn the only true God, and what kind of a being we have got to worship."[39]

Since the nineteenth century, Joseph Smith's theological views regarding this council have provided the focus of considerable criticism for many Christians. However, in recent years, Biblical scholars have followed the Prophet's lead in devoting substantial consideration to the role of the divine council in the Hebrew Bible.[40] In an important article published in 1975, biblical scholar N.L.A. Tidwell provided a useful definition of the biblical council genre as

> a narrative of events in the heavenly council on an occasion when the council is gathered to make some fateful decision concerning the affairs of men. In fact, wherever in the OT the activities of the council are described, or the deliberations of the council may by thought to be alluded to, some decision of great moment is always involved.[41]

Significantly, prior to its explicit reference to the Gods working together to create the world, the Book of Abraham presents a story that reflects Tidwell's definition of a council drama:

> And there stood one among them [the premortal intelligences] that was like unto God, and he said unto those who were with him: We will go down, for there is space there, and we will take of these materials, and we will make an earth whereon these may dwell; And we will prove them herewith, to see if they will do all things whatsoever the Lord their God shall command them; And they who keep their first estate shall be added upon; and they who keep not their first estate shall not have glory in the same kingdom with those who keep their first estate; and they who keep their second estate shall have glory added upon their heads for ever and ever. And the Lord said: Whom

---

38. Ibid., 84 note 10.

39. Smith, *Teachings of Joseph Smith*, 349–50.

40. See David E. Bokovoy, "'Ye Really Are Gods': A Response to Michael Heiser Concerning the LDS Use of Psalm 82 and the Gospel of John," 267–313.

41. N.L.A. Tidwell, "*Wā'ōmar* (Zech 3:5) and the Genre of Zechariah's Fourth Vision," 352.

shall I send? And one answered like unto the Son of Man: Here am I, send me. (Abr. 3:24–27)

With the words, "Here am I, send me," Latter-day Saints generally believe that Jesus Christ stepped forward in the council and volunteered to save humanity from the challenges associated with mortal probation (Abr. 3:27).

The story told in the Book of Abraham parallels council traditions in the ancient Near East. Stories of the divine council typically begin with a crisis in which the head God calls together the gods of the council to resolve the dilemma. During the council, a series of proposals are offered. Finally, a "savior" or "messenger" steps forward, offering his services to the council. The individual then receives a commission to perform his redemptive role.[42] This common Near Eastern pattern is seen, for example, in the Enūma Elish.[43] In this Babylonian myth, the head god of the pantheon calls together the gods in a council to resolve a dilemma created by the goddess Tiamat. Following a series of proposals, Marduk, the chief god of Babylon, receives a commission as savior. Marduk agrees to perform the role of savior on the condition that his father, Ea, the head god of the council, grant Marduk all power and glory. The same pattern appears in the Assyrian myth of Anzu. However, in this version, the god Ninurta agrees to serve as council savior while allowing his father to retain his position within the council. Thus the Book of Abraham story conceptually reflects a general Near Eastern pattern.

In the council story in the Book of Abraham, the account refers to beings called "intelligences" that were "organized before the world was" (3:22). In this setting, God "stood among those that were spirits, and he saw that they were good" (v. 23) and identifies those beings in his assembly as his rulers. This view accords with the Prophet's teaching that "every man who has a calling to minister to the inhabitants of the world was ordained to that very purpose in the grand council of heaven."[44]

Though not a direct cognate, the notion of God assigning members of his council to assume important positions of administrative responsibility appears in its earliest form in Deuteronomy 32:8: "When the Most High apportioned the nations, when he divided humankind, he fixed the boundaries of the peoples according to the number of the gods" (NRSV). This verse reflects an ancient Israelite belief concerning the council in

---

42. This summary is based upon the pattern identified by Simon B. Parker, "Council," 39–98.

43. See Chapter 5.

44. Smith, *Words of Joseph Smith*, 367.

which each nation received its deity as an assignment from the Most High God and parallels the council story featured in the Book of Abraham.

Significantly, in the context of assigning these "gods" a leadership position, the Book of Abraham specifically notes that God "stood in the midst of" these souls (Abr. 3:23). This reference to God *standing* among divine beings in a heavenly council setting finds important parallels with biblical tradition, including Psalms 82:1, which refers to God standing in the council and passing judgment.[45]

The motif has its origin in a secular cultural context. From an analysis of the legal material in the Hebrew Bible, it appears that in a traditional judicial setting, judges sat while plaintiffs stood.[46] This distinction provides a significant clue for interpreting Moses as judge in Exodus 18:13–14:

> And it came to pass on the morrow, that Moses sat to judge the people: and the people stood by Moses from the morning unto the evening. And when Moses' father in law saw all that he did to the people, he said, What is this thing thou doest to the people? why sittest thou thyself alone, and all the people stand by thee from morning unto even?[47]

Biblical scholar Simon Parker has shown that the distinction between sitting and standing in judicial settings also operates in the biblical view of the divine council.[48] This observation, for instance, sheds light on passages such as Isaiah 3:13 where Yahweh "stands up to plead a cause, He rises to champion peoples" (JPS). Thus, it is interesting the Book of Abraham records God "stood" amongst those premortal beings and passed judgment that they were "good."

This council story in the Book of Abraham and the subsequent creation narrative appears with a preface in which Abraham receives a vision concerning stars.

> And I saw the stars, that they were very great, and that one of them was nearest unto the throne of God; and there were many great ones which were near unto it; And the Lord said unto me: These are the governing ones; and the name of the great one is Kolob, because it is near unto me, for I am the

---

45. See Bokovoy, "Ye Really Are Gods," 272.

46. Hans J. Boecker, *Redeformen des Rechtslebens im Alten Testament*, 85–86.

47. For additional examples of the practice of sitting for judgment, see Judges 4:5; Joel 3:2; Psalms 22:5; Proverbs 20:8; Daniel 7:9–10.

48. See, for example, 1 Kings 22:19, 21; Job 1:6; 2:1; Daniel 7:9–10; see also Simon B. Parker, "The Beginning of the Reign of God—Psalm 82 as Myth and Liturgy," 537.

Lord thy God: I have set this one to govern all those which belong to the same order as that upon which thou standest. (Abr. 3:2–3)

When read in context, this vision can be seen as creating a thematic link between the council drama at the end of Abraham 3 and the story of the Gods creation in Abraham 4. When interpreted from this perspective, the "stars" may serve as types for members of the heavenly assembly. Kolob, for instance, as a type for Christ is "the great one" situated nearest unto the throne of God whereas the other stars are described as "great ones" assigned to govern.[49] This description conceptually links these stars with the intelligences defined as "great ones" assigned to "rule" in verses 22 and 23.

We see a similar idea reflected in Matthew's story of the Magi who come to visit Jesus after his birth. The account reads:

Now when Jesus was born in Bethlehem of Judaea in the days of Herod the king, behold, there came wise men from the east to Jerusalem, Saying, Where is he that is born King of the Jews? for we have seen his star in the east, and are come to worship him (Matt. 2:1–2).

The idea that Jesus had a personal star associated with his birth finds parallels with many ancient traditions.[50] For instance, in his classic work *Timaeus* (written circa 360 BC), the Greek philosopher Plato refers to stars connected with each human soul in a discussion concerning pre-mortal human existence:

[The Creator of this universe] turned once more to the bowl he had used previously to mix and blend the soul of the universe. He poured into it what was left of the ingredients he had used before and mixed them in the same way . . . Once he had a complete mixture, he divided it up into as many souls as there are stars and he assigned each soul to a star. Then with each soul mounted on its chariot, so to speak, he showed it the nature of the universe. He told them the laws of their destinies—how it was ordained that the first incarnation they would undergo would be the same for all of them, so that none of them would suffer any disadvantage at his hands, and how, after he

---

49. For an analysis of Kolob as a type for Christ, see Alonzo L. Gaskill, *The Lost Language of Symbolism* (Salt Lake City: Deseret Book, 2003).

50. The Roman Poet, Quintus Horatius Flaccus, who lived during the reign of Caesar Augustus, refers to the idea of stars connected with each human soul; the more famous or important the individual, the brighter his star: "The Genius alone knows—that companion who rules our star of birth, the god of human nature, though mortal for each single life, and changing in countenance, white or black Horace," Epistles 2.2 (187); as cited in Henry Rushton Fairclough, *Horace Satires, Epistles and Ars Poetica*, 439.

had planted each of them in the appropriate instrument of time, they were to be born as the most god-fearing of creatures.[51]

This statement is part of Plato's account of the formation of the universe. It parallels the Book of Abraham's vision of the pre-mortal existence of the human soul and the connection it makes between souls and stars. Some scholars speculate that these types of traditions may have influenced Matthew's account of the Magi seeking Jesus' birth star.[52] Reading Abraham's astronomy lesson in the Book of Abraham as typology for the intelligences in God's assembly links Jesus with the brightest star nearest the very throne of God.

Stars serve a similar purpose in the Hebrew Bible. They are part of what is often described as "the Host of Heaven," a term which biblical scholar Lowell Handy has explained "is widely understood" by scholars as a designation referring to "the gods who made up the heavenly court in Judah and Israel."[53] Moreover, the actual term "morning stars" appears in the Book of Job as a parallel expression for the "sons of God" who comprise the assembly in biblical and general Northwest Semitic traditions (Job 38:7). As members of His assembly, the council stars were "counted" by God and each one given a name (Ps. 147:4). According to the book of Judges, these are the divine beings who, as "stars fought from heaven, from their courses they fought against Sisera" (Judg. 5:20). A similar link between human beings and divine stars appears in Daniel's statement concerning the final judgment:

> Many of those that sleep in the dust of the earth will awake, some to eternal life, others to reproaches, to everlasting abhorrence. And the knowledgeable

---

51. Plato, *Timaeus*, 41e, as translated by Robin Waterfield Oxford World's Classics, 2008, 31.

52. "In Hellenistic sources there are reports . . . of comets or other light phenomena at the birth of gods. On coins of Alexander, of the Diadochi, of Caesar, of Augustus, but also of Alexander Jannaeus and of Herod a star appears as the symbol of the king. Furthermore, the idea is widespread that every person has a star—important and wealthy people a bright star, the others a dim one—that comes into existence at birth and is extinguished at death. This idea is the basis of the popular astrology of that day. In the Jewish tradition a star appears in the story of Abraham's child who is persecuted by Nimrod." Ulrich Luz, *Matthew 1–7: A Commentary on Matthew 1–7*, 104.

53. Lowell K. Handy, *Among the Host of Heaven: The Syro-Palestinian Pantheon as Bureaucracy*, 120.

will be radiant like the bright expanse of sky, and those who lead the many to righteousness will be like the stars forever and ever. (Dan. 12:2–3; JPS)

Since the stars are gods in biblical and Near Eastern thought, this passage provides hints of a type of apotheosis in the Book of Daniel.

The issue of divine stars appears as an important motif within the biblical story of Abraham, where God takes Abraham outside and tells him, "Look toward heaven and count the stars, if you are able to count them," adding, "So shall your offspring be" (Gen. 15:5). This promise can be interpreted as a reference to Abraham's offspring being like the stars, both in number and divinity.

Though obscured in the King James Version, the concept of "great stars" appears in the biblical promise God made Abraham concerning eternal progeny: "I will make your seed *great like the stars of heaven*, and assign to your seed all these lands, so that all the nations of the earth shall bless themselves by your heirs" (Gen. 26:4). Significantly, this promise declares that Abraham's seed will be "great like the stars of heaven" and that God will assign them to provide a "blessing" to the nations of the earth. These concepts appear thematically connected with the governing stars and intelligence imagery in the Book of Abraham. Even the gods whom the Most High assigned to govern the nations in Deuteronomy 32:8 first appear textually as "stars":

> And when you look up to the sky and behold the sun and the moon and the stars, the whole heavenly host, you must not be lured into bowing down to them or serving them. These the LORD your God assigned to other peoples everywhere under heaven; but you the LORD took and brought out of Egypt. (Deut. 4:19–20)

Through a sequential reading of the Book of Abraham, we can see a similar cosmological and typological vision that compares stars with divinities. Its astronomical account transitions to a story of a heavenly council that follows the basic narrative structure of a traditional council story in the ancient Near East. In this setting, God stood among the heavenly host and passed judgment on those among them who would be his rulers—including Jesus, the Savior. The account presents these Gods of the assembly working together to create the world. Finally, the Book of Abraham concludes with a depiction of Abraham experiencing a type of apotheosis through an adaptation of a traditional Egyptian presentation scene with thematic ties to the LDS temple endowment. This reading suggests that even when interpreted as a modern adaptation of Egyptian symbols that produces a pseudepigraphic account of Abraham's life, the

Book of Abraham is a profound theological text, which is central to Joseph Smith's revelatory work in organizing ancient paradigms into an inspired theological structure.

Conclusion

For Latter-day Saints, the Book of Abraham can be a challenging text in light of modern Egyptological scholarship and Higher Criticism. Fundamental to Joseph Smith's theology, however, is the notion of a restoration and revelation of religious truths that bind together past generations. Producing a book of Abraham with spiritual and doctrinal ideas (some of which can be found in ancient Near Eastern religious paradigms) facilitated that process in a way that a modern Doctrine and Covenants' revelation would not. By working with the papyri in accordance with the spiritual gift as "translator," the Prophet's mind was opened to produce a profound scriptural account of the biblical patriarch, Abraham. His role in religious history is paramount to Judaism, Christianity, and even Islam. Joseph's Book of Abraham creates a direct link between this important icon and the Restoration.

While the conclusions of Higher Criticism make a literal attribution to Abraham difficult to accept, approaching the Book of Abraham as inspired pseudepigraphy places it directly into the traditions of ancient scripture and religious texts. Not only does it place the Book of Abraham into a sphere not subject to Historical Critical objection, it allows the Book of Abraham to speak as revelatory scripture, drawing upon the past as a theological pattern that typifies human progression toward divinity.

Chapter Nine

Higher Criticism and the Book of Mormon

Introduction

The Book of Mormon stands out as Joseph Smith's greatest scriptural achievement. In the March 26, 1830, edition of the *Wayne Sentinel*, a small printing company located in Palmyra, New York published the title page of the Book of Mormon, announcing: "The above work, containing about 600 pages, large Deuodecimo, is now for sale, wholesale and retail, at the Palmyra Bookstore, by E. B. Grandin."[1] Instantly, Joseph Smith, the uneducated farm boy from upstate New York, had become one of the most famous Americans in the nineteenth century.

Although the Book of Mormon is an independent historical record of an indigenous people from ancient America, its story begins in the city of Jerusalem shortly before the Babylonian captivity in 586 BC. It recounts how this small group journeyed through the ancient Near East to a land called Bountiful where they constructed a vessel that allowed passage to the New World. The Book of Mormon itself cites various passages from the Hebrew Bible and even gives emphasis to a collection of books written by the Prophet Moses. Thus, like the books of Moses and Abraham, the Book of Mormon may also be approached utilizing the insights scholars have gained through Historical Criticism.[2]

The Book of Mormon itself invites readers to ponder carefully over the truthfulness of its claims. As discussed in the prologue of this volume, Elder B. H. Roberts recognized this fact, writing:

---

1. As cited in Richard L. Bushman, *Joseph Smith and the Beginnings of Mormonism*, 110.

2. The chapter focuses on the issues raised thus far concerning the authorship of the Pentateuch. The topic of Deutero-Isaiah (another important observation made through Higher Criticism) will be considered in the subsequent volume.

The Book of Mormon of necessity must submit to every test, to literary criticism, as well as to every other class of criticism; for our age is above all things critical, and especially critical of sacred literature, and we may not hope that the Book of Mormon will escape closest scrutiny; neither, indeed, is it desirable that it should escape. It is given to the world as a revelation from God. It is a volume of American scripture. Men have a right to test it by the keenest criticism, and to pass severest judgment upon it, and we who accept it as a revelation from God have every reason to believe that it will endure every test; and the more thoroughly it is investigated, the greater shall be its ultimate triumph. Here it is in the world; let the world make the most of it, or the least of it. It is and will remain true. But it will not do for those who believe it to suppose that they can dismiss objections to this American volume of scripture by the assumption of a lofty air of superiority, and a declaration as to what is enough for us or anybody else to know. The Book of Mormon is presented to the world for its acceptance; and the Latter-day Saints are anxious that their fellow men should believe it. If objections are made to it, to the manner of its translation, with the rest, these objections should be patiently investigated, and the most reasonable explanations possible, given.[3]

The tenets of Higher Criticism certainly create some challenges for the Book of Mormon. However, rather than being simply dismissed or ignored, these issues should receive careful consideration. The following chapter provides a basic introduction to the Book of Mormon in light of the insights scholars have gained into the Pentateuch through Historical Criticism. Even though Historical Criticism (and by extension, Higher/Source Criticism) presents some difficulties for the Book of Mormon's claims, a careful reading of the text and a consideration of the work as revelatory literature can resolve some of these issues.

Book of Mormon Versus Biblical Narrators

From the beginning, Joseph Smith and his associates insisted that rather than a mere revelatory text, the Book of Mormon was a translation of an ancient record written in a reformed Egyptian script.[4] It was history that conveyed a deep spiritual message, presented primarily through the

---

3. B. H. Roberts, "The Translation of the Book of Mormon," 435–36.

4. The term "reformed" seems to simply serve as an adjective meaning "altered." "Both hieratic and demotic [Egyptian scripts] were in use in Lehi's time and can properly be termed 'reformed Egyptian.'" John A. Tvedtnes and Stephen D. Ricks, "Jewish and Other Semitic Texts Written in Egyptian Characters," 158.

voices of three ancient narrators, Nephi, Mormon, and Moroni.[5] As one of those narrators states in the book's Title Page, the Book of Mormon has two primary objectives: to show unto the remnant of the House of Israel what great things the Lord has done for their fathers through covenant, and to convince both Jew and Gentile that Jesus is the Christ.[6] Thus, more than just being an ancient historical record, this volume of scripture's spiritual purpose ought to take precedent over any other approach to the text.

The Book of Mormon is comparable to the Bible in that it presents itself as a scribal compilation of a historical narrative and is a literary example of ethnogenesis, meaning the formation or emergence of an ethnic group put to narrative. However, instead of omniscient, anonymous narrators who tell the story of the rise and fall of *Israel*, named Book of Mormon narrators document the rise and fall of the *Nephite* nation. It follows the basic pattern of the Documentary Hypothesis with an editor or redactor taking various records (some of which cover the exact same time period and events, albeit from a different perspective) and organizing these sources into a single literary work.

Despite its biblical-like feel and the book's claims for an original Near Eastern connection, the fact that identifiable narrators serve as primary characters in the account makes the Book of Mormon different than the Hebrew Bible. For instance, the Book of Mormon's opening lines emphasize Nephi as an author through a common Judean scribal technique that appears in the Hebrew Bible—the growing phrase:[7] "I make a record; I make a record *which I know is true*; I make a record *with my own hand*; and I make a record *according to my knowledge*." Through this technique, readers of the Book of Mormon immediately begin the record learning that Nephi's record is true, that the text's first primary character himself made the account, and that it imparts his own authorial knowledge.

To illustrate the difference, we can also compare the Book of Chronicles, which is a scribal compilation of various sources brought together to tell the history of the House of Israel. Unlike the Book of Mormon, Chronicles follows the same pattern witnessed in the Documentary Hypothesis. It is a record written by an anonymous author (or perhaps even authors in the

---

5. See the summary provided by Grant Hardy in *Understanding the Book of Mormon: A Reader's Guide*, 10.

6. For a consideration on one of the ways in which the Book of Mormon articulates this dual theme of Christ and covenants, see David E. Bokovoy, "On Christ and Covenants: An LDS Reading of Isaiah's Prophetic Call," 29–49.

7. On the "growing phrase" as scribal technique, see J. Magonet, *Form and Meaning: Studies in Literary Techniques in the Book of Jonah*, 31–33.

plural). Yet like the Book of Mormon, Chronicles places considerable emphasis upon its merit as a historical record. Though anonymous, the author emphasizes that his history is a "work of scholarship" through constant references to his sources.[8] He claims to draw his information from "the book [*seper*] of the Kings of Israel" (1 Chr. 9:10); "The Words of Samuel" (29:29); "the Words of Nathan" (12:15); "the Words of Jehu" (2 Chr. 20:34); "The Prophecy of Isaiah" (32:32); "the Lamentations" (35:25); as well as other titles. "To a large extent," writes Karel van der Toorn, "these references are 'mere show' of wide learning; both by the actual mode of production and by self-conscious parading of scholarship, Chronicles is evidently a product from the scribal workshop."[9] Many scholars believe that these sources serve as a type of false footnoting system designed to provide Chronicles with a real historical feel. And yet, even this biblical book, which shares the Book of Mormon's emphasis on historicity, follows the general Near Eastern and specifically biblical trend of anonymous narrators.

Simply put, we do not have any type of record from the world of the Bible comparable to the Book of Mormon in which named narrators present their *true* history as a type of autobiographical narrative. Even the sections from the Hebrew Bible that feature stories of the prophets in the books named after these figures are not comparable. For example, commenting upon the autobiographical features in the Book of Jeremiah (a Judean prophetic contemporary of Nephi), van der Toorn explains:

> [Jeremiah] is a scribal composition as opposed to a prophetic memoir; those parts of the book that present themselves as a genuine autobiographical document by Jeremiah, namely the so-called Confessions, are in fact the works of scribes. . . . If indeed authentically autobiographical, [the Confessions of Jeremiah] are truly unique. There is nothing like them in the ancient Near East. No one kept this kind of personal diary. . . . The ancient Near East has no documented parallel to a private record of inner struggle with one's destiny.[10]

This observation is certainly not enough to sustain an argument against the Book of Mormon's claims for ancient authenticity, but it is an important distinction. The Book of Mormon presents itself in a manner that reflects the way scholars believe the Pentateuch came together in terms of

---

8. Karel van der Toorn, *Scribal Culture and the Making of the Hebrew Bible*, 117.

9. Ibid.

10. van der Toorn, 189. The Confessions of Jeremiah appear in 1:4–19, 6:8–11, 6:27–30, 9:1–6, 11:18–12:6, 15:10–21, 17:14–18, 18:18–23, 20:7–18. It is worth noting that Lehi was a contemporary of Jeremiah. Thus the personal accounts by Nephi are scripturally connected to his father's contemporary.

edited documentary sources, but it does so through the voice of narrators that serve as primary characters in the account.

Book of Mormon Narrators as Genuine Authors

When read critically, the characters in the Book of Mormon have a feel of genuineness. There is an intrinsic logic to their accounts. This point can be illustrated by a careful reading of the Book of Mormon's opening verses. For example, as author, Nephi begins his record by stating that he had been born of "goodly parents." He then immediately shifts to a focus on his father Lehi, as if Lehi is the sole parent to whom Nephi refers: I was born of goodly parents (in the plural), "therefore I was taught somewhat in the learning of my father" (1 Ne. 1:1). This patriarchal focus is certainly paralleled by general Near Eastern conventions. Moreover, it conveys one of the central themes in Nephi's writings: Nephi is the political and religious heir to Lehi's prophetic teachings.

As a witness of the character's authenticity, Nephi's love and respect for his Mother as teacher comes through almost unexpectedly in the narrative. We see this, for example, when comparing Nephi's response to a difficult challenge with that of his mother, Sariah. Toward the beginning of his record, Nephi draws a parallel for his readers between speaking with the Lord and speaking with his father in a tent (1 Ne. 3:1). Lehi is the Lord's representative, his mouthpiece for the family. Thus, when Lehi asks Nephi to return to Jerusalem and obtain "the record of the Jews" and a genealogy of their family, Nephi records a heroic response:

> I will go and do the things which the Lord hath commanded, for I know that the Lord giveth no commandments unto the children of men, save he shall prepare a way for them that they may accomplish the thing which he commandeth them. (1 Ne. 3:7)

From a literary perspective, Nephi's declaration "I will *go*," serves as a sign of his complete fidelity to the specific command of his Father: "the Lord hath commanded me that thou and thy brothers should *go*. . . . Therefore *go*, my son. . . . And I Nephi said, 'I will *go*'" (3:4, 6–7). However, this heroic testimony that pays homage to Nephi's "goodly parents" directly parallels the words spoken by Nephi's mother when her sons successfully return from the venture:

> Now *I know* of a surety that *the Lord hath commanded* my husband to flee into the wilderness; yea, and I also know of a surety that the Lord hath protected my sons, and delivered them out of the hands of Laban, and given

them power whereby *they could accomplish the thing which the Lord hath commanded them.* (1 Ne. 5:8)

Almost unwittingly, therefore, Nephi reveals that his heroic qualities are not simply a result of having been born of goodly parents that taught him his father's language. Nephi's qualities of faith were learned from his mother's language as well.

Continuing this theme of authenticity, in the text's initial verse, Nephi repeats the expression "my days" a total of three times. Though redundant and unnecessary from a contemporary western literary perspective, this type of repetition served an essential purpose in ancient texts.[11] As narrator, Nephi tells his readers that his days were filled with "many afflictions"; his days were filled with the Lord's "favor"; and that he will make "a record" of his days (1 Ne. 1:1). Therefore, readers will experience an account which shows that afflictions and favor work together as a blessing in the lives of the faithful. To quote Nephi, his record will show readers "that the tender mercies of the Lord are over all those whom he hath chosen, because of their faith, to make them mighty even unto the power of deliverance" (v. 20).

The second verse in Nephi's account begins with the archaic English term "yea," a word that "enforces the sense of something preceding" as in "not only so, but more."[12] From a literary perspective, this conveys an *a fortiori* argument, meaning "an argument from a yet stronger reason" (biblical scholars James Kugel and Robert Alter have argued that the same type of conceptual rhetoric appears in biblical parallelism).[13] Thus, this verse gives emphasis to the idea that the author's record in the language of his father and teacher is a spiritual account designed to present the theological message that afflictions can be a blessing to those who experience God's tender mercies. In so doing, the text can be shown to feature a subtle yet consistent literary message.

It is interesting that in verses 2 and 3, Nephi expresses an immediate need to explain his ability to produce a record. As we have discussed throughout this study, prior to the Babylonian destruction of Jerusalem, Israelite and Judean societies placed greater emphasis on orality than tex-

---

11. On repetition as literary device, see Robert Alter, *The Art of Biblical Poetry*, 111–42.

12. Noah Webster, *American Dictionary of the English Language*.

13. Alter, *The Art of Biblical Poetry*, 3–26; James Kugel, *The Ideal of Biblical Poetry: Parallelism and its History* (Baltimore: John Hopkins University Press, 1998).

tuality.[14] Literacy in the ancient world was always restricted to a small segment of the social elite.[15] Thus, Nephi's explanation that he had been taught "the language" of his father, and that he had an ability to "make a record," provides an appropriate historical introduction to his work. Nephi possessed a very unusual skill. As author, Nephi received a scribal education and had an ability to produce a record in the language of his father. While it is difficult to know precisely what Nephi intended by the statement that his record reflects a combination of Jewish learning and Egyptian language, the declaration seems primarily to serve as an aside to Nephi's education. His greater focus is spiritual; his is a *true* record and a continuation of Lehi's teachings.

The expression "my father" in 1 Nephi 1:2 is given repeated emphasis throughout Nephi's introduction. It appears ten times in 1 Nephi 1. Significantly, Lehi's name occurs three times in the initial chapter, but it never appears without the additional descriptive, "my father." The mere fact that Nephi repeats the phrase with so much frequency shows that Lehi looms as a pivotal figure in Nephi's thoughts. Moreover, this repeated reference may carry a dual meaning: (1) in ancient Israel, the term "my father" was used as an honorific title for a leading prophetic figure (see, for example, 2 Kings 2:12);[16] and (2) in both ancient and modern Hebrew, when combined with the first-person common singular pronominal suffix ("my"), the noun "father" functions as a term of endearment equivalent to "poppa" or "daddy" in English.[17] Thus, through repetition, Nephi's emphasis conveys his love for Lehi and a deep respect for the figure to whom Nephi's people will look toward as a pivotal patriarchal figure.

This brief analysis of the opening authorial lines in the Book of Mormon illustrates that despite the fact that named authorial narrators is a technique foreign to biblical patterns, the accounts attributed to these characters in the Book of Mormon carry a strong sense of authenticity. One further illustration of this idea should suffice. Reading carefully the

---

14. William M. Schniedewind, *How the Bible Became a Book*, 81–82.

15. Though Mesopotamians were the first people to develop a writing system, it is estimated that less than five percent of the populations were actually literate. The number in Egypt was slightly higher at about seven percent. Even ancient Greece had only about a ten percent literacy rate; see van der Toorn, *Scribal Culture and the Making of the Hebrew Bible*, 10.

16. See, James G. Williams, "The Prophetic Father: A Brief Explanation of the Term Sons of the Prophets," 345.

17. Robert Alter, *Genesis: Translation and Commentary*, 105.

words of the Book of Mormon's named authors reveals that these narrators often had a difficult time closing their accounts.[18] Granted, such an effect could be attributed to a highly sophisticated author, however, it could also be argued that if Joseph Smith were the true and only author behind the text, moving onto a new authorial voice would have been an easier task.

This point can be illustrated by considering the conclusion to the account attributed to the book's second author and brother of Nephi, Jacob. As author, Jacob reveals his intent to conclude his contribution to the Book of Mormon in Jacob 6. Creating a clear sense of closure, he writes:

> O then, my beloved brethren, repent ye, and enter in at the strait gate and continue in the way which is narrow, until ye shall obtain eternal life. O be wise; what can I say more? Finally, I bid you farewell, until I shall meet you before the pleasing bar of God, which bar striketh the wicked with awful dread and fear. Amen. (vv. 11–13)

With these words, the Book of Mormon's second named authorial voice shows that he personally believes that his record is over. Then, following these verses, which include an official farewell to his readers, Jacob adds one final story to his account. When approached synchronically, the text reads as if this authentic narrator finished his record and then years later had an experience that for some reason he felt needed to be added.

After his initial conclusion, Jacob presents a story of an encounter that he had at the end of his life with Sherem, a man described as an "anti-Christ" who preaches to Jacob's people that there is no Messiah figure.[19] Jacob depicts Sherem as the epitome of pride. He was "learned," writes Jacob, and "he had a perfect knowledge of the language of the people; wherefore, he could use much flattery, and much power of speech" (Jacob 7:4). Jacob then illustrates this assessment by presenting Sherem's words in a speech that clearly carries a sense of intellectual and religious arrogance:

> Brother Jacob, I have sought much opportunity that I might speak unto you; for I have heard and also know that thou goest about much, preaching that which ye call the gospel, or the doctrine of Christ. And ye have led away much of this people that they pervert the right way of God, and keep not the law of Moses which is the right way; and convert the law of Moses into the worship of a being which ye say shall come many hundred years hence.

---

18. This point appears well articulated by Grant Hardy in *Understanding the Book of Mormon*, 217–67.

19. For an analysis of this exchange in terms of ancient legal constructs, see John W. Welch, "The Case of Sherem," 107–38.

And now behold, I, Sherem, declare unto you that this is blasphemy; for no man knoweth of such things; for he cannot tell of things to come. (vv. 6–7)

Sherem's words are dripping with sarcasm. The question that critical readers of the text must ask, however, is why Jacob, the narrator of his own book, felt prompted to add this account to a record that he had already completed.

The answer to this question is derived by paying close attention to Sherem's pride and his specific message. Sherem accused Jacob of having "converted the law of Moses" into a false religious system that worshiped a Christ or Messiah figure. In so doing, Sherem inadvertently personifies the two primary themes Jacob focuses on as an authorial figure in the Book of Mormon.

In his writings, Jacob explores two basic themes, the sinfulness of pride and the connection between the Law of Moses and Christ. Jacob's concern with pride appears at the beginning of his narrative in a sermon delivered to his people at the temple. Jacob records his words of warning in this way:

Ye are lifted up in the *pride* of your hearts. . . . [L]et not this *pride* of your hearts destroy your souls. . . . And now, my brethren, I have spoken unto you concerning *pride*; and those of you which have afflicted your neighbor, and persecuted him because ye were *proud* in your hearts. . . . I make an end of speaking unto you concerning this *pride*. (Jacob 2:13–22)

Thus, in Jacob's foundational literary sermon, "pride" functions as a biblical-like *leitwort* or theme word.[20] Its repetition illustrates one of Jacob's primary concerns as religious author.

This emphasis on pride is matched by Jacob's focus on the connections he sees between the Law of Moses and the Messiah. Concerning this theme, Jacob writes that Israelite patriarchs "believed in Christ and worshiped the Father in his name." He then adds:

and also we worship the Father in his name. And for this intent we keep the law of Moses, it pointing our souls to him; and for this cause it is sanctified unto us for righteousness, even as it was accounted unto Abraham in the wilderness to be obedient unto the commands of God in offering up his son Isaac, which is a similitude of God and his Only Begotten Son. (Jacob 4:5)

---

20. For an introduction to this important literary technique, see Martin Buber, "Leitwort Style in Pentateuch Narrative," 114–28. As literary scholar Robert Alter notes in his analysis of the convention, "This kind of word-motif, as a good commentators have recognized, is one of the most common features of the narrative art of the Bible," Alter, *The Art of Biblical Narrative*, 92.

Thus, two of Jacob's primary themes include the wickedness of pride and the role of the Law of Moses as a system that points souls to the coming Messiah.

The account of Sherem is depicted as a personal, albeit dramatic encounter Jacob experienced after he initially concluded his authorial contribution to the Book of Mormon. As author, Jacob had finished his record, bid his readers farewell, and even written the line, "O be wise; what can I say more?" (Jacob 6:12). Why did he feel inspired, therefore, to pick up his record and recount one last story that happened several years later?

Jacob's encounter with Sherem personified the very concerns Jacob focused on earlier in his narrative. Jacob *feels* like a real character; a real *author*. Granted, such a technique could be produced by a highly sophisticated writer such as Joseph Smith, but again, reading the text carefully gives the impression that Book of Mormon narrators were real people who could be touched by an experience to the point that it unexpectedly shaped the course of their narrative. Book of Mormon authors are therefore nothing like anonymous biblical narrators. But as characters, they certainly come across as genuine people.

The Book of Mormon and the Brass Plates

In terms of the insights scholars have obtained through Higher Criticism, the most significant challenge the Book of Mormon faces is not that it is a work produced by named autobiographical authors. The greatest challenge the Book of Mormon faces is its reference to scriptural records that most critical scholars believe were produced after the Nephite exodus.

According to the Book of Mormon, these records were recorded on "brass plates" (1 Ne. 3:3) and written in the "language of the Egyptians" (Mosiah 1:4). Thus, it is specifically Higher Criticism and the analysis of biblical sources that presents the most difficult test for the Book of Mormon's historical claims. 1 Nephi 5 provides a glimpse of the contents of the "biblical" material Lehi and his family had access to through these records. The account states that once Lehi obtained the plates, he "did search them from the beginning" (v. 11). This phrase seems to function as a type of wordplay on the opening line of the Pentateuch, "in *the beginning* God created the heaven and the earth" (Gen. 1:1). It suggests that Lehi began his study of this material with the Priestly account of creation. However, Nephi's description of the record continues suggesting that in addition to an account of "the beginning," his father had access through the Brass Plates to much more material:

And he beheld that they did contain the five books of Moses, which gave an account of the creation of the world, and also of Adam and Eve, who were our first parents; And also a record of the Jews from the beginning, even down to the commencement of the reign of Zedekiah, king of Judah; And also the prophecies of the holy prophets, from the beginning, even down to the commencement of the reign of Zedekiah; and also many prophecies which have been spoken by the mouth of Jeremiah. And it came to pass that my father, Lehi, also found upon the plates of brass a genealogy of his fathers; wherefore he knew that he was a descendant of Joseph; yea, even that Joseph who was the son of Jacob, who was sold into Egypt, and who was preserved by the hand of the Lord, that he might preserve his father, Jacob, and all his household from perishing with famine. And they were also led out of captivity and out of the land of Egypt, by that same God who had preserved them. And thus my father, Lehi, did discover the genealogy of his fathers. (1 Ne. 5:11–16)

As we have learned through this study, most scholars who adhere to the views of Higher Criticism do not imagine that the Pentateuchal sources were compiled together and attributed to Moses as author until the Persian era.[21]

Moreover, given our current understanding of the development of the Hebrew Bible, it is difficult to imagine that the Pentateuch could have been combined in a single volume of plates with the historical books recounting Israelite history and the writings of the prophets. This view reflects the contemporary understanding of the Christian Old Testament that begins with the Pentateuch, followed by the history of Israel (Joshua–Chronicles), and then the prophets (Isaiah–Malachi). Significantly, this is not even the sequence that the current Hebrew Bible used in Judaism follows. Instead, as a collection, the modern Hebrew Bible begins with the Torah, then the prophetic material, and the final section is the Writings.[22] Although the current Christian structure for the collection serves to emphasize the

---

21. See Chapter 4 for dating of documentary sources.

22. As Marc Brettler points out, "The 'Hebrew Bible' and the 'Old Testament' differ in more than name only. They comprise different numbers of books, which they place in a different order. (The ordering matters because it alters the context in which we understand the text; a book's meaning can shift depending upon which books we read before and after it.) More significantly, the term 'Hebrew Bible' suggests a corpus that is self-standing, whereas the 'Old Testament' does not. The meaning of many passages in the 'Old Testament' changes when one views them as part of a larger whole that includes the New Testament." Marc Zvi Brettler, *How to Read the Bible*, 9.

fact that the prophetic material points toward the New Testament (since these books immediately precede the Gospels in the Bible), the structure that the description of the Brass Plates seems to apply to the collection is an original Jewish construct. But even this construct did not develop for several centuries after Lehi's exodus from Jerusalem.

Still, there is no hint in the Book of Mormon's references to the Brass Plates that these records were a "book" in the modern sense.[23] The first reference to these texts appears in Lehi's description: "For behold, Laban hath the record of the Jews and also a genealogy of my forefathers, and they are engraven upon plates of brass" (1 Ne. 3:3). Although subsequent verses in the Book of Mormon will use the expression "*the* plates of brass," this initial reference to these texts simply refers to material as documents that appear on "plates of brass" without the definite article. The word "the" seems to imply a collection, whereas "plates of brass" need not convey that nuance.[24]

Though the construct of the Brass Plates in 1 Nephi 5 seems to reflect the later Christian understanding of the Old Testament rather than individual documentary sources, a careful reading of Nephi's description of the Brass Plates does not suggest that all of this material existed in a single "book." In fact, the text seems to indicate that the books of Moses were a separate collection from "the record of the Jews from the beginning, even down to the commencement of the reign of Zedekiah, king of Judah" (v. 12). This suggests, perhaps, two separate collections,

---

23. However, the Book of Mormon does show signs of conceptualizing the Bible as a "book." Note, for instance, 1 Nephi 13:23: "And he said: Behold it proceedeth out of the mouth of a Jew. And I, Nephi, beheld it; and he said unto me: The book that thou beholdest is a record of the Jews, which contains the covenants of the Lord, which he hath made unto the house of Israel; and it also containeth many of the prophecies of the holy prophets; and it is a record like unto the engravings which are upon the plates of brass, save there are not so many; nevertheless, they contain the covenants of the Lord, which he hath made unto the house of Israel; wherefore, they are of great worth unto the Gentiles."

24. Even the subsequent expression "the plates of brass" might conceptually employ the definite article with the adjective "brass" to refer to groups of brass plates—as in phrases such as "the rich," "the poor," and "the young," which are all examples of English expressions that use the definite article as a designation of groups of people.

the Pentateuch and what biblical scholars refer to as the Deuteronomistic History (Joshua–Kings).[25]

The Old Testament contains three main sources that recount the tale of Israel's past. These compilations consist of what scholars refer to as the Tetrateuch (Genesis–Numbers), the Deuteronomistic History (Deuteronomy, Joshua, Judges, Samuel, and Kings), and the Chronicles complex (1–2 Chronicles and Ezra–Nehemiah).[26] The Deuteronomistic History tells a version of Israel's story beginning at the plains of Moab that eventually concludes much like the Book of Mormon with the destruction and scattering of the covenant people. As a collection, this was a major literary work, much larger than anything else known to have existed in the ancient Near East.

Presently, most scholars believe that there existed both a pre-exilic and later post-exilic version of the Deuteronomistic History. Therefore, the idea that Lehi could have access to such a work is not a difficult challenge. The concept of five Mosaic books, however, is clearly anachronistic. Moreover, it is extremely difficult to imagine that these books could have existed as an Egyptian translation. There's no historical evidence that Judean scribes translated what would become biblical texts into a foreign language until the second century BC; and when they did, it was the Greek Septuagint.[27]

Thus far, the most helpful proposal concerning this material by an LDS scholar is John Welch's suggestion that perhaps the Brass Plates might have been produced for King Josiah himself, after the discovery of Deuteronomy.[28] Although the Book of Mormon refers to a collection of sources as the five Books of Moses, this claim does not directly challenge the validity of the Documentary Hypothesis. It simply suggests that if taken literally, five books attributed to Moses would have existed prior

---

25. The Deuteronomistic History will be addressed in greater detail in the subsequent study, *Authoring the Old Testament: The Prophets*.

26. See Martin Noth, "The Deuteronomistic History," 13. Steven L. McKenzie, "The Deuteronomistic History," 2:160.

27. Tvedtnes and Ricks have pointed to the *Papyrus Amherst 63* as a "Bible passage, in its Aramaic translation, written in late Egyptian characters;" see Tvedtnes and Ricks, "Jewish and Other Semitic Texts." However, this document from the second century BC cannot claim to be a translation of Psalm 20. Though related, it has too many differences, including references to multiple non-Israelite deities other than Yahweh (i.e., the focus of the biblical Psalm). See the analysis provided by K.A.D. Smelik, "The Origin of Psalm 20," 75–81.

28. John W. Welch, "Authorship of the Book of Isaiah," 430–32.

to the Babylonian exile.[29] These need not have been identical, however, to the present form of the Pentateuch put together after the exilic period (i.e., the form that appears in contemporary Bible's today).

Unfortunately, most students of the Book of Mormon have ignored its relationship to the claims of Higher Criticism. There have been, however, exceptions to this trend. The first LDS scholar to seriously engage the Documentary Hypothesis and the Book of Mormon was anthropologist John L. Sorenson. In 1977, Sorenson wrote an article suggesting that the Brass Plates may have been the original source for the Elohist tradition. Sorenson theorized that the Book of Mormon (particularly in its first portion), could be interpreted as a "manifestation" of the Elohist scribal school.[30] Since the E source reflects a pro-Northern perspective, Sorenson's theory would work well with the fact Lehi is identified as a member of the Northern tribe of Manasseh and that the only major Book of Mormon figure and line of ancestry from a southern tribe is the Zarahemla/Mulek connection. When the two distinct groups encounter each other, the smaller Lehite clan became the dominant political force (there is simply no return to a Davidic king and an acceptance of J's pro-Judean perspective despite Zarahemla's claim to being a direct descendant of David).

Additionally, Sorenson identified what he believed were examples of the Book of Mormon relying upon the E narrative rather than J. He referred to such issues as the fact that the Book of Mormon seems to ignore the Davidic covenant emphasized in J, and instead focuses its attention upon the Abrahamic covenant to the patriarchs. Like the Book of Mormon, E refers to Jacob by his proper name; whereas in J, Jacob

---

29. In the original Book of Mormon manuscript, 1 Nephi 5:11 refers to the "five books of Moses." It is possible, however, as Kevin Barney has suggested that "five" is simply a translational gloss by Joseph Smith produced in the course of the original translation; see Kevin L. Barney, "Reflections on the Documentary Hypothesis," 57–99. In 1 Nephi 19:23 there exists a different reading in the printer's manuscript than later editions. There the text refers not to "books of Moses" in the plural, but rather "book of Moses" in the singular. The original manuscript, however, reads "books" in the plural. Oliver Cowdery appears to have simply miscopied the term into the printer's manuscript, the result being that "book" in the singular appeared in the1830 edition of the Book of Mormon. This was later changed, however, back to "books" in the subsequent 1837 edition. Thus, Skousen's *The Book of Mormon: The Earliest Text* reads "books" in the plural. For his analysis, see Royal Skousen, *Analysis of Textual Variants of the Book of Mormon, Part One: 1 Nephi 1-2 Nephi 10*, 421–22.

30. John L. Sorenson, "The Brass Plates and Biblical Scholarship," 36.

typically appears referred to as "Israel." Sorenson also noted that the inhabitants of Jerusalem are "branded as evil in the strongest terms," a reflection of a pro-Northern bias like the one reflected throughout the Elohist source. The Book of Mormon also follows the pattern in E by placing special emphasis upon Joseph being sold into Egypt and saving the entire House of Israel.

In addition to Sorenson's observations, additional points could be used to support a connection between the Book of Mormon and E. For example, Nephi depicts the account of Moses striking the rock and providing water for the children of Israel as a positive event that occurred "according to the power of God" (1 Ne. 17:29). The Old Testament presents two different versions of this story regarding Moses answering the needs of the thirsty Israelites in the wilderness. The first one appears in Exodus 17:1–7. According to the account, after the Israelites had crossed the sea, but before they arrived at God's mountain, the people complained to Moses that they had nothing to drink. In response, Moses struck a rock that produced water, and the location of the miracle was named Massah and Meribah. Later, after the Israelites left the mountain and once again journeyed in the wilderness, the people complained to Moses that they had nothing to drink. He responded by striking a rock to provide them with water (Num. 20:2–13). And once again, the place was named "the waters of Meribah."

Critical scholars attribute the first version of the story to E and the second to P. E's version of the story presents Moses striking the rock at Massah and Meribah as an obedient response to God's instruction (Ex. 17:5–7). This reflects E's thematic tendency to depict Moses as a prophet and in a very positive light. In contrast, P's version is quite critical of Moses. In P, God rebukes Moses for the act of striking the rock, stating "because ye believed me not, to sanctify me in the eyes of the children of Israel, therefore ye shall not bring this congregation into the land which I have given them" (Num. 20:12). Thus one version of the story (P) views Moses' act of providing water at Meribah as a negative event, and the other (E) interprets it as a positive miracle. Taking Sorenson's argument seriously, readers could assume that Nephi's positive interpretation of the story of Moses striking a rock and providing the thirsting Israelites with water derives from his familiarity with E.

At first, these arguments seem quite compelling. Nephi may have received his scribal training by members of the Elohist school. Whether right or wrong, Sorenson certainly deserves credit for attempting to reconcile the Book of Mormon with the Documentary Hypothesis. Ultimately, however, the notion that the Book of Mormon relies upon E instead of the other documentary sources is not a compelling proposal. Again, according to Nephi's depiction of the Brass Plates, they contained "the five books of Moses, which gave an account of the creation of the world, and also of Adam and Eve, who were our first parents" (1 Ne. 5:11). Thus, the Nephites had access to the J source, and it appears cited throughout the Book of Mormon. The Book of Mormon refers to the Cain and Abel story, which is unique to J (Hel. 6:27, Ether 8:15), and it also uses the name "Sinai" rather than "Horeb" for the mountain of God (Mosiah 12:33; 13:5; only J and P use "Sinai"; E and D use "Horeb"). Additionally, an Elohist source from the North would certainly not describe itself as "a record of the Jews," which is the term used for the scriptural material on the Brass Plates (1 Ne. 5:12). E was a northern source, at least initially connected with Israelite rather than Judean scribes.

In fact, a careful reading of the Book of Mormon clearly shows a literary reliance upon not just J, but also P and D. To provide one illustration of this fact, King Benjamin's sermon encouraging his people to serve God includes a statement featuring literary allusions to both P and J's creation narratives: "If ye should serve him who has created you from the beginning, and is preserving you from day to day, by lending you breath, that ye may live, . . . ye would be unprofitable servants" (Mosiah 2:21). References to the verb "created" and the prepositional phrase "from the beginning" seem to reflect the opening verse of P's creation account: "In the beginning, God created heaven and earth" (Gen. 1:1). Allusion to "day to day" in this context reminds readers of the "day to day" creative acts in P's narrative. However, an allusion to "lending breath" and man *serving* God specifically reflects J's creation story in which Yahweh breathed into man's nostrils "the breath of life" (Gen. 2:7), and man was created to "serve" Yahweh by "dressing" and "keeping" the garden (Gen. 2:15). The statement, therefore, shows a reliance upon these distinct documentary sources to the point that it treats both narratives as a single account. Ultimately, whatever Nephi's relationship might have been to the Elohist scribal school, the Book of Mormon shows an awareness of all four documentary sources. This material, according to the Book of Mormon's claims, was accessible as the "five books of Moses" on the Brass Plates.

This brief summary of the relationship between the Book of Mormon and the Documentary Hypothesis is not meant to be exhaustive. Much more can and should be done in terms of analyzing the book's use of Pentateuchal sources to the point that it treats various documentary sources as a single account. Such a study, however, would extend beyond the scope of the present focus, which is designed as a basic introduction to Historical Criticism and the Pentateuch. It seems appropriate at this point to simply quote from LDS scholar Kevin Barney's important study on this topic: "In the case of the Book of Mormon I see no necessary conflict between that book's essential historicity and the Documentary Hypothesis; the dating of the sources raises a potential conflict, if one accepts a late date."[31] Barney is correct. It really is the dating of the Pentateuchal sources that presents the only major challenge for the Book of Mormon's claims for ancient authenticity, not the hypothesis itself. The Documentary Hypothesis actually parallels the way the Book of Mormon presents its own literary development.

Historical Criticism: Questions And Answers

Although some Latter-day Saints might feel concerned by the process of applying Higher Criticism to the Book of Mormon, some of the critical perspectives scholars hold can be comfortably reconciled with the text. This fact was illustrated in the first chapter of the present study, which compared the Documentary Hypothesis to the way the Book of Mormon presents itself as a redacted religious work. To choose another illustration, even though the Book of Mormon's views on the Devil or Satan seem historically anachronistic from the perspective of Historical Criticism, a careful reading shows that they reflect critical paradigms.

Throughout the Book of Mormon, Satan appears as a character who personifies evil, a fallen angel who "leads away" human hearts "to do all manner of iniquity" (3 Ne. 6:16). This notion is central to traditional Jewish and Christian beliefs. However, the Devil, as such, does not appear in the Old Testament. Historically, the idea of a devil or Satan began to emerge in Judaism during the Hellenistic period (323 to 30 BC). Critical scholars maintain that Judaism eventually adopted the idea as a result of Persian influence.[32] Thus, one of the earliest historical references connecting the snake in Eden with Satan is the apocryphal book the Wisdom of Solomon, ca. 200 BC.[33]

---

31. Barney, "Reflections on the Documentary Hypothesis," 73.

32. John J. Collins, "Cosmology: Time and History," 62.

33. For an analysis of later Jewish and Christian interpretations of the snake in contrast to the original idea a mere clever animal, see James Kugel, *The Bible as it Was,* 72–75.

In the King James Bible, the term "Satan" only appears in 1 Chronicles 21:1, Job 1:6–9, 12; 2:1–4, 6–7; Psalm 109:6, and Zechariah 3:1–2 (the term "devil" in the singular never occurs). However, the word *satan* in Hebrew means simply "the accuser" or the "adversary."[34] Texts such as Job 1, which refer to "satan" indicate that this figure is one of the divine beings in Yahweh's court. The fact that he is referred to with the definite article "the" (*ha-* in Hebrew) means that the text does not refer to a proper noun "Satan," the later Devil of Judean-Christian thought, but rather *the* "adversary" who represents the side of justice. The adversary or "opponent" opposing Yahweh's desire to bless Job on the grounds that his righteousness may simply reflect the fact that Job had never experienced anything difficult in his life. The divine being in this story does not personify evil. He is one of the "sons of God" or divine council deities who in this story personifies justice. Even the snake or serpent in J's creation story is never depicted as a devil figure. He is simply a literal serpent who talks with the woman in Eden.

This historical approach to the concept of Satan as an evolutionary theological development in Judaism raises the question of whether the Book of Mormon's references to the Devil should be seen as anachronistic. A careful reading of the Book of Mormon, however, shows that in this instance, the Book of Mormon seems to reflect the way biblical scholars who read the Hebrew Bible critically understand this issue.

One of the key texts for understanding the Book of Mormon's view of Satan is 2 Nephi 2:17. This passage derives from Lehi's final sermons to his sons. The text reads:

> And I, Lehi, according to the things which I have read, must needs suppose that an angel of God, according to that which is written, had fallen from heaven; wherefore, he became a devil, having sought that which was evil before God.

According to this passage, it was through the things he had read that Lehi learned about a fallen angel of God who became a devil. The notion of a Satan figure was something that Lehi was not taught before leaving Jerusalem around 600 BC. Moreover, the text even goes so far as to suggest that it was a doctrine that Lehi "supposed" to be true, a term that in Joseph Smith's day meant:

---

34. Ludwig Koehler and Walter Baumgartner, *The Hebrew and Aramaic Lexicon of the Old Testament*, 2:1317. See also see Welch, "The Case of Sherem," 107–38.

To lay down or state as a position or fact that may exist or be true, though not known or believed to be true or to exist; or to imagine or admit to exist, for the sake of argument or illustration.[35]

This passage, then, presents Lehi proposing his own interpretation that was otherwise not known or believed to be true.

Reading through the Old Testament texts cited by Lehi and Nephi shows which sources Lehi most likely used to put together his supposition concerning Satan. His same sermon indicates that one of the texts Lehi used to create his understanding of Satan was J's Garden of Eden account. Lehi refers to this fallen angel as

that old serpent, who is the devil, who is the father of all lies, wherefore he said: Partake of the forbidden fruit, and ye shall not die, but ye shall be as God, knowing good and evil. (2 Ne. 2:18)

However, given the fact that J's myth simply presents a serpent similar to the view of the serpent in the Epic of Gilgamesh (i.e., as a literal snake), it would take more for Lehi to come to this interpretation. He would need to have a text that described a fallen angel. Such a view appears in Isaiah 14. This biblical passage is a lament, mocking the death of an Assyrian king from the time of Isaiah. Many scholars assume that the fallen figure in this text is Sargon II who was killed in battle in 705 BC. The text reads:

How art thou fallen from heaven, O Lucifer, son of the morning! how art thou cut down to the ground, which didst weaken the nations! For thou hast said in thine heart, I will ascend into heaven, I will exalt my throne above the stars of God: I will sit also upon the mount of the congregation, in the sides of the north: I will ascend above the heights of the clouds; I will be like the most High. Yet thou shalt be brought down to hell, to the sides of the pit. They that see thee shall narrowly look upon thee, and consider thee, saying, Is this the man that made the earth to tremble, that did shake kingdoms. (vv. 12–16)

Even though this text refers directly to an Assyrian monarch who tried to make himself a divine being like the most High God, the taunt is based upon an ancient Canaanite motif of a literal divinity who tried to ascend to the throne of El, the highest god in the divine assembly.[36] Moreover, despite the lack of an explicit Satan figure, Israelite traditions concerning a divine being falling from heaven appear in a variety of biblical texts, including Psalms 82; Genesis 6:1–4; Ezekiel 28; Isaiah 14:12, 24:21; and

---

35. Noah Webster, *American Dictionary of the English Language*.

36. Michael S. Heiser, "The Mythological Provenance of Isa. XIV 12-15: A Reconsideration of the Ugaritic Material," 354–69.

Zechariah 3:1–2.[37] It is significant, however, that Lehi's son Nephi cites the Isaiah 14 taunt in 2 Nephi 24. Lehi's statement that he gained a "supposition" concerning a fallen angel from the things he had read suggests that Lehi put texts such as Genesis 2–3 and Isaiah 14 together in a way to understand the theological notion of Satan before it later developed in Jewish history.

Historical Criticism presents some challenges to the Book of Mormon's claims for ancient authenticity. However, oftentimes these issues can be resolved through a careful, critical reading of the text. This is certainly true, for example, with the Book of Mormon's anachronistic understanding of Satan as a fallen angel who opposes God's work. However, one of the challenges Higher Criticism raises that cannot be resolved through a careful reading of the text is actually its greatest religious strength.

Related to the issue of the Book of Mormon's historically anachronistic view of Satan is the text's understanding of Jesus as the Christ. In terms of its theology, the Book of Mormon possesses what scholars would refer to as an advanced or "high" Christology.[38] Book of Mormon prophets had an awareness of not only Jesus' name, but that he was God's divine son. We see this view, for example, in Book of Mormon texts such as Mosiah 15, which presents a prophet by the name of Abinadi teaching:

> God himself shall come down among the children of men, and shall redeem his people. And because he dwelleth in flesh he shall be called the Son of God, and having subjected the flesh to the will of the Father, being the Father and the Son—The Father, because he was conceived by the power of God; and the Son, because of the flesh; thus becoming the Father and Son. (vv. 1–3)

Book of Mormon prophets show a familiarity with Jesus' mission as a Messiah who will come to earth to suffer and die. Critical scholars believe, however, that this understanding of Christ did not develop amongst Jesus' followers until after his death.

LDS scholar Robert Millet points to this dissonance when he writes: "the Old Testament prophecies of Christ are often veiled, [whereas] the prophets of the plates of brass [i.e., Israelite prophets cited in the Book of Mormon but not in the Bible] are bold in testifying of the coming of Jesus Christ and are specific as to his ministry."[39] Thus, from an historical-

---

37. Sang Youl Cho, *Lesser Deities in the Ugaritic Texts and the Hebrew Bible*, 125.

38. For an introduction to the distinctions historians makes in terms of "Christology," high and low, see Bart D. Ehrman, *The New Testament: A Historical Introduction to the Early Christian Writings*, 177.

39. Robert Millet, "The Plates of Brass: A Witness of Christ," *Ensign* Jan. (1988).

critical perspective, the Book of Mormon's greatest religious message (i.e., that Jesus is the Christ, the Savior of the human race) is also a sign of its modern influences.

However, given the book's extraordinary origins, the Book of Mormon's high Christology need not indicate that the book lacks an authentic ancient core. This point was acknowledged by non-LDS scholar James Charlesworth, a scholar famous for his work with second-temple Jewish sources. Regarding this issue, Charlesworth observed:

> Mormons acknowledge that the Book of Mormon could have been edited and expanded on at least two occasions that postdate the life of Jesus of Nazareth. It is claimed that the prophet Mormon abridged some parts of the Book of Mormon in the fourth century A.D. And likewise it is evident that Joseph Smith in the nineteenth century had the opportunity to redact the traditions that he claimed to have received.[40]

Charlesworth recognized that by its own claims, the Book of Mormon comes to us as a heavily redacted document. Historical anachronisms, therefore, such as the text's advanced Christology, must be interpreted in accordance with the book's intrinsic claim to be an ancient document produced as modern revelation.

The Book of Mormon as Modern Expansion

Even though the Book of Mormon presents itself as a historical narrative, it is without question a revelatory document. And like all revelation, the Book of Mormon comes to us through a human filter. It would seem impossible, therefore, for such a work not to carry the imprint of Joseph Smith. As "translated" material, the Book of Mormon was not produced in the way contemporary linguists analyze a document and then render it into another language.[41] The Prophet did not know any ancient languages at the time he dictated the text. He was a seer, and the work was revelatory. Joseph did not seem to have directly used the plates while producing his translation.[42] Instead, he would look into a seerstone while the plates lay

---

40. James Charlesworth, "Messianism in the Pseudigrapha and the Book of Mormon," 125.

41. For the translation process see Tim Rathbone and John W. Welch, "Book of Mormon Translation by Joseph Smith," 210–13.

42. The Church's official website recently posted the following statement concerning the translation of the Book of Mormon:

hidden upon the table and typically dictate approximately eighteen words of text at a time.[43]

Thus, for those who accept the Book of Mormon's claims, one of the ways believers make sense of the presence of historical anachronisms in the text is through the theory of modern expansion through the imprint of Joseph Smith.[44] Blake Ostler explains this approach:

> The presence of translator anachronisms or expansions in the book show that Joseph imposed an interpretation on the text which was foreign to the ancient text, but not an interpretation alien to his revelatory experiences which produced the book. In other words, he did not perceive the ancient text and then consciously interpret it as he pleased; rather, the text is the revelation he experienced within his own conceptual paradigms.[45]

This approach, which suggests that the Book of Mormon we possess is the revelation Joseph Smith experienced through his own intellectual framework, allows believers in the book's ancient authenticity to explain such issues as references to Moses' five books, as well as citations of biblical passages that would have been unavailable to Lehi and his family.

In his analysis of the Book of Mormon, Terryl Givens refers to this method of interpreting the text as "one of the most appealing products

---

Joseph Smith and his scribes wrote of two instruments used in translating the Book of Mormon. . . . One instrument, called in the Book of Mormon the "interpreters," is better known to Latter-day Saints today as the "Urim and Thummim." . . . The other instrument, which Joseph Smith discovered in the ground years before he retrieved the gold plates, was a small oval stone, or "seer stone." As a young man during the 1820s, Joseph Smith, like others in his day, used a seer stone to look for lost objects and buried treasure. As Joseph grew to understand his prophetic calling, he learned that he could use this stone for the higher purpose of translating scripture. Apparently for convenience, Joseph often translated with the single seer stone rather than the two stones bound together to form the interpreters.

There is no historical evidence that Joseph used any other device other than the seerstone after the loss of 116 pages of the original manuscript. See "Book of Mormon Translation," available at http://www.lds.org/topics/book-of-mormon-translation?lang=eng.

43. Also, see the commentary on translation at the beginning of Chapter 8.

44. In terms of translation theory, the most helpful analysis thus far is Brant A. Gardner, *The Gift and Power: Translating the Book of Mormon* (Salt Lake City: Greg Kofford Books, 2011).

45. Blake T. Ostler, "The Book of Mormon as a Modern Expansion of an Ancient Source," 111–12.

of the new détente in the Book of Mormon wars."[46] Givens goes on to note that historian Richard Bushman has observed that this interpretation is now "attracting more and more fairly faithful church members."[47] Yet despite his own apparent acceptance of the model, Givens is quick to note that the concept of modern expansion does not solve all of the challenges the Book of Mormon faces in terms of its claims for ancient authenticity. As Givens observes, the problem with this approach to the Book of Mormon is that many of the book's historical anachronisms appear "synthesized seamlessly" into the book as a whole. As an illustration, Givens writes that "it is hard to see the pervasive Christology in the narrative as mere insertions into a preexistent account."[48] This same observation is true for the Book of Mormon's use of Old Testament texts, particularly sections of Isaiah that critical scholars believe were written long after Lehi and his family left Jerusalem.[49]

Still, those who accept the Book of Mormon as an English translation of ancient scripture must allow for historical anachronisms as part of the revelatory process. Even Brigham Young was open to the idea that external forces influenced the present form in which the Book of Mormon appears. On this subject, Brigham Young taught: "I will even venture to say that if the Book of Mormon were now to be rewritten, in many instances it would materially differ from the present translation."[50] Taking this idea even further, LDS scholar Mark Thomas suggests that "the Book of Mormon uses the Bible as proof text, as a springboard to new revelation and creativity."[51] From this perspective, Joseph was doing the very thing that the ancient authors of the Hebrew Bible did by taking a previous source and making it relevant for a contemporary audience. Nephi, Mormon, Moroni, and Joseph Smith were all continuing the tradition of using archaic sources to create new scripture.

However ancient in its core, the Book of Mormon is not a traditional translation. It is a revelatory document designed to bring its readers closer to divinity. Ultimately, therefore, the Book of Mormon's ability to fulfill

---

46. Terryl Givens, *By the Hand of Mormon: The American Scripture that Launched a New World Religion*, 173.

47. Ibid., 173–74.

48. Ibid., 173.

49. See the forthcoming analysis in *Authoring the Old Testament: The Prophets*.

50. Brigham Young, July 13, 1862, *Journal of Discourses*, 9:311.

51. Mark Thomas, *Digging in Cumorah*, 17.

this objective is independent from how much or how little of the work can truly be considered ancient.

Conclusion

At a Church conference in 1831, the Prophet's brother Hyrum invited Joseph to explain how the Book of Mormon came forth. Joseph Smith responded that "it was not intended to tell the world all the particulars of the coming forth of the Book of Mormon; and . . . it was not expedient for him to relate these things."[52] Given the revelatory nature of the text and Joseph's evolving views regarding divinity, it seems likely that this statement was not a mere attempt to keep hidden the details concerning translation. Joseph himself most likely did not understand the exact manner by which he translated the Book of Mormon.

As understood in the Book of Mormon itself, translation is the gift of seeing hidden things and making them known to the world. The Book of Mormon is a spiritual text with a historical claim. Its historicity must be assessed critically in light of the way scholars have come to understand the authorship of the Bible. Though some of the conclusions scholars reach through Higher Criticism certainly create some challenges for the Book of Mormon's ancient claims, Latter-day Saint students should not be afraid to give these matters careful consideration. Often times issues such as the book's use of Satan and its reliance upon named authors are resolved through a close, critical reading of the text. Other matters, however, including the text's references to the "five books of Moses" and its advanced Christology prove more difficult to reconcile with the notion that the Book of Mormon is simply a literal translation of an ancient source. However, as with all scripture, the Book of Mormon's spiritual validity is a matter that transcends questions of historicity.

---

52. Joseph Smith, *History of the Church*, 1:220.

Chapter Ten

Conclusion

The Hebrew Bible (or Christian Old Testament) is a compilation of scribal material written over a thousand year period in Israelite and Judean history. It is an extraordinary compilation, both in scope and in terms of its impressive historical impact. The Hebrew Bible is scripture to both Jews and Christians, although admittedly, these distinct religious movements understand "scripture" quite differently. However one interprets scripture, one thing is certain: the Bible is imperfect. It possesses competing statements on nearly every single topic of significance: creation, the history of Israel, questions of ethics and moral behavior, the nature and will of God, etc. In this diversity, the Bible presents statements on issues such as genocide, slavery, and marriage that most people in the modern era would rightfully deem immoral. Therefore, it is essential for all those who consider the Bible to be scripture to understand the insights scholars have gained through Historical Criticism.

Recently, the editors of the 2012 book, *The Bible and the Believer*, expressed this same point. In the introduction to the volume, the authors explain that seeking to understand the original historical context of the Bible and assessing its accuracy "allow(s) those who take the Bible seriously to make informed judgments about its current meaning and significance (or insignificance)."[1]

Throughout our history, Mormons have frequently approached the Bible from a Historical Critical perspective. We find this view at a very early stage in Church history through a letter written by Benton Pixley to

---

1. Marc Zvi Brettler, Peter Enns, and Daniel J. Harrington, S.J., *The Bible and the Believer: How to Read the Bible Critically and Religiously*, 3; for additional perspectives on the way critical study may be combined with religious engagement, see Robert A. Orsi, *Between Heaven and Earth: The Religious Worlds that People Make and the Scholars Who Study Them* (Princeton, N.J.: Princeton University Press, 2005).

the editor of the *Christian Watchman*, October 12, 1832.[2] Concerning the Mormon approach to the Bible taught by Church leaders, Pixley wrote:

> Their first, best, great and celebrated preacher, Elder Rigdon, tells us the Epistles are not and were not given for our instruction, but for the instruction of people of another age and country, far removed from ours, of different manners and habits, and needing different teaching; and that it is altogether inconsistent for us to take the Epistles written for that people, at that age of the world, as containing suitable instruction for this people, at this age of the world. The gospels, too, we are given by them to understand, are so mutilated and altered, as to convey little of the instruction, which they should convey. Hence we are told a new revelation is to be sought, —is to be expected; indeed is coming forthwith. Our present Bible is to be altered and restored to its primitive purity, by Smith, the present prophet of the Lord, and some books to be added of great importance, which have been lost.[3]

This statement suggests that in Mormonism, early Church leader Sydney Rigdon was openly teaching the Saints that the Bible must be read in accordance with its historical setting and that it contains errors.

Joseph Smith himself recognized these same points. "There are many things in the Bible," he once declared, "which do not, as they now stand, accord with the revelations of the Holy Ghost to me."[4] Joseph believed that the Bible had been subject to scribal editing and that it contained internal inconsistencies that required explanation. Moreover, he looked to scholars to learn more about the Bible, including its ancient languages and historical context. In a contemporary approach to the Old Testament, Latter-day Saint readers would do well to follow the Prophet's lead.

As a philosophy, Mormonism rejects the religious notion of dogma, meaning a principle set up by an authority as incontrovertibly true. Describing the religion of the Latter-day Saints, John Taylor said:

> [It] embraces every principle of truth and intelligence pertaining to us as moral, intellectual, mortal and immortal beings, pertaining to this world and the world that is to come. We are open to truth of every kind, no matter whence it comes, where it originates or who believes it . . . A man in search of the truth has no particular system to sustain, no particular dogma to defend or theory to uphold.[5]

---

2. This letter was later reprinted in *Independent Messenger*, November 29, 1832.

3. http://www.sidneyrigdon.com/dbroadhu/NE/miscne01.htm#112932. I'm grateful to Christopher Smith for drawing my attention to this source.

4. Joseph Smith, *Teachings of the Prophet Joseph Smith*, 310.

5. *Journal of Discourses*, 16:369.

This perspective is seen in the Article of Faith statement "[we believe God] will yet reveal many great and important things pertaining to the Kingdom of God" (Article of Faith 9). The idea of continuing revelation within Mormonism allows for the possibility of inspired correction of religious doctrines once held true.[6] Brigham Young explained this concept with these words:

> I do not even believe that there is a single revelation, among the many God has given to the Church that is perfect in its fullness. . . . [I]t is impossible for the poor, weak, low, groveling, sinful inhabitants of the earth to receive a revelation from the Almighty in all its perfections. He has to speak to us in a manner to meet the extent of our capacities. . . . [W]e are not capacitated to throw off in one day all our traditions, and our prepossessed feelings and notions, but have to do it little by little. . . . [I]f we continue so to grow we shall be prepared eventually to receive the Son of Man, and that is what we are after.[7]

For Brigham, revelation was given line upon line, precept upon precept. This is just as true for individuals and institutions today as it was in ancient Israel. For believers in the scriptural authenticity of the Bible, its diversity of religious views attests to the evolutionary nature of divine disclosure.

Revelation is far from complete. It must be interpreted. Divine insights, therefore, always pass through human filters. No matter how inspired, prophets are tied to their time and culture. Eugene England once expressed the matter in this way:

> Even after a revelation is received and expressed by a prophet, it has to be understood, taught, translated into other languages, and expressed in programs,

---

6. The validity of this point was recently brought home for many Latter-day Saints through the Church's online publication, "Race and the Priesthood." In the context of assessing past and present views on the topic of racism, the LDS Church officially declared:

> Today, the Church disavows the theories advanced in the past that black skin is a sign of divine disfavor or curse, or that it reflects actions in a premortal life; that mixed-race marriages are a sin; or that blacks or people of any other race or ethnicity are inferior in any way to anyone else. Church leaders today unequivocally condemn all racism, past and present, in any form.

For many years, a variety of Church leaders had presented authoritative views regarding skin color as a curse from God. As explained in this official publication, however, these religious views were a product of their time and incorrect. See "Race and the Priesthood," Website for the Church of Jesus Christ of Latter-day Saints, http://www.lds.org/topics/race-and-the-priesthood (accessed December 23, 2013).

7. Brigham Young, July 8, 1855, *Journal of Discourses*, 2:309–17.

manuals, sermons, and essays—in a word, interpreted. And that means that at least one more set of limitations of language and world-view enters in. I always find it perplexing when someone asks a teacher or speaker if what she is saying is the pure gospel or merely her own interpretation. Everything anyone says is essentially an interpretation. Even simply reading the scriptures to others involves interpretation, in choosing both what to read in a particular circumstance and how to read it (tone and emphasis). Beyond that point, anything we do becomes less and less 'authoritative' as we move into explication and application of the scriptures, that is, as we teach 'the gospel.'

For England, the fact that revelation always passes through human filters does not mean that individuals cannot receive insights that transcend certain boundaries. He did recognize, however, that in so doing, revelation does not supersede agency; that God gives revelation to his servants "in their weakness, after the manner of their language, that they might come to understanding" (D&C 1:24). England continues:

> Yes, I know that the Holy Ghost can give strokes of pure intelligence to the speaker and bear witness of truth to the hearer. I have experienced both of these lovely, reassuring gifts. But such gifts, which guarantee the overall guidance of the Church in the way the Lord intends and provide guidance, often of a remarkably clear nature, to individuals, still do not override individuality and agency. They are not exempt from the limitations of human language and moral perception that the Lord describes in [D&C 1:24], and thus they cannot impose universal acceptance and understanding.[8]

Since this process is true for modern revelation, Latter-day Saints must allow for the same approach to exist in the Old Testament. Historical Criticism allows readers to uncover this process in the development of biblical sources.

Human beings have always had an influence on the development of sacred texts. Allowing for human agency in the production of scripture has an analogy with Jesus Christ himself (i.e., the "Word of God"). The Gospel of John depicts Jesus in these terms:

> In the beginning was the Word, and the Word was with God, and the Word was God. . . . And the Word was made flesh, and dwelt among us, (and we beheld his glory, the glory as of the only begotten of the Father,) full of grace and truth. (John 1:1, 14)

---

8. Eugene England, "Why the Church is as True as the Gospel," 62.

Like Jesus himself, scripture is a divine word made flesh among us.[9] Evangelical scholar Peter Enn expresses the analogy this way:

> As Christ is both God and human, so is the Bible. In other words, we are to think of the Bible in the same way that Christians think about Jesus. Christians confess that Jesus is both God and human at the same time. He is not half-God and half-human. He is not sometimes one and other times the other. He is not essentially one and only apparently the other. . . . Jesus is 100 percent God and 100 percent human—at the same time. This way of thinking of Christ is analogous to thinking about the Bible. In the same way that Jesus is—must be—both God and human the Bible is also a divine and human book.[10]

The traditional LDS understanding of the Bible and scripture takes the metaphor of divine word being made flesh even further. As Joseph Smith once explained, Mormons "believe the Bible to be the word of God as far as it is translated correctly" (A of F 8). Implicit with the belief that the Bible contains errors introduced by humans, is the belief that there are portions of the Bible that are fully human and cannot be said to be divine. There is error; there is weakness; there is flesh. Historical Criticism allows Latter-day Saint readers to identify both attributes in the written word. Sacred words must pass through a human filter; there is therefore no such thing as the pure, unadulterated word of God. It is both human and divine.

It's important to note that the Bible is not alone as inspired, yet imperfect scripture. The Book of Mormon goes out of its way to remind readers that it is written by imperfect human beings. Its narrators constantly attest to the fact that they struggled to put into words their spiritual feelings. Moroni refers to this matter through the expression "my weakness in writing" (Ether 12:23, 25, 40). Moreover, fully aware that revelatory insights must always pass through imperfect human vessels, Nephi informs his readers,

> I do not write anything upon plates save it be that I think it be sacred. And now, if I do err, even did they err of old; not that I would excuse myself

---

9. This analogy has been expressed in Catholicism this way: "For the words of God, expressed in human language, have become like unto speech, just as the Word of the eternal Father, when he took on himself the flesh of human weakness, became like unto human beings" (*Der Verbum* 13).

10. Peter Enns, *Inspiration and Incarnation: Evangelicals and the Problem of the Old Testament*, 17–18. I am grateful to Benjamin Spackman for drawing my attention to this source.

because of other men, but because of the weakness which is in me, according to the flesh, I would excuse myself. (1 Ne. 19:6)

At the conclusion of his record, Nephi returned to this same theme, testifying that despite the weakness of his written record, Christ approved his words:

And I know that the Lord God will consecrate my prayers for the gain of my people. And the words which I have written in weakness will be made strong unto them; for it persuadeth them to do good; it maketh known unto them of their fathers; and it speaketh of Jesus, and persuadeth them to believe in him, and to endure to the end, which is life eternal. . . And if they are not the words of Christ, judge ye—for Christ will show unto you, with power and great glory, that they are his words, at the last day; and you and I shall stand face to face before his bar; and ye shall know that I have been commanded of him to write these things, notwithstanding my weakness. (2 Ne. 33:4, 11)

As Nephi attests, revelatory insights, no matter how inspired, must always pass through weak human vessels. In this process, mistakes are inevitably made, notwithstanding the sacred nature of religious texts. For this reason, in the title page of the Book of Mormon, Moroni explicitly recognized the possibility of error: "And now, if there are faults they are the mistakes of men; wherefore, condemn not the things of God, that ye may be found spotless at the judgment-seat of Christ." As Latter-day Saints, we must allow room for such error as we seek to expand our understanding through revelatory and scholarly insights.

This human-divine nature of scripture that can be understood through Historical Criticism requires us to alter our traditional LDS assumptions concerning the Old Testament. Historical Criticism also requires Latter-day Saints to shift some of our paradigms concerning modern revelatory texts. This shift, however, need not lead to the conclusion that these texts are somehow devoid of inspiration.

In his efforts to combine his revelatory work with past dispensations, Joseph, as a seer and translator, had the ability to create new scriptural texts. But these texts were never traditional translations that resulted from directly working with another language.[11] Instead, in the creation of scripture, Joseph's work reflects his understanding of divine creation. It is a process whereby structure or order is given to preexistent chaos. In translating, Joseph was imitating God and His creative work. The Prophet understood "translation" as a process whereby something (or even someone)

---

11. See Richard van Wagoner and Steven Walker, "Joseph Smith: 'The Gift of Seeing,'" 48–68.

was "carried off" or "moved from one place to another."[12] For example, in his revised version of Genesis, Joseph referred to ancient men of faith who entered into the order of the Son of God and were "translated and taken up into heaven" (JST, Gen. 14:32). Thus, in "translating," the Prophet took something that existed in the physical or temporal world (such as the Egyptian papyri or even the Bible itself) and translated that material to a higher, spiritual plane.

Moreover, Joseph's revisions of his United Firm documents into revelations received by the biblical prophet Enoch shows how the Prophet had the ability to create inspired scriptural material attributed to, but not truly written by ancient authors. Instead of reproducing what these individuals literally wrote, Joseph's texts create a link between previous religious dispensations and his own revelations. In so doing, Joseph's revelations use ancient prophetic figures from the Bible as mediators for establishing this bond.

The books of Moses and Abraham in the LDS canon offer not only correction, but additions to the sources from the Bible Latter-day Saints hold as both inspired and imperfect. The Book of Moses, for instance, provides the opening chapters of Genesis with a new *Sitz im Leben* as temple-based revelation. The Book of Abraham takes the beginning of Genesis and adds ancient theological paradigms such as a divine council of gods and the premortal existence of the human soul. These scriptural texts serve an essential role in Joseph's effort to not only correct some of the Bible's errors as he saw them, but to spiritually bind previous dispensations with the modern era. Through these books, we see that as a translator of religious texts, the Prophet Joseph Smith was a seer who made known that which was hidden from the world.

This perspective on translation and the production of scripture is important to conceptualize. It allows LDS readers who engage in Historical Criticism to see Joseph's work as inspired scripture, even when the Prophet may not have literally recreated ancient writings from biblical prophets. Texts such as the books of Moses and Abraham that revise ancient Judean scribal sources into revelatory documents for our day accomplish something more significant than a restoration of ancient writings. They combine ancient and modern paradigms into an organized religious construct that allows believers to place themselves spiritually into God's work and glory—past, present, and future.

---

12. Noah Webster, *American Dictionary of the English Language* (1828), s.v. "translation."

Ultimately, scripture finds its spiritual worth in the process of actualization, bringing something from the past into the present. It is the power to act rather than theorize. For Joseph Smith, the Bible was a collection of sacred religious texts with imperfections and human error. It needed, therefore, to be "translated correctly." From the Book of Mormon to the books of Moses and Abraham, Joseph's scriptural texts were designed to actualize the Bible in the lives of Latter-day Saints.

Historical Criticism (i.e., the act of interpreting the Bible in its original context while paying attention to its various authorial voices) allows Latter-day Saints to make informed judgments about the Bible's current meaning and significance (or insignificance) in their lives. From this angle, Historical Criticism is a spiritual quest. It can be an ally in the search for truth.

Recommended Readings
for Further Study

Joel Baden, *The Composition of the Pentateuch: Renewing the Documentary Hypothesis* (New Haven, Conn.: Yale University Press, 2012).

A comprehensive argument for the Documentary Hypothesis, this book presents textual case studies that illustrate the validity of source analysis as a practical model for the study of the text.

Adele Berlin, Marc Zvi Brettler, and Michael Fishbane, *The Jewish Study Bible* (Oxford: Oxford University Press, 2004).

An excellent modern translation of the Hebrew Bible, the Jewish Study Bible features essays and commentary from many of the premier Jewish scholars in biblical studies.

Marc Zvi Brettler, *How to Read the Bible* (Philadelphia: The Jewish Publication Society, 2005).

A general survey of the entire Hebrew Bible from a historical-critical perspective written for a Jewish audience. Brettler concludes the volume explaining how he is able to reconcile Historical Criticism with the fact that he is an observant Jew.

Michael D. Coogan, *The Old Testament: A Historical and Literary Introduction to the Hebrew Scriptures* (Oxford: Oxford University Press, 2010).

Designed as a textbook for college courses on the Hebrew Bible, this book provides a helpful introduction to the way scholars interpret the Old Testament from a historical-critical perspective.

Bart D. Ehrman, *The Bible: A Historical and Literary Introduction* (Oxford: Oxford University Press, 2014).

Designed as a textbook for college courses, Ehrman's book serves as a basic introduction to reading the entire Bible (Old and New Testament) from a historical-critical perspective.

Richard Elliot Friedman, *The Bible with Sources Revealed: A New View into the Five Books of Moses* (San Francisco: HarperSanFrancisco, 2003).

A visual presentation of the Pentateuch divided into its historical sources with different colors and type styles. Though not all scholars agree with some of the specific decisions Friedman makes concerning source attribution, this is a helpful recourse for students wishing to read through each documentary tradition.

Richard Elliot Friedman, *Who Wrote the Bible?* (HarperOne, 1987).

A basic introduction to the history and validity of the Documentary Hypothesis, including Friedman's own views concerning the historical development of the sources.

Richard Neitzel Holzapfel, Dana M. Pike, and David Rolph Seely, *Jehovah and the World of the Old Testament* (Salt Lake City: Deseret Book, 2009).

Written from an LDS perspective, this book contains pictures, graphs, and commentary that provide a helpful introduction to reading the Old Testament in its historical context.

William M. Schniedewind, *How the Bible Became a Book: The Textualization of Ancient Israel* (Cambridge: Cambridge Unversity Press, 2004).

This book focuses upon recent archaeological and textual discoveries that document the transition in Judean and Israelite cultures from orality to textuality during the late Iron Age (eighth through sixth centuries BC).

Bibliography

Abusch, Tzvi. "Biblical Accounts of Prehistory: Their Meaning and Formation." In *Bringing the Hidden to Light: The Process of Interpretation: Studies in Honor of Stephen A. Geller*, edited by Kathryn Kravitz. Winona Lake, Ind.: Eisenbrauns/Jewish Theological Seminary, 2007.

———. "Ghost and God: Some Observations on a Babylonian Understanding of Human Nature." In *Self, Soul, and Body in Religious Experience*, edited by Albert Baumgarten. Leiden: Brill, 1998.

———. "Marduk." In *Dictionary of Deities and Demons in the Bible*, edited by Karel van der Toorn, Bob Becking, and Pieter W. van der Horst. Leiden: Brill, 1995.

Albertz, Rainer. *A History of Israelite Religion in the Old Testament Period: From the Beginnings to the End of the Monarchy*. Westminster John Knox Press, 1994.

Alexander, Patrick H. and Shirley Decker-Lucke. *The Society of Biblical Literature Handbook of Style: For Ancient Near Eastern, Biblical, and Early Christian Studies*. Peabody: Hendrickson, 1999.

Alster, B. "Tiamat." In *Dictionary of Deities and Demons in the Bible*, edited by Karel van der Toorn, Bob Becking, Pieter W. van der Horst. Leiden: Brill, 1995.

Alter, Robert. *Genesis: Translation and Commentary*. New York: W.W. Norton & Company, 1997.

———. *The Art of Biblical Poetry*. New York: Basic Books, 1985.

Andersen, F. I. *The Sentence in Biblical Hebrew*. The Hague and Paris: Mouton, 1974.

Buber, Martin. "Leitwort Style in Pentateuch Narrative." In *Scripture and Translation*, edited by Martin Buber and Franz Rosenzweig; translated by Lawrence Rosenwald and Everett Fox. Bloomington: Indiana University Press, 1994.

Bachman, Danel W. "New Light on an Old Hypothesis: The Ohio Origins of the Revelation on Eternal Marriage." *Journal of Mormon History* 5 (1978): 19–32.

Bachvarova, Mary R. "Relations Between God and Man in the Hurro-Hittite 'Song of Release.'" *Journal of the American Oriental Society* 125 (2005): 45–58.

Baden, Joel S. *The Composition of the Pentateuch: Renewing the Documentary Hypothesis*. New Haven: Yale University Press, 2012.

_____. *J, E, and the Redaction of the Pentateuch*. Tübingen: Mohr Siebeck, 2009.

Barlow, Phillip L. *Mormons and the Bible: The Place of the Latter-day Saints in American Religion*. Oxford: Oxford University Press, 1991.

_____. "The Uniquely True Church." In *A Thoughtful Faith: Essays on Belief by Mormon Scholars*, edited by Philip L. Barlow. Centerville, Utah: Canon Press, 1986.

Barney, Kevin L. "The Facsimiles and Semitic Adaptation of Existing Sources." In *Traditions About the Early Life of Abraham*, edited by John A. Tvedtnes, Brian M. Hauglid, and John Gee. Provo, Utah: FARMS, 2001.

_____. "Joseph Smith's Emendation of Hebrew Genesis 1:1." *Dialogue: A Journal of Mormon Thought* 30, no. 4 (Winter 1997): 103–35.

_____. "Reflections on the Documentary Hypothesis." *Dialogue: A Journal of Mormon Thought* 33 (2000): 57–99.

Brettler, Marc Zvi. *Biblical Hebrew for Students of Modern Israeli Hebrew*. New Haven: Yale University Press, 2002.

_____. *How to Read the Bible*. Philadelphia: JPS, 2005.

_____. "Torah." In *The Jewish Study Bible*. Oxford: Oxford University Press, 2004.

Brettler, Marc Zvi, Peter Enns, and Daniel J. Harringon, S.J. *The Bible and the Believer: How to Read the Bible Critically and Religiously*. Oxford: Oxford University Press, 2012.

Berlin, Adele and Marc Zvi Brettler, eds. *The Jewish Study Bible*. Oxford: Oxford University Press, 2004.

_____, eds. "The Modern Study of the Bible." In *The Jewish Study Bible*. Oxford: Oxford University Press.

Blomberg, Craig L. and Stephen E. Robinson. *How Wide the Divide? A Mormon and an Evangelical in Conversation*. Downders Grove, Ill.: InterVarsity, 1997.

Boecker, Hans J. *Redeformen des Rechtslebens im Alten Testament*. Neukirchen: Neukirchener Verlag, 1964.

Bonino, José Miquez, Solomon Avotri, and Choan-Seng Song. "Genesis 11:1–9: A Latin-American Perspective." In *Return to Babel: Global Perspectives on the Bible*, edited by Priscilla Pope-Levison and John R. Levison. Louisville: Westminster John Knox, 1999.

Bokovoy, David E. "Invoking the Council as Witness." *Journal of Biblical Literature* 127 (2008): 37–51.

_____. "On Christ and Covenants: An LDS Reading of Isaiah's Prophetic Call." *Studies in the Bible and Antiquity* 3 (2011): 29–49.

_____. "'Ye Really Are Gods': A Response to Michael Heiser Concerning the LDS Use of Psalm 82 and the Gospel of John." *FARMS Review* 19 (2007): 267–313.

Bokovoy, David E. and John A. Tvedtnes. *Testaments: Links Between the Book of Mormon and the Hebrew Bible*. Tooele: Heritage Press, 2003.

"Book of Mormon Translation." Website for the Church of Jesus Christ of Latter-day Saints. Available at http://www.lds.org/topics/book-of-mormon-translation?lang=eng (accessed January 8, 2014).

Burnett, Joel. *A Reassessment of Biblical Elohim*. Atlanta: Scholars, 2001.

Bushman, Richard L. *Joseph Smith and the Beginnings of Mormonism*. Chicago: University of Illinois Press, 1984.

_____. *Joseph Smith: Rough Stone Rolling*. New York: Vintage, 2007.

Campbell, Anthony F. and Mark A. O'Brien. *Sources of the Pentateuch*. Minneapolis: Fortress Press, 2000.

_____. *Sources of the Pentateuch: Texts, Introductions, Annotations*. Minneapolis: Fortress Press, 1993.

Carr, David McLain. *The Formation of the Hebrew Bible: A New Reconstruction*. Oxford: Oxford University Press, 2011.

_____. "Response to W.M. Schniedewind, *How the Bible Became a Book: The Textualization of Ancient Israel*," *Journal of Hebrew Studies* 5 no. 18 (2004–2005):1–20.

_____. "The Tel Zayit Abecedary in (Social) Context." In *Literature Culture and Tenth-Century Canaan: The Tel Zayit Abecedary in Context*, edited by Ron E. Tappy, P. Kyle, and Jr. McCarter. Winona Lake, Ind.: Eisenbrauns, 2008.

Cassuto, Umberto. *A Commentary on the Book of Genesis Part II: From Noah to Abraham*. Jerusalem: Magnes, 1964.

Charlesworth, James. "Messianism in the Pseudepigrapha and the Book of Mormon." In *Reflections on Mormonism: Judaeo-Christian Parallels*. Provo, Utah: Religious Studies Center, 1978.

_____. *Old Testament Pseudepigrapha*. 2 vols. Garden City, N.Y.: Doubleday, 1983–87.

Cho, Sang Youl. *Lesser Deities in the Ugaritic Texts and the Hebrew Bible*. New Jersey: Gorgias Press, 2007.

Clark, James R. *Messages of the First Presidency of the Church of Jesus Christ of Latter-day Saints*. Vol. 5. Salt Lake City: Bookcraft, 1971.

Collins, John J. *The Bible After Babel: Historical Criticism in a Postmodern Age*. Grand Rapids: Eerdmans, 2005.

_____. "Cosmology: Time and History." In *Religions of the Ancient World: A Guide*, edited by Sarah Iles Johnson. Cambridge: Belknap Press of Harvard University Press, 2004.

_____. *Introduction to the Hebrew Bible*. Minneapolis: Fortress Press, 2004.

Coogan, Michael D. "In the Beginning: The Earliest History." In *The Oxford History of the Biblical World*, edited by Michael D. Coogan. Oxford: Oxford University Press, 1998.

_____. *The Old Testament: A Historical and Literary Introduction to the Hebrew Scriptures*. Oxford: Oxford University Press, 2010.

Dalley, Stephanie. "The Influence of Mesopotamia upon Israel and the Bible." In *The Legacy of Mesopotamia*, edited by Stephanie Dalley. Oxford: Oxford

University Press, 1998.

Davis, Ryan Conrad and Paul Y. Hoskisson. "Usage of the Title Elohim." In *Bountiful Harvest: Essays in Honor of S. Kent Brown*, edited by Andrew C. Skinner, D. Morgan Davis, and Carl Griffin. Provo, Utah: Neal A. Maxwell Institute for Religious Scholarship, 2011.

Delitzsch, Friedrich. *Babel and Bible; Two Lectures Delivered Before the Members of the Deutsche Orient-Gesellschaft in the Presence of the German Emperor.* New York: G. P. Putnam's Sons, 1903.

Dever, William. *Did God Have a Wife? Archaeology and Folk Religion in Ancient Israel.* Grand Rapids, Mich.: Eerdmans, 2005.

de Pury, Albert. "Yahwist ("J") Source." *Anchor Bible Dictionary* 6 (1992): 1013.

Dunn, J. D. G. "Pseudepigraphy." In *Dictionary of the Later New Testament and its Development*, edited by Ralph Martin and Peter Davids. IVP, 1997.

Ehat, Andrew F. and Lyndon W. Cook. *The Words of Joseph Smith: The Contemporary Accounts of the Nauvoo Discourses of the Prophet Joseph.* Bookcraft, 1980.

Ehrman, Bart D. *Forged: Writing in the Name of God—Why the Bible's Authors Are Not Who We Think They Are.* New York: HarperOne, 2011.

_____. *The New Testament: A Historical Introduction to the Early Christian Writings.* Oxford: Oxford University Press, 2007.

Eichler, B. L. "Literary Structure in the Laws of Eshnunna." In *Language, Literature, and History: Philological and Historical Studies Presented to Erica Reiner*, edited by F. Rochberg-Halton. New Haven: AOS, 1987.

Emerton, J. A. "An Examination of Some Attempts to Defend the Unity of the Flood Narrative in Genesis: Part II." *Vetus Testamentum* 38 (1988): 1–21.

England, Eugene. "Why the Church is as True as the Gospel." *Sunstone* (June 1999): 61–69.

Enns, Peter. *Inspiration and Incarnation: Evangelicals and the Problem of the Old Testament.* Grand Rapids, Mich.:Maker Academic, 2005.

Fairclough, Henry Rushton. *Horace Satires, Epistles and Ars Poetica.* Cambridge: Harvard University Press, 1939.

Fewell, Danna Nolan. "Building Babel." In *Postmodern Interpretations of the Bible: A Reader*, edited by A.K.M. Adam. St. Louis: Chalice, 2001.

Fishbane, Michael A. *Biblical Interpretation in Ancient Israel.* Oxford: Oxford University Press, 1984.

_____. *Biblical Myth and Rabbinic Mythmaking.* Oxford: Oxford University Press, 2003.

Fokkelmann, J. P. *Reading Biblical Narrative: An Introductory Guide.* Translated by Ineke Smit. Louisville, Ky.: Westminster John Knox, 1999.

Foster, Benjamin R., trans. *Before the Muses: An Anthology of Akkadian Literature.* Bethesda, Md.: CDL Press, 2005.

Fox, Nili S. "Leviticus: Introduction." In *The Jewish Study Bible*, edited by Adele Berlin and Marc Zvi Brettler. Oxford: Oxford University Press, 2004.

Friedman, Richard Elliott. *The Bible with Sources Revealed: A New View into the Five Books of Moses.* San Francisco, Calif.: HarperSanFrancisco, 2003.

————. *Commentary on the Torah.* New York: HarperOne, 2003.

————. "Current Thoughts About the Documentary Hypothesis." In *Empirical Models for Biblical Criticism.* Eugene, Ore.: Wipf & Stock Pub, 2005.

————. *Who Wrote the Bible?* San Francisco: HarperSanFrancisco, 1997.

Frymer-Kensky, Tikva. "The Atrahasis Epic and Its Significance for Our Understanding of Genesis 1–9." *The Biblical Archaeologist* 40 (1977): 147–55.

Gardner, Brant A. *The Gift and Power: Translating the Book of Mormon.* Salt Lake City: Greg Kofford Books, 2011.

————. "Musings on the Makings of Mormon's Book: Preliminary: Nephi as Author." *Interpreter: A Journal of Mormon Scripture* (blog). http://www.mormoninterpreter.com/musings-on-the-making-of-mormons-book-preliminary-nephi-as-author/#more-3075 (accessed October 22, 2013).

Gaskill, Alonzo L. *The Lost Language of Symbolism.* Salt Lake City: Deseret Book, 2003.

Gee, John. *A Guide to the Joseph Smith Papyri.* Provo, Utah: FARMS, 2000.

————. "New Light on the Joseph Smith Papyri." FARMS Review 19, no. 2 (2007): 245–59.

————. "A Tragedy of Errors." In *Review of Books on the Book of Mormon* 4, no. 1 (1992): 93–119.

Gee, John and Stephen D. Ricks. "Historical Plausibility: The Historicity of the Book of Abraham as a Case Study." In *Historicity and the Latter-day Saint Scriptures,* edited by Paul Y. Hoskisson. Provo, Utah: BYU Religious Studies Center, 2001.

Geller, Stephen A. "Fiery Wisdom: Logos and Lexis in Deuteronomy 4." *Prooftexts* 14 (1994): 116.

Givens, Terryl. *By the Hand of Mormon: The American Scripture that Launched a New World Religion.* Oxford: Oxford University Press, 2003.

Givens, Terryl and Fiona Givens. *The God Who Weeps: How Mormonism Makes Sense of Life.* Salt Lake City: Ensign Peak, 2012.

Gottwald, Norman K. *The Hebrew Bible: A Socio-Literary Introduction.* Fortress Press, 1985.

Graupner, Axel. *Der Elohist: Gegenwart und Wirksamkeit des transzendenten Gottes in der Geschichte.* Neukirchen-Vluyn: Neukirchener Verglag, 2002.

Griggs, C. Wilfred. *Apocryphal Writings and the Latter-day Saints.* Salt Lake City: Kofford Books, 2007.

Hallo, William H. and Lawson K. Younger, ed. *The Context of Scripture.* Leiden: Brill, 2003.

Handy, Lowell K. *Among the Host of Heaven: The Syro-Palestinian Pantheon as Bureaucracy.* Winona Lake: Eisenbrauns, 1994.

Hardy, Grant. *Understanding the Book of Mormon: A Reader's Guide.* Oxford: Oxford University Press, 2010.

Harrell, Charles R. *This is My Doctrine: The Development of Mormon Theology.*

Draper, Utah: Greg Kofford Books, 2011.

Hauglid, Brian M. *A Textual History of the Book of Abraham: Manuscripts and Editions*. Provo, Utah: Maxwell Institute, 2010.

Heidel, Alexander. *The Babylonian Genesis*. Chicago: The University of Chicago Press, 1951.

_____. *The Gilgamesh Epic and Old Testament Parallels*. Chicago: University of Chicago Press, 1963.

Heiser, Michael S. "The Mythological Provenance of Isa. XIV 12–15: A Reconsideration of the Ugaritic Material." *Vetus Testamentum* 51, no. 3 (2001): 354–69.

Hendel, Ronald S. "Leitwort Style and Literary Structure in the J Primeval Narrative." In *Sacred History, Sacred Literature: Essays on Ancient Israel, the Bible, and Religion in Honor of R.E. Friedman on his Sixtieth Birthday*, edited by Shawn Dolansky. Winona Lake: Eisenbrauns, 2008.

Herion, Gary A. "Why God Rejected Cain's Offering: The Obvious Answer." In *Fortunate the Eyes that See: Essays in Honor of David Noel Freedman in Celebration of his Seventieth Birthday*, edited by Astrid Beck. Grand Rapids, Mich.: Eerdmans, 1995.

Hinckley, Gordon B. "The Great Things Which God Has Revealed." *Ensign*, May 2005, 80–83.

Hobbes, Thomas. *Leviathan with Selected Variants from the Latin of 1668*. Edited by Edwin Curley. Indianapolis: Hackett Publishing Company, 1994.

Hoskisson, Paul Y. "Where Was Ur of the Chaldees?" In *The Pearl of Great Price: Revelations from God*, edited by Donl Peterson. Provo, Utah: BYU Religious Studies Center, 1989.

Hurowitz, Victor. "The Genesis of Genesis: Is the Creation Story Babylonian?" *Bible Review* 21 (2005): 36–48.

_____. "P—Understanding the Priestly Source." *Bible Review* June (1996): 30.

Jackson, Kent P. *The Book of Moses and the Joseph Smith Translation Manuscripts*. http://rsc.byu.edu/es/archived/book-moses-and-joseph-smith-translation-manuscripts/history-book-moses (accessed November 25, 2013).

Jacobsen, Thorkild. *The Harps that Once: Sumerian Poetry in Translation*. New Haven: Yale University Press, 1987.

_____. "Sumerian Mythology: A Review Article." *Journal of Near Eastern Studies* 5 (1946): 136.

Jenks, Alan W. "Elohist." In *The Anchor Bible Dictionary*, edited by David Noel Freedman. New York: Doubleday, 1992.

Jensen, Robin Scott, Robert J. Woodford, and Steven C. Harper, eds. *Revelations and Translations, Volume 1: Manuscript Revelation Books*. Vol. 1 of the Revelations and Translations series of *The Joseph Smith Papers*, edited by Dean C. Jessee, Ronald K. Esplin, and Richard Lyman Bushman. Salt Lake City: Church Historian's Press, 2011.

Jessee, Dean C. "Early Accounts of Joseph Smith's First Vision." *BYU Studies* 9

(1969): 275–94.

_____., ed. and comp. *The Personal Writings of Joseph Smith*. Salt Lake City: Deseret Book, 1984.

Joüon, Paul and T. Muraoka. *A Grammar of Biblical Hebrew*. Subsidia Biblica 14. Roma: Editrice Pontificio Instituto Biblico, 1991.

Journal of Discourses, 26 vols. London and Liverpool: LDS Booksellers Depot, 1854–86.

Klostermann, August. *Der Pentateuch*. Leipzig, 1893.

Knohl, Israel. *The Sanctuary of Silence: The Priestly Torah and the Holiness School*. Minneapolis: Fortress Press, 1995.

Koehler, Ludwig and Walter Baumgartner. *The Hebrew and Aramaic Lexicon of the Old Testament*. Study Edition. 2 vols. Leiden: Brill, 1988.

Kramer, Samuel Noah. "Mythology of Sumer and Akkad." In *Mythologies of the Ancient World*, edited by Samuel Noah Kramer. New York: Anchor, 1960.

Kraus, Hans-Joachim. *Theology of the Psalms*. Edited by Keith Crim. Minneapolis: Fortress Press, 1992.

Kugel, James. *The Bible as it Was*. Cambridge: Belknap Press, 1999.

_____. *The Ideal of Biblical Poetry: Parallelism and its History*. Baltimore: John Hopkins University Press, 1998.

Larsen, Mogens Trolle. "The 'Babel/Bible' Controversy and its Aftermath." In *Civilizations of the Ancient Near East*, edited by Jack M. Sasson. Vol 1. Peabody: Hendrickson, 2000.

Larson, Charles M. *By His Own Hand Upon Papyrus: A New Look at the Joseph Smith Papyri*. Grand Rapids, Mich.: Institute for Religious Research, 1992.

Levenson, Jon D. "Genesis: Introduction." In *The Jewish Study Bible*, edited by Adele Berlin and Marc Zvi Brettler. Oxford: Oxford University Press, 2004.

Levinson, Bernard M. *Deuteronomy and the Hermeneutics of Legal Innovation*. New York: Oxford University Press, 1997.

_____. "Deuteronomy: Introduction." In *The Jewish Study Bible*, edited by Adele Berlin and Marc Zvi Brettler. Oxford: Oxford University Press, 2004.

_____. *Legal Revision and Religious Renewal in Ancient Israel*. Cambridge: Cambridge University Press, 2008.

Lichtheim, Miriam. "Instruction of Amenemope (1.47)." In *The Context of Scripture*, edited by William H. Hallo and Lawson K. Younger, 1:115. Leiden: Brill, 2003.

Lohfink, N. "Hate and Love in Osee 9, 15." *Catholic Biblical Quarterly* 25, no. 4 (1963): 417.

Ludlow, Jared W. *Abraham Meets Death: Narrative Humor in the Testament of Abraham*. New York: Sheffield Academic Press, 2002.

_____. "Reinterpretation of the Judgment Scene in the Testament of Abraham."

In *Proceedings of the Evolving Egypt: Innovation, Appropriation and Reinterpretation*, edited by John Gee and Kerry Muhlestein. Oxford: British Archaeological Reports, 2012.

Luz, Ulrich. *Matthew 1–7: A Commentary on Matthew 1–7*. Translated by James E. Crouch. Edited by Helmut Koester. Minneapolis: Fortress Press, 2007.

Magonet, J. *Form and Meaning: Studies in Literary Techniques in the Book of Jonah*. Sheffield: Almond Press, 1983.

Margueron, Jean-Cl. "Ur." In *The Anchor Bible Dictionary*. Translated by Stephen Rosoff. New York: Doubleday, 1992.

Marquardt, H. Michael. *The Joseph Smith Revelations Text and Commentary*. Salt Lake City: Signature Book, 1999.

Matthews, Victor Harold and Don C. Benjamin. *Old Testament Parallels: Laws and Stories from the Ancient Near East*. Mahwah, N.J.: Paulist Press, 2007.

McKenzie, Steven L. "The Deuteronomistic History." *Anchor Bible Dictionary* 2:160.

Miller, Patrick D. "Cosmology and World Order in the Old Testament." In *Israelite Religion and Biblical Theology; Collected Essays*. Sheffield: Sheffield Academic Press, 2000.

Millet, Robert. "How Should Our Story Be Told." In *To Be Learned is Good If: A Response by Mormon Educators to Controversial Religious Questions*. Salt Lake City: Bookcraft, 1987.

_____. "The Plates of Brass: A Witness of Christ." *Ensign*, Jan. 1988, 26–29.

Moran, William L. "The Ancient Near Eastern Background of the Love of God in Deuteronomy." *Catholic Biblical Quarterly* 25 (1963): 77–87.

_____. *The Most Magic Word: Essays on Babylonian and Biblical Literature*. Edited by Ronald S. Hendel. Washington, DC: Catholic Biblical Association of America, 2002.

Muhlestein, Kerry. "Abraham, Isaac, and Osiris-Michael: The Use of Biblical Figures in Egyptian Religion, a Survey." *Achievements and Problems of Modern Egyptology: Proceedings of the International Conference Held in Moscow on September 29–October 2, 2009*, edited by Galina A. Belova. Moscow: 2011.

_____. "Egyptian Papyri and the Book of Abraham: Some Questions and Answers." *Religious Educator* 11 (2010): 91–108.

Nibley, Hugh. *Message of the Joseph Smith Papyri: An Egyptian Endowment*. Edited by John Gee and Michael D. Rhodes. Salt Lake City: Deseret Book, 2005.

Nickelsburg, George W. E. *1 Enoch 1: A Commentary of the Book of Enoch Chapters 1–36, 81–108*. Hermeneia; Minneapolis: Fortress, 2001.

_____. "The Nature and Function of Revelation in 1 Enoch, Jubilees, and Some Qumranic Documents." In *Pseudepigraphic Perspectives: The Apocrypha and Pseudepigrapha in Light of the Dead Sea Scrolls*, edited by Esther G. Chazon, et al. Leiden: Brill, 1999.

_____. "Revealed Wisdom as a Criterion for Inclusion and Exclusion: From Jewish Sectarianism to Early Christianity." In *To See Ourselves as Others See*, edited by J. Neusner and E. S. Frerichs. Atlanta: Scholars Press, 1985.

North, Martin. The Deuteronomistic History. *Journal for the Study of the Old Testament* 15; JSOT Press, 1881/1991.

Noth, Martin. *Exodus: A Commentary*. Philadelphia: The Westminster Press, 1962.

Oppenheim, A. L. et al., eds. *Chicago Assyrian Dictionary of the Oriental Institute of the University of Chicago*. Chicago: University of Chicago Press, 1956–2011.

Orsi, Robert A. *Between Heaven and Earth: The Religious Worlds that People Make and the Scholars Who Study Them*. Princeton, N.J.: Princeton University Press, 2005.

Ostler, Blake T. "The Book of Mormon as a Modern Expansion of an Ancient Source." *Dialogue: A Journal of Mormon Thought* 20, no. 1 (Spring 1987): 66–123.

Otto, Eckart. "Political Theology in Judah and Assyria: The Beginning of the Hebrew Bible as Literature." *Svensk Exegetisk Årsbok* 65 (2000): 72–75.

Paine, Thomas. *The Age of Reason, Being an Investigation of True and Fabulous Theology (Part 1 and 2)*. Thomas Paine Foundation, 2009.

Parker, Simon B. "Council." In *Dictionary of Deities and Demons in the Bible*, edited by Karel van der Toorn et al. 2nd ed. Grand Rapids, Mich.: Eerdmans, 1999.

Parker, Simon B. "The Beginning of the Reign of God—Psalm 82 as Myth and Liturgy." *Revue Biblique* 102, no. 4 (1995): 532–59.

Pettinato, Giovanni. *Das altorientalische Menschenbild und die sumerischen und akkadischen Schopfungsmythen*. Heidelberg: Carl Winter Universitatsverlag, 1971.

Plato. *Timaeus*, Translated by Robin Waterfield. Oxford World's Classics. Oxford: Oxford University Press 2008.

Pritchard, James B., ed. *Ancient Near Eastern Texts Relating to the Old Testament*. Princeton University Press, 1969.

Propp, William Henry. *Exodus 19–40: A New Translation with Introduction and Commentary*. New York: Doubleday, 2006.

_____. "The Priestly Source Recovered Intact?" *Vetus Testamentum* 46 (1996): 458–78.

Rathbone, Tim and John W. Welch. "Book of Mormon Translation by Joseph Smith." In *Encyclopedia of Mormonism*, edited by Daniel H. Ludlow. 4 Vols., 1:210–13. New York : Macmillan, 1992.

Reed, Annette Yoshiko. "Pseudepigraphy, Authorship and the Reception of 'the Bible' in Late Antiquity." In *The Reception and Interception of the Bible in Late Antiquity*, edited by L. DiTommason and L. Turcescu. Leiden: Brill, 2008.

Rhodes, Michael. *The Hor Book of Breathings: A Translation and Commentary*.

Provo, Utah: FARMS, 2002.

Ritner, Robert K. *The Joseph Smith Egyptian Papyri*. Salt Lake City: Signature Book, 2011.

Roberts, B. H. *The Seventy's Course of Theology*. Vol. V. Salt Lake City: The Deseret News, 1912.

_____. "The Translation of the Book of Mormon." *Improvement Era* 9 (April 1906): 435–36.

Roux, George. *Ancient Iraq*. New York: Penguin History, 1993.

Saaenz-Badillos, Angel. *A History of the Hebrew Language*. Cambridge: Cambridge University Press, 1996.

Saggs, H. W. F. *The Encounter with the Divine in Mesopotamia and Israel*. London: London Athlone Press, 1978.

Sandberg, Karl C. "The Book of Abraham and Joseph Smith as Translator." *Dialogue: A Journal of Mormon Thought* 22, no. 4 (Winter 1989): 19–56.

Sanders, Seth L. *The Invention of Hebrew*. Urbana: University of Illinois Press, 2009.

Schmid, Konrad. "Has European Scholarship Abandoned the Documentary Hypothesis? Some Reminders on Its History and Remarks on Its Current Status." In *The Pentateuch: International Perspectives on Current Research*, edited by Thomas Dozeman et al. Tübingen: Mohr Siebeck, 2011.

Schmidt, Werner H. *Die Schöpfungsgeschichte der Priesterschaft*. BWANT 17; Neukirchen: Neukirchener Verlag, 1964.

Schniedewind, William M. *How the Bible Became a Book: The Textualization of Ancient Israel*. Cambridge: Cambridge Unversity Press, 2004.

Schramm, Gene M. "Languages (Hebrew)." In *The Anchor Bible Dictionary*, edited by David Noel Freedman. New York: Doubleday, 1992.

Schwartz, Baruch J. "Leviticus Introduction." In *The Jewish Study Bible*, edited by Adele Berlin and Marc Zvi Brettler. Oxford: Oxford University Press, 2004.

_____. "The Pentateuch as Scripture and the Challenge of Biblical Criticism: Responses Among Modern Jewish Thinkers and Scholars." In *Jewish Concepts of Scripture a Comparative Introduction*, edited by Benjamin D. Sommer. New York and London: New York University Press, 2012.

_____. "The Visit of Jethro: A Case of Chronological Displacement?: The Source-Critical Solution." In *Mishneh Todah: Studies in Deuteronomy and Its Cultural Enviornment in Honor of Jeffrey H. Tigay*, edited by Nili Sacher and David Glatt-gilad. Winona Lake, Ind.: Eisenbrauns, 2009.

Seidel, Moshe. "Parallels between Isaiah and Psalms." *Sinai* 38 (1955–56): 149–72, 272–80, 335–55.

Seixas, Joshua. Certificate. 30 March 1836. http://josephsmithpapers.org/paper-Summary/certificate-from-joshua-seixas-30-march-1836?p=1 (accessed on November 15, 2012).

Ska, Jean Louis. "From History Writing to Library Building: The End of History and the Birth of the Book." In *The Pentateuch as Torah: New Models for Understanding Its Promulgation and Acceptance*, edited by Gary

Knoppers and Jon Levenson. Winona Lake, Ind.: Eisenbrauns, 2007.

Skousen, Royal. *Analysis of Textual Variants of the Book of Mormon, Part One: 1 Nephi 1–2 Nephi 10*. Provo, Utah: Foundation for Ancient Research & Mormon Studies, 2004.

_____., ed. *The Book of Mormon: The Earliest Text*. New Haven, Conn.: Yale University Press, 2009.

Smelik, K.A.D. "The Origin of Psalm 20." *Journal for the Study of the Old Testament* 31 (1985): 75–81.

Smith, Christopher C. "The Inspired Fictionalization of the 1835 United Firm Revelations." *The Claremont Journal of Mormon Studies* 1 (2011): 15–31.

Smith, Mark S. *The Memoirs of God: History, Memory, and the Experience of the Divine in Ancient Israel*. Minneapolis: Fortress Press, 2004.

_____. *The Priestly Vision of Genesis 1*. Minneapolis: Fortress Press, 2009.

Smith, Joseph, et al. *History of the Church of Jesus Christ of Latter-day Saints*, edited by B. H. Roberts, 7 vols., 2nd ed. rev. Salt Lake City: Deseret Book, 1948 printing.

_____. "Journal, December 1841–December 1842," Joseph Smith Papers, http://josephsmithpapers.org/paperSummary/journal-december-1841-december-1842?p=25 (accessed on November 25, 2013).

_____. *Teachings of the Prophet Joseph Smith*. Compiled and edited by Joseph Fielding Smith. Salt Lake City: Deseret Book, 1977.

_____. *The Words of Joseph Smith: The Contemporary Accounts of the Nauvoo Discourses of the Prophet Joseph*. Edited by Andrew F. Ehat and Lyndon W. Cook. Provo, Utah: BYU Religious Studies Center, 1980.

Sorensen, John L. "The Brass Plates and Biblical Scholarship." *Dialogue: A Journal of Mormon Thought* 10 (1977): 36.

Speiser, E.A. *Genesis: Introduction, Translation, and Notes*. New York: Doubleday, 1964.

Stackert, Jeffrey. *Rewriting the Torah: Literary Revision in Deuteornomy and the Holiness Legislation (Forschunmgen Zum Alten Testament)*. FAT 52; Tübingen: Mohr Siebeck, 2007.

Stolz, F. "Sea." In *Dictionary of Deities and Demons in the Bible*, edited by Karen van der Toorn, et al. 2nd ed. Grand Rapids, Mich.: Eerdmans, 1999.

Talon, Philippe. *The Standard Babylonian Creation Myth: Enuma Elish*. SAACT 4; Helsinki: The Neo-Assyrian Text Corpus Project, 2005.

Tatian. *The Diatessaron of Tatian*. Translated by Hope W. Hogg. Nabu Press, 2009.

Thomas, Matthew A. *These Are the Generations: Identity, Covenant, and the 'Toledot' Formula*. New York: T&T Clark, 2011.

Tidwell, N.L.A. "*Wāōmar* (Zech 3:5) and the Genre of Zechariah's Fourth Vision." *Journal of Biblical Literature* 94 (1975): 343–55.

Tigay, Jeffrey H. *Deuteronomy; JPS Torah Commentary*. Philadelphia: The Jewish Publication Soceity, 1996.

_____. "Documentary Hypothesis Confirmed," *Biblical Archeology Review*

Sept/Oct (2008): 8–10.

_____. "The Documentary Hypothesis, Empirical Models and Holistic Interpretation." In *Modernity and Interpretations of Ancient Texts: The Collapse and Remaking of Traditions*, edited by Jun Ikeda, et al. International Institute of Advanced Studies, Kizugawa-City: Kyoto, Japan, 2012.

_____. *Empirical Models for Biblical Criticism*. Eugene, Ore.: Wipf & Stock Pub, 2005.

_____. *The Evolution of the Gilgamesh Epic*. Wauconda, Ill.: Bolchazy-Carducci Publishers, Inc., 2002.

_____. "Exodus: Introduction." In *The Jewish Study Bible*, edited by Adele Berlin and Marc Zvi Brettler. Oxford: Oxford University Press, 2004.

_____. "On Evaluating Claims of Literary Borrowing." In *The Tablet and the Scroll: Near Eastern Studies in Honor of William W. Hallo*, edited by Mark Cohen et al. Bethesda, Md.: CDL Press, 1993.

Todd, Jay M. *The Saga of the Book of Abraham*. Salt Lake City: Deseret Book Company, 1969.

Tvedtnes, John A. and Stephen D. Ricks. "Jewish and Other Semitic Texts Written in Egyptian Characters." *Journal of Book of Mormon Studies* 5, no. 2 (1996): 156–63.

VanderKam, James C. *From Revelation to Canon: Studies in the Hebrew Bible and Second Temple Literature*. Leiden: Brill, 1999.

van der Toorn, Karel. *Scribal Culture and the Making of the Hebrew Bible*. Cambridge: Harvard University Press, 2007.

_____. "Yahweh." In *Dictionary of Deities and Demons in the Bible*. Edited by Karel van der Toorn, Bob Becking, and Pieter W. van der Horst. Leiden: Brill, 1995.

van Wagoner, Richard and Steven Walker. "Joseph Smith: 'The Gift of Seeing.'" *Dialogue* 15 (Summer 1982): 48–68.

Vater, Johann Severin. *Commentar über den Pentateuch: Mit Einleitungen zu den einzelnen Abschnitten, der eingeschalteten Übersetzung von Dr. Alexander Geddes's merkwurdigeren critischen und exegetischen Anmerkungen, und einer Abhandlung über Moses und Verfasser des Pentateuchs*. Halle: Waisenhaus-Buchhandlung, 1802–1805.

Waltke, Bruce K. and M. O'Connor. *An Introduction to Biblical Hebrew Syntax*. Winona Lake: Eisenbrauns, 1990.

Walton, Michael T. "Professor Seixas, the Hebrew Bible and the Book of Abraham." *Sunstone* March/April 43 (1981): 41–43.

Watson, John A. *Ancient Israelite Literature in its Cultural Context*. Grand Rapids, Mich.: Zondervan, 1994.

Webster, Noah. *American Dictionary of the English Language* (1828). Facsimile edition. Anaheim, Calif.: Foundation for American Christian Education, 1967.

Weinfeld, Moshe. *Deuteronomy and the Deuteronomic School*. Winona Lake, Ind.:

Eisenbrauns, 1992.

Welch, John W. "Authorship of the Book of Isaiah." In *Isaiah in the Book of Mormon*, edited by Donald W. Parry and John Welch. Provo, Utah: FARMS, 1988.

————, ed. *Chiasmus in Antiquity: Structures, Analysis, Exegesis*. Provo, Utah: FARMS, 1998.

————. "The Case of Sherem." In *The Legal Cases in the Book of Mormon*, 107–38. Provo, Utah: Brigham Young University Press and the Neal A. Maxwell Institute for Religious Scholarship, 2008.

————. *The Legal Cases in the Book of Mormon*. Provo, Utah: Brigham Young University Press and the Neal A. Maxwell Institute for Religious Scholarship, 2008.

Wenham, G. J. "The Coherence of the Flood Narrative." *Vetus Testamentum* 28 (1978): 336–48.

Westenholz, Joan Goodnick. "Review: *In The Shadow of the Muses a View of Akkadian Literature*." *Journal of the American Oriental Society* 119 (1999): 83–84.

Whisenant, J. "Review—Literate Culture and Tenth-Century Canaan: The Tel Zayit Abecedary in Context," *Journal of the American Oriental Society* 129 (2009): 550–52.

Widtsoe, John A. *Evidences And Reconciliations*. Salt Lake City: Bookcraft, 1987.

————. *In Search of Truth: Comments on the Gospel and Modern Thought*. Salt Lake City: Deseret Book, 1930.

Williams, James G. "The Prophetic Father: A Brief Explanation of the Term Sons of the Prophets." *Journal of Biblical Literature* 85 (1966): 345.

Winter, Irene J. "The King and the Cup: Iconography of the Royal Presentation Scene on Ur III Seals." *Insight Through Images: Studies in Honor of Edith Porada*. Malibu: Undena Publications, 1986.

Woods, Christopher. "The Practice of Egyptian Religion at 'Ur of the Chaldees'?" In Robert K. Ritner, *The Joseph Smith Egyptian Papyri*. Salt Lake City: Signature Book, 2011.

Wright, David P. "Holiness in Leviticus and Beyond." *Interpreter* 53, no. 4 (1999): 351–63.

————. "Holiness, Sex and Death in the Garden of Eden." *Biblica* 77 (1996): 312–22.

————. *Inventing God's Law: How the Covenant Code of the Bible Used and Revised the Laws of Hammurabi*. Oxford: Oxford University Press, 2013.

————. "Profane Versus Sacrifical Slaughter: The Priestly Recasting of the Yahwist Flood Story." In *Current Issues in Priestly and Related Literature: The Legacy of Jacob Milgrom and Beyond*, edited by Roy Gane and Ada Taggar-Cohen. Place: Publisher, forthcoming.

Wright, G. E. *The Old Testament Against Its Environment*. London: SCM Press LTD, 1950.

Wyatt, Nicholas. "Degrees of Divinity: Some Mythical and Ritual Aspects of West Semitic Kingship." *Ugarit-Forschungen* 3 (1999): 853–87.

Wyrick, Jed. *The Ascension of Authorship: Attribution and Canon Formation in Jewish, Hellenistic, and Christian Traditions.* Cambridge: Department of Comparative Literature, 2004.

Yerushalmi, Yosef Hayim. *Zakhor: Jewish History and Jewish Memory.* Seattle: University of Washington Press, 1982.

Yoreh, Tzemah. *The First Book of God.* Berlin: de Gruyter, 2010.

Zanovello, Luciano. "Enuma Elish e Bibbia Ebraica." *Bibbia e Oriente* 48 (2006): 205–22.

Zucker, Louis C. "Joseph Smith as a Student of Hebrew." *Dialogue: A Journal of Mormon Thought* 3 (1968): 41–55.

Scripture Index

Subject Index

Also available from
GREG KOFFORD BOOKS

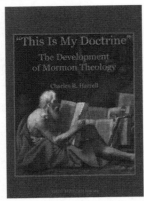

"This is My Doctrine":
The Development of Mormon Theology

Charles R. Harrell

Hardcover, ISBN: 978-1-58958-103-6

The principal doctrines defining Mormonism today often bear little resemblance to those it started out with in the early 1830s. This book shows that these doctrines did not originate in a vacuum but were rather prompted and informed by the religious culture from which Mormonism arose. Early Mormons, like their early Christian and even earlier Israelite predecessors, brought with them their own varied culturally conditioned theological presuppositions (a process of convergence) and only later acquired a more distinctive theological outlook (a process of differentiation).

In this first-of-its-kind comprehensive treatment of the development of Mormon theology, Charles Harrell traces the history of Latter-day Saint doctrines from the times of the Old Testament to the present. He describes how Mormonism has carried on the tradition of the biblical authors, early Christians, and later Protestants in reinterpreting scripture to accommodate new theological ideas while attempting to uphold the integrity and authority of the scriptures. In the process, he probes three questions: How did Mormon doctrines develop? What are the scriptural underpinnings of these doctrines? And what do critical scholars make of these same scriptures? In this enlightening study, Harrell systematically peels back the doctrinal accretions of time to provide a fresh new look at Mormon theology.

"*This Is My Doctrine*" will provide those already versed in Mormonism's theological tradition with a new and richer perspective of Mormon theology. Those unacquainted with Mormonism will gain an appreciation for how Mormon theology fits into the larger Jewish and Christian theological traditions.

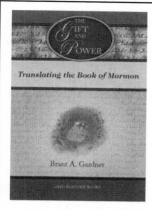

The Gift and Power: Translating the Book of Mormon

Brant A. Gardner

Hardcover, ISBN: 978-1-58958-131-9

From Brant A. Gardner, the author of the highly praised *Second Witness* commentaries on the Book of Mormon, comes *The Gift and Power: Translating the Book of Mormon*. In this first book-length treatment of the translation process, Gardner closely examines the accounts surrounding Joseph Smith's translation of the Book of Mormon to answer a wide spectrum of questions about the process, including: Did the Prophet use seerstones common to folk magicians of his time? How did he use them? And, what is the relationship to the golden plates and the printed text?

Approaching the topic in three sections, part 1 examines the stories told about Joseph, folk magic, and the translation. Part 2 examines the available evidence to determine how closely the English text replicates the original plate text. And part 3 seeks to explain how seer stones worked, why they no longer work, and how Joseph Smith could have produced a translation with them.

Second Witness: Analytical and Contextual Commentary on the Book of Mormon

Brant A. Gardner

Second Witness, a new six-volume series from Greg Kofford Books, takes a detailed, verse-by-verse look at the Book of Mormon. It marshals the best of modern scholarship and new insights into a consistent picture of the Book of Mormon as a historical document. Taking a faithful but scholarly approach to the text and reading it through the insights of linguistics, anthropology, and ethnohistory, the commentary approaches the text from a variety of perspectives: how it was created, how it relates to history and culture, and what religious insights it provides.

The commentary accepts the best modern scholarship, which focuses on a particular region of Mesoamerica as the most plausible location for the Book of Mormon's setting. For the first time, that location—its peoples, cultures, and historical trends—are used as the backdrop for reading the text. The historical background is not presented as proof, but rather as an explanatory context.

The commentary does not forget Mormon's purpose in writing. It discusses the doctrinal and theological aspects of the text and highlights the way in which Mormon created it to meet his goal of "convincing . . . the Jew and Gentile that Jesus is the Christ, the Eternal God."

Praise for the *Second Witness* series:

"Gardner not only provides a unique tool for understanding the Book of Mormon as an ancient document written by real, living prophets, but he sets a standard for Latter-day Saint thinking and writing about scripture, providing a model for all who follow. . . . No other reference source will prove as thorough and valuable for serious readers of the Book of Mormon."

-Neal A. Maxwell Institute, Brigham Young University

1. 1st Nephi: 978-1-58958-041-1
2. 2nd Nephi–Jacob: 978-1-58958-042-8
3. Enos–Mosiah: 978-1-58958-043-5
4. Alma: 978-1-58958-044-2
5. Helaman–3rd Nephi: 978-1-58958-045-9
6. 4th Nephi–Moroni: 978-1-58958-046-6

Hugh Nibley:
A Consecrated Life

Boyd Jay Petersen

Hardcover, ISBN: 978-1-58958-019-0

Winner of the Mormon History Association's Best Biography Award

As one of the LDS Church's most widely recognized scholars, Hugh Nibley is both an icon and an enigma. Through complete access to Nibley's correspondence, journals, notes, and papers, Petersen has painted a portrait that reveals the man behind the legend.

Starting with a foreword written by Zina Nibley Petersen and finishing with appendices that include some of the best of Nibley's personal correspondence, the biography reveals aspects of the tapestry of the life of one who has truly consecrated his life to the service of the Lord.

Praise for *A Consecrated Life*:

"Hugh Nibley is generally touted as one of Mormonism's greatest minds and perhaps its most prolific scholarly apologist. Just as hefty as some of Nibley's largest tomes, this authorized biography is delightfully accessible and full of the scholar's delicious wordplay and wit, not to mention some astonishing war stories and insights into Nibley's phenomenal acquisition of languages. Introduced by a personable foreword from the author's wife (who is Nibley's daughter), the book is written with enthusiasm, respect and insight. . . . On the whole, Petersen is a careful scholar who provides helpful historical context. . . . This project is far from hagiography. It fills an important gap in LDS history and will appeal to a wide Mormon audience."
　　　　—Publishers Weekly

"Well written and thoroughly researched, Petersen's biography is a must-have for anyone struggling to reconcile faith and reason."
　　　　—Greg Taggart, Association for Mormon Letters

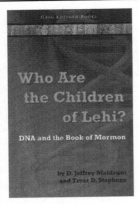

Who Are the Children of Lehi? DNA and the Book of Mormon

D. Jeffrey Meldrum and Trent D. Stephens

Hardcover, ISBN: 978-1-58958-048-0
Paperback, ISBN: 978-1-58958-129-6

How does the Book of Mormon, keystone of the LDS faith, stand up to data about DNA sequencing that puts the ancestors of modern Native Americans in northeast Asia instead of Palestine?

In *Who Are the Children of Lehi?* Meldrum and Stephens examine the merits and the fallacies of DNA-based interpretations that challenge the Book of Mormon's historicity. They provide clear guides to the science, summarize the studies, illuminate technical points with easy-to-grasp examples, and spell out the data's implications.

The results? There is no straight-line conclusion between DNA evidence and "Lamanites." The Book of Mormon's validity lies beyond the purview of scientific empiricism—as it always has. And finally, inspiringly, they affirm Lehi's kinship as one of covenant, not genes.

Mormon Women Have Their Say:
Essays from the Claremont
Oral History Collection

Edited by Claudia L. Bushman
and Caroline Kline

Paperback, ISBN: 978-1-58958-494-5

The Claremont Women's Oral History Project has collected hundreds of interviews with Mormon women of various ages, experiences, and levels of activity. These interviews record the experiences of these women in their homes and family life, their church life, and their work life, in their roles as homemakers, students, missionaries, career women, single women, converts, and disaffected members. Their stories feed into and illuminate the broader narrative of LDS history and belief, filling in a large gap in Mormon history that has often neglected the lived experiences of women. This project preserves and perpetuates their voices and memories, allowing them to say share what has too often been left unspoken. The silent majority speaks in these records.

This volume is the first to explore the riches of the collection in print. A group of young scholars and others have used the interviews to better understand what Mormonism means to these women and what women mean for Mormonism. They explore those interviews through the lenses of history, doctrine, mythology, feminist theory, personal experience, and current events to help us understand what these women have to say about their own faith and lives.

Praise for *Mormon Women Have Their Say*:

"Using a variety of analytical techniques and their own savvy, the authors connect ordinary lives with enduring themes in Latter-day Saint faith and history." --Laurel Thatcher Ulrich, author of *Well-Behaved Women Seldom Make History*

"Essential. . . . In these pages, Mormon women will find *ourselves*." --Joanna Brooks, author of *The Book of Mormon Girl: A Memoir of an American Faith*

"The varieties of women's responses to the major issues in their lives will provide many surprises for the reader, who will be struck by how many different ways there are to be a thoughtful and faithful Latter-day Saint woman." --Armand Mauss, author of *All Abraham's Children: Changing Mormon Conceptions of Race and Lineage*

Common Ground—Different Opinions:
Latter-day Saints and Contemporary Issues

Edited by Justin F. White
and James E. Faulconer

Paperback, ISBN: 978-1-58958-573-7

There are many hotly debated issues about which many people disagree, and where common ground is hard to find. From evolution to environmentalism, war and peace to political partisanship, stem cell research to same-sex marriage, how we think about controversial issues affects how we interact as Latter-day Saints.

In this volume various Latter-day Saint authors address these and other issues from differing points of view. Though they differ on these tough questions, they have all found common ground in the gospel of Jesus Christ and the latter-day restoration. Their insights offer diverse points of view while demonstrating we can still love those with whom we disagree.

Praise for *Common Ground—Different Opinions*:

"[This book] provide models of faithful and diverse Latter-day Saints who remain united in the body of Christ. This collection clearly demonstrates that a variety of perspectives on a number of sensitive issues do in fact exist in the Church. . . . [T]he collection is successful in any case where it manages to give readers pause with regard to an issue they've been fond of debating, or convinces them to approach such conversations with greater charity and much more patience. It served as just such a reminder and encouragement to me, and for that reason above all, I recommend this book." — Blair Hodges, Maxwell Institute

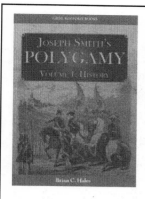

Joseph Smith's Polygamy, 3 Vols.

Brian Hales

Hardcover
Volume 1: History 978-1-58958-189-0
Volume 2: History 978-1-58958-548-5
Volume 3: Theology 978-1-58958-190-6

Perhaps the least understood part of Joseph Smith's life and teachings is his introduction of polygamy to the Saints in Nauvoo. Because of the persecution he knew it would bring, Joseph said little about it publicly and only taught it to his closest and most trusted friends and associates before his martyrdom.

In this three-volume work, Brian C. Hales provides the most comprehensive faithful examination of this much misunderstood period in LDS Church history. Drawing for the first time on every known account, Hales helps us understand the history and teachings surrounding this secretive practice and also addresses and corrects many of the numerous allegations and misrepresentations concerning it. Hales further discusses how polygamy was practiced during this time and why so many of the early Saints were willing to participate in it.

Joseph Smith's Polygamy is an essential resource in understanding this challenging and misunderstood practice of early Mormonism.

Praise for *Joseph Smith's Polygamy*:

"Brian Hales wants to face up to every question, every problem, every fear about plural marriage. His answers may not satisfy everyone, but he gives readers the relevant sources where answers, if they exist, are to be found. There has never been a more thorough examination of the polygamy idea."
—Richard L. Bushman, author of *Joseph Smith: Rough Stone Rolling*

"Hales's massive and well documented three volume examination of the history and theology of Mormon plural marriage, as introduced and practiced during the life of Joseph Smith, will now be the standard against which all other treatments of this important subject will be measured." —Danel W. Bachman, author of "A Study of the Mormon Practice of Plural Marriage before the Death of Joseph Smith"

From Above and Below: The Mormon Embrace of Revolution, 1840–1940

Craig Livingston

Paperback, ISBN: 978-1-58958-621-5

Praise for *From Above and Below*:

"In this engaging study, Craig Livingston examines Mormon responses to political revolutions across the globe from the 1840s to the 1930s. Latter-day Saints saw utopian possibilities in revolutions from the European tumults of 1848 to the Mexican Revolution. Highlighting the often radical anti-capitalist and anti-imperialist rhetoric of Mormon leaders, Livingston demonstrates how Latter-day Saints interpreted revolutions through their unique theology and millennialism."
--Matthew J. Grow, author of *Liberty to the Downtrodden: Thomas L. Kane, Romantic Reformer*

"Craig Livingston's landmark book demonstrates how 21st-century Mormonism's arch-conservatism was preceded by its pro-revolutionary worldview that was dominant from the 1830s to the 1930s. Shown by current opinion-polling to be the most politically conservative religious group in the United States, contemporary Mormons are unaware that leaders of the LDS Church once praised radical liberalism and violent revolutionaries. By this pre-1936 Mormon view, 'The people would reduce privilege and exploitation in the crucible of revolution, then reforge society in a spiritual union of peace' before the Coming of Christ and His Millennium. With profound research in Mormon sources and in academic studies about various social revolutions and political upheavals, Livingston provides a nuanced examination of this little-known dimension of LDS thought which tenuously balanced pro-revolutionary enthusiasms with anti-mob sentiments."
--D. Michael Quinn, author of *Elder Statesman: A Biography of J. Reuben Clark*

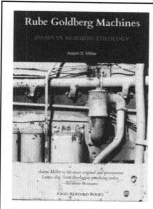

Rube Goldberg Machines:
Essays in Mormon Theology

Adam S. Miller

Paperback, ISBN: 978-1-58958-193-7

"Adam Miller is the most original and provocative Latter-day Saint theologian practicing today."

—Richard Bushman, author of *Joseph Smith: Rough Stone Rolling*

"As a stylist, Miller gives Nietzsche a run for his money. As a believer, Miller is as submissive as Augustine hearing a child's voice in the garden. Miller is a theologian of the ordinary, thinking about our ordinary beliefs in very non-ordinary ways while never insisting that the ordinary become extra-ordinary."

—James Faulconer, Richard L. Evans Chair of Religious Understanding,Brigham Young University

"Miller's language is both recognizably Mormon and startlingly original. . . . The whole is an essay worthy of the name, inviting the reader to try ideas, following the philosopher pilgrim's intellectual progress through tangled brambles and into broad fields, fruitful orchards, and perhaps a sacred grove or two."

—Kristine Haglund, editor of *Dialogue: A Journal of Mormon Thought*

"Miller's Rube Goldberg theology is nothing like anything done in the Mormon tradition before."

—Blake Ostler, author of the EXPLORING MORMON THOUGHT series

"The value of Miller's writings is in the modesty he both exhibits and projects onto the theological enterprise, even while showing its joyfully disruptive potential. Conventional Mormon minds may not resonate with every line of poetry and provocation—but Miller surely afflicts the comfortable, which is the theologian's highest end."

—Terryl Givens, author of *By the Hand of Mormon: The American Scripture that Launched a New World Religion*

Fire on the Horizon:
A Meditation on the Endowment and
Love of Atonement

Blake T. Ostler

Paperback, ISBN: 978-1-58958-553-9

Blake Ostler, author of the groundbreaking Exploring Mormon Thought series, explores two of the most important and central aspects of Mormon theology and practice: the Atonement and the temple endowment. Utilizing observations from Søren Kierkegaard, Martin Buber, and others, Ostler offers further insights on what it means to become alienated from God and to once again have at-one-ment with Him.

Praise for *Fire on the Horizon*:

"*Fire on the Horizon* distills decades of reading, argument, and reflection into one potent dose. Urgent, sharp, and intimate, it's Ostler at his best." — Adam S. Miller, author of *Rube Goldberg Machines: Essays in Mormon Theology*

"Blake Ostler has been one of the most stimulating, deep, and original thinkers in the Latter-day Saint community. This book continues and consolidates that status. His work demonstrates that Mormonism can, and indeed does, offer profound nourishment for reflective minds and soul-satisfying insights for thoughtful believers." — Daniel C. Peterson, editor of *Interpreter: A Journal of Mormon Scripture*

Dead Wood and Rushing Water: Essays on Mormon Faith, Culture, and Family

Boyd Jay Petersen

Paperback, ISBN: 978-1-58958-658-1

For over a decade, Boyd Petersen has been an active voice in Mormon studies and thought. In essays that steer a course between apologetics and criticism, striving for the balance of what Eugene England once called the "radical middle," he explores various aspects of Mormon life and culture—from the Dream Mine near Salem, Utah, to the challenges that Latter-day Saints of the millennial generation face today.

Praise for *Dead Wood and Rushing Water*:

"*Dead Wood and Rushing Water* gives us a reflective, striving, wise soul ruminating on his world. In the tradition of Eugene England, Petersen examines everything in his Mormon life from the gold plates to missions to dream mines to doubt and on to Glenn Beck, Hugh Nibley, and gender. It is a book I had trouble putting down." — Richard L. Bushman, author of *Joseph Smith: Rough Stone Rolling*

"Boyd Petersen is correct when he says that Mormons have a deep hunger for personal stories—at least when they are as thoughtful and well-crafted as the ones he shares in this collection." — Jana Riess, author of *The Twible* and *Flunking Sainthood*

"Boyd Petersen invites us all to ponder anew the verities we hold, sharing in his humility, tentativeness, and cheerful confidence that our paths will converge in the end." — Terryl. L. Givens, author of *People of Paradox: A History of Mormon Culture*

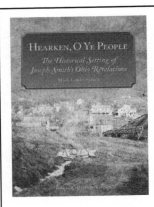

Hearken, O Ye People:
The Historical Setting of Joseph
Smith's Ohio Revelations

Mark Lyman Staker

Hardcover, ISBN: 978-1-58958-113-5

2010 Best Book Award - John Whitmer Historical Association

2011 Best Book Award - Mormon History Association

More of Mormonism's canonized revelations originated in or near Kirtland than any other place. Yet many of the events connected with those revelations and their 1830s historical context have faded over time. Mark Staker reconstructs the cultural experiences by which Kirtland's Latter-day Saints made sense of the revelations Joseph Smith pronounced. This volume rebuilds that exciting decade using clues from numerous archives, privately held records, museum collections, and even the soil where early members planted corn and homes. From this vast array of sources he shapes a detailed narrative of weather, religious backgrounds, dialect differences, race relations, theological discussions, food preparation, frontier violence, astronomical phenomena, and myriad daily customs of nineteenth-century life. The result is a "from the ground up" experience that today's Latter-day Saints can all but walk into and touch.

Praise for *Hearken O Ye People*:

"I am not aware of a more deeply researched and richly contextualized study of any period of Mormon church history than Mark Staker's study of Mormons in Ohio. We learn about everything from the details of Alexander Campbell's views on priesthood authority to the road conditions and weather on the four Lamanite missionaries' journey from New York to Ohio. All the Ohio revelations and even the First Vision are made to pulse with new meaning. This book sets a new standard of in-depth research in Latter-day Saint history."

-Richard Bushman, author of *Joseph Smith: Rough Stone Rolling*

"To be well-informed, any student of Latter-day Saint history and doctrine must now be acquainted with the remarkable research of Mark Staker on the important history of the church in the Kirtland, Ohio, area."

-Neal A. Maxwell Institute, Brigham Young University

Made in the USA
San Bernardino, CA
17 December 2017